AAT
INTERACTIVE TEXT

Intermediate Unit 6

Cost Information

In this May 2002 edition

- Text updated in the light of the assessor's review of the previous edition of this text

- New guidance on the preparation of portfolios

- Icons to guide you through a 'fast track' approach if you wish

- Numerous activities throughout the text to reinforce learning

- Thorough reliable updating of material to 1 April 2002

- **FOR 2002 AND 2003 SKILLS BASED AND EXAM BASED ASSESSMENTS**

BPP Publishing
May 2002

First edition 1998
Fifth edition May 2002

ISBN 0 7517 6276 8 (Previous edition 0 7517 6509 0)

British Library Cataloguing-in-Publication Data
A catalogue record for this book
is available from the British Library

Published by

BPP Publishing Limited
Aldine House, Aldine Place
London W12 8AW

www.bpp.com

Printed in Great Britain by Ashford Colour Press

We are grateful to the Lead Body for Accounting for permission to reproduce extracts from the Standards of Competence for Accounting, and to the AAT for permission to reproduce extracts from the mapping and Guidance Notes.

Page

BPP
PUBLISHING

HOW TO USE THIS INTERACTIVE TEXT

Aims of this Interactive Text

To provide the knowledge and practice to help you succeed in the devolved and central assessments for Intermediate Unit 6 *Recording Cost Information*.

To complete the assessments successfully you need a thorough understanding in all areas covered by the standards of competence.

To tie in with the other components of the BPP Effective Study Package to ensure you have the best possible chance of success.

Interactive Text

This covers all you need to know for assessment for Unit 6 *Recording Cost Information*. Icons clearly mark key areas of the text. Numerous activities throughout the text help you practise what you have just learnt.

Assessment Kit

When you have understood and practised the material in the Interactive Text, you will have the knowledge and experience to tackle the Assessment Kit for Unit 6 *Cost Information*. This aims to get you through the assessments, whether in the form of the AAT simulation or in the workplace. It contains the AAT's sample simulation and sample Central Assessment for Unit 6 plus other simulations.

Passcards

These short memorable notes are focused on key topics for Unit 6, designed to remind you of what the Interactive Text has taught you.

Recommended approach to this Interactive Text

(a) To achieve competence in Unit 6 (and all the other units), you need to be able to do **everything** specified by the standards. Study the text very carefully and do not skip any of it.

(b) Learning is an **active** process. Do **all** the activities as you work through the text so you can be sure you really understand what you have read. Depending on their difficulty, the activities are graded as pre-assessment or assessment.

(c) After you have covered the material in the Interactive Text, work through the **Assessment Kit**.

(d) Before you take the assessments, check that you still remember the material using the following quick revision plan for each chapter.

    (i) Read through the **chapter learning objectives**. Are there any gaps in your knowledge? If so, study the section again.

    (ii) Read and learn the **key terms**.

    (iii) Look at the **assessment alerts**. These show the sort of things that are likely to come up.

    (iv) Read and learn the **key learning points**, which are a summary of the chapter.

    (v) Do the **quick quiz** again. If you know what you're doing, it shouldn't take long.

(vi)   Go through the **Passcards** as often as you can in the weeks leading up to your assessment.

This approach is only a suggestion. Your college may well adapt it to suit your needs.

Remember this is a **practical** course.

(a)   Try to relate the material to your experience in the workplace or any other work experience you may have had.

(b)   Try to make as many links as you can to your study of the other Units at Intermediate level.

(c)   Keep this Text - you will need it as you move on to Technician, and (hopefully) you will find it invaluable in your everyday work too!

Stop press

The AAT is planning to change the terminology used for assessments in the following ways:

(a)   Central assessments to be called exam based testing
(b)   Devolved assessments to be called skills based testing

As the plans had not been finalised at the time of going to press, the 2002 editions of BPP titles will continue to refer to central and devolved assessments.

INTERMEDIATE QUALIFICATION STRUCTURE

The competence-based Education and Training Scheme of the Association of Accounting Technicians is based on an analysis of the work of accounting staff in a wide range of industries and types of organisation. The Standards of Competence for Accounting which students are expected to meet are based on this analysis.

The Standards identify the **key purpose** of the accounting occupation, which is **to operate, maintain and improve systems to record, plan, monitor and report on the financial activities of an organisation**, and a number of **key roles** of the occupation. Each key role is subdivided into **units of competence**, which are further divided into **elements of competences**. By successfully completing assessments in specified units of competence, students can gain qualifications at NVQ/SVQ levels 2, 3 and 4, which correspond to the AAT Foundation, Intermediate and Technician stages of competence respectively.

On the following page, we set out the overall structure of the Intermediate (NVQ/SVQ Level 3) stage, indicating how competence in each Unit is assessed. In the next two sections there is more detail about the Standards of Competence and the Assessment Strategy for Unit 6.

BPP PUBLISHING

NVQ/SVQ **Level 3 - Intermediate**

All units are mandatory

Unit of competence	**Elements of competence**

Unit 5 Maintaining financial records and preparing accounts

Central *and* Devolved Assessment

5.1	Maintain records relating to capital acquisition and disposal
5.2	Record income and expenditure
5.3	Collect and collate information for the preparation of financial accounts
5.4	Prepare the extended trial balance account

Unit 6 Recording cost information

Central *and* Devolved Assessment

6.1	Record and analyse information relating to direct costs
6.2	Record and analyse information relating to the allocation, apportionment and absorption of overhead costs
6.3	Prepare and present standard cost reports

Unit 7 Preparing reports and returns

Devolved Assessment *only*

7.1	Prepare and present periodic performance reports
7.2	Prepare reports and returns for outside agencies
7.3	Prepare VAT returns

Unit 21 Using information technology

Devolved Assessment *only*

21.1	Obtain information from a computerised Management Information System
21.2	Produce spreadsheets for the analysis of numerical information
21.3	Contribute to the quality of the Management Information System

Unit 22 Monitor and maintain a healthy, safe and secure workplace (ASC)

Devolved Assessment *only*

22.1	Monitor and maintain health and safety within the workplace
22.2	Monitor and maintain the security of the workplace

UNIT 6 STANDARDS OF COMPETENCE

The structure of the Standards for Unit 6

The Unit commences with a statement of the **knowledge and understanding** which underpin competence in the Unit's elements.

The unit of Competence is then divided into **elements of competence** describing activities which the individual should be able to perform.

Each element includes:

(a) A set of **performance criteria** which define what constitutes competent performance

(b) A **range statement** which defines the situations, contexts, methods etc in which competence should be displayed

(c) **Evidence requirements**, which state that competence must be demonstrated consistently, over an appropriate time scale with evidence of performance being provided from the appropriate sources

(d) **Sources of evidence**, being suggestions of ways in which you can find evidence to demonstrate that competence. These fall under the headings: 'observed performance; work produced by the candidate; authenticated testimonies from relevant witnesses; personal account of competence; other sources of evidence.' They are reproduced in full in our Assessment Kit for Unit 6.

The elements of competence for Unit 6: *Recording Cost Information* are set out below. Knowledge and understanding required for the unit as a whole are listed first, followed by the performance criteria, and range statements for each element. Performance criteria are cross-referenced below to chapters in this Unit 6 *Cost Information* Interactive Text.

Unit 6:   Recording Cost Information

What is the unit about?

This unit is concerned with recording, analysing and reporting information relating to both direct and indirect costs. It involves the identification, coding and analysis of all costs, the apportionment and absorption of indirect costs and the presentation of all the information in standard cost reports. The candidate is required to carry out variance analyses, different methods of allocation, apportionment and absorption and adjustments for under/over recovered indirect costs. There is also a requirement for information to be systematically checked and any unusual or unexpected results to be communicated to management.

BPP PUBLISHING

Knowledge and understanding

The business environment

- Main types of materials: raw materials; part finished goods; materials issued from stores within the organisation; deliveries (Elements 6.1 & 6.2)

- Methods of payment for labour: salaried labour; performance related pay; profit related pay (Elements 6.1 6.2)

- Main types of expenses: expenses directly charged to cost units; indirect expenses; depreciation charges (Elements 6.1 & 6.2)

Accounting techniques

- Basic analysis of variances: usage; price; rate; efficiency; expenditure; volume; capacity (Elements 6.1, 6.2 & 6.3)

- Procedures for establishing standard materials costs, use of technical and purchasing information (Element 6.1)

- Methods of analysing materials usage: reasons for wastage (Element 6.1)

- Procedures for establishing standard labour costs: use of information about labour rates (Element 6.1)

- Analysis of labour rate and efficiency: idle time; overtime levels; absenteeism; sickness rates (Element 6.1)

- Methods of stock control (Element 6.1)

- Methods of setting standards for expenses (Elements 6.1 & 6.2)

- Procedures and documentation relating to expenses (Elements 6.1 & 6.2)

- Allocation of expenses to cost centres (Elements 6.1 & 6.2)

- Analysis of the effect of changing activity levels on unit costs (Elements 6.1 & 6.2)

- Procedures for establishing standard absorption rates (Element 6.2)

- Bases of allocating and apportioning indirect costs to responsibility centres: direct; reciprocal allocation; step down method (Element 6.2)

- Activity based systems of allocating costs: cost drivers; cost pools (Element 6.2)

- Bases of absorption (Element 6.2)

- Methods of presenting information orally and in written reports (Element 6.3)

- Control ratios of efficiency, capacity and activity (Element 6.3)

Accounting principles and theory

- Relationship between technical systems and costing systems - job, batch, unit, systems (Elements 6.1 & 6.2)

- Principles and objectives of standard costing systems: variance reports (Elements 6.1, 6.2 & 6.3)

- Relationships between the materials costing system and the stock control system (Element 6.1)

- Relationships between the labour costing system and the payroll accounting system (Element 6.1)

- Relationships between the expenses costing system and the accounting system (Elements 6.1 & 6.2)

- Objectives of depreciation accounting (Elements 6.1 & 6.2)

- The distinction between fixed, semi-fixed and variable costs (Elements 6.1 & 6.2)

- Effect of changes in capacity levels (Element 6.2)

- Arbitrary nature of overhead apportionments (Element 6.2)

- The significance of and possible reasons for variances (Elements 6.1, 6.2 & 6.3)

The organisation

- Understanding of the ways the accounting systems of an organisation are affected by its organisational structure, its administrative systems and procedures and the nature of its business transactions (Elements 6.1, 6.2 & 6.3)

- The reporting cycle of the organisation (Element 6.3)

Element 6.1 Record and analyse information relating to direct costs

Performance criteria	Chapters in this Text
1 Direct costs are identified in accordance with the organisation's costing procedures	2-4,9
2 Information relating to direct costs is clearly and correctly coded, analysed and recorded	2-4, 7-9
3 Direct costs are calculated in accordance with the organisation's policies and procedures	2-4, 9
4 Standard costs are compared against actual costs and any variances are analysed	10, 11
5 Information is systematically checked against the overall usage and stock control practices	10, 11
6 Queries are either resolved or referred to the appropriate person	2-4, 7

Range statement

1   Direct costs: standard and actual material costs; standard and actual labour costs; standard and actual expenses

- Materials: raw materials; part finished goods; materials issued from stores within the organisation; deliveries

- Labour: employees of the organisation on the payroll; sub-contractors; agency staff

- Expenses: direct revenue expenditure

2   Variance analysis: Materials variances: usage, price; Labour variances: rate, efficiency

BPP PUBLISHING

Element 6.2 Record and analyse information relating to the allocation, apportionment and absorption of overhead costs

Performance criteria		Chapters in this Text
1	Data are correctly coded, analysed and recorded	2-4, 7
2	Overhead costs are established in accordance with the organisation's procedures	2-4, 9
3	Information relating to overhead costs is accurately and clearly recorded	2-4, 7-9
4	Overhead costs are correctly attributed to producing and service cost centres in accordance with agreed methods of allocation, apportionment and absorption	5
5	Adjustments for under or over recovered overhead costs are made in accordance with established procedures	5
6	Standard costs are compared against actual costs and any variances are analysed	10
7	Methods of allocation, apportionment and absorption are reviewed at regular intervals in discussions with senior staff, and agreed changes to methods are implemented	5
8	Staff working in operational departments are consulted to resolve any queries in the data	2-4, 7

Range statement

1 Overhead costs: standard and actual indirect material costs; standard and actual indirect labour costs; indirect expenses; depreciation charges

2 Methods of allocation and apportionment: direct; reciprocal allocation; step down method

3 Variance analysis: Overhead variances: expenditure, efficiency, volume, capacity; Fixed overhead variances: expenditure, volume, capacity, efficiency

Element 6.3 Prepare and present standard cost reports

Performance criteria	Chapters in this Text
1 Standard cost reports with variances clearly identified are presented in an intelligible form	11
2 Unusual or unexpected results are identified and reported to managers	11
3 Any reasons for significant variances from standard are identified and the explanations presented to management	11
4 The results of the analysis and explanations of specific variances are produced for management	11
5 Staff working in operational departments are consulted to resolve any queries in the data	11

Range statement

1   Methods of presentation: written report containing analysis and explanation of specific variances; further explanations to managers

2   Types of variances: Overhead variances: expenditure, efficiency, volume, capacity; Materials variances: usage, price; Labour variances: rate, efficiency

BPP
PUBLISHING

ASSESSMENT STRATEGY

This unit is assessed by both **central assessment** (exam based testing) and **devolved assessment** (skills based testing).

Central Assessment/Exam based testing

A central assessment is a means of collecting evidence that you have the **essential knowledge and understanding** which underpins competence. It is also a means of collecting evidence across the **range of contexts** for the standards, and of your ability to **transfer skills**, knowledge and understanding to different situations. Thus, although central assessments contain practical tests linked to the performance criteria, they also focus on the underpinning knowledge and understanding. You should in addition expect each central assessment to contain tasks taken from across a broad range of the standards.

Each Unit 6 central assessment will last for **three hours** *plus fifteen minutes' reading time and will be divided into two sections.* The two sections will normally take the same time to complete.

Section 1

This section will assess competence in element 6.1 and will also include standard cost reporting relating to direct costs as detailed in element 6.3 of this unit. Examples of tasks which may be assessed in this section include the following.

(a)   Calculation of material price and usage variances.

(b)   Calculation of labour rate and efficiency variances.

(c)   Calculation of control ratios such as the labour efficiency ratio.

(d)   Consideration of the different types of standard costs and the procedures to be adopted in establishing those standard costs.

(e)   Methods of stock control and pricing of materials to include first-in-first-out, last-in-first-out and standard cost.

(f)   The use of actual costs for materials and labour and the analysis of those costs.

(g)   Application of different cost behaviours to direct costs.

(h)   Preparation of cost accounting entries from payroll and stock control systems.

(i)   Preparation of standard cost reports for direct materials, which will include an assessment of knowledge and understanding relating to standard cost variances.

Section 2

This section will assess competence in element 6.2 and will also include standard cost reporting relating to indirect costs as detailed in element 6.3 of this unit. Examples of tasks which may be assessed in this section include the following.

(a)   The allocation and apportionment of indirect costs to cost centres.

(b)   Procedures for the calculation of departmental absorption rates using different absorption bases.

(c)   The application of different cost behaviours to indirect costs.

(d)   The separation of variable costs from fixed costs and the impact of changing capacity levels.

(e) Comparison of budgeted indirect cost data with actual data and the calculation of indirect cost variances.

(f) The calculation of fixed overhead expenditure and volume variances and the division of the volume variance into efficiency and capacity variances.

(g) Preparation of cost accounting entries for indirect costs.

(h) Preparation of standard cost reports for indirect costs, which will include an assessment of knowledge and understanding relating to standard cost variances.

The tasks detailed above are indicative of those which may be assessed but are not exhaustive. It is important to understand that the Central Assessment is based on the Standards of Competence for this unit and that all areas included in the Standards are assessable.

Students will now be required to prepare a report in both sections. Since competence must be demonstrated in both sections, it is important that students practise their report writing.

(a) Plan the report and check that the plan deals with the tasks set.

(b) Be aware of the context in which the report is written. (A common scenario will be used for both sections.)

(c) Use appropriate headings.

(d) Use clear and concise English.

Devolved Assessment/Skills based testing

Devolved assessment is a means of collecting evidence of your ability to carry out **practical activities** and to **operate effectively in the conditions of the workplace** to the standards required. Evidence may be collected at your place of work or at an Approved Assessment Centre by means of simulations of workplace activity, or by a combination of these methods.

If the Approved Assessment Centre is a **workplace**, you may be observed carrying out accounting activities as part of your normal work routine. You should collect documentary evidence of the work you have done, or contributed to, in an **accounting portfolio**. Evidence collected in a portfolio can be assessed in addition to observed performance or where it is not possible to assess by observation.

Where the Approved Assessment Centre is a **college or training organisation**, devolved assessment will be by means of a combination of the following.

(a) Documentary evidence of activities carried out at the workplace, collected by you in an **accounting portfolio**.

(b) Realistic **simulations** of workplace activities. These simulations may take the form of case studies and in-tray exercises and involve the use of primary documents and reference sources.

(c) **Projects and assignments** designed to assess the Standards of Competence.

If you are unable to provide workplace evidence you will be able to complete the assessment requirements by the alternative methods listed above.

BUILDING YOUR PORTFOLIO

What is a portfolio?

A portfolio is a collection of work that demonstrates what the owner can do. In AAT language the portfolio demonstrates **competence**.

A painter will have a collection of his paintings to exhibit in a gallery, an advertising executive will have a range of advertisements and ideas that she has produced to show to a prospective client. Both the collection of paintings and the advertisements form the portfolio of that artist or advertising executive.

Your portfolio will be unique to you just as the portfolio of the artist will be unique because no one will paint the same range of pictures in the same way. It is a very personal collection of your work and should be treated as a **confidential** record.

What evidence should a portfolio include?

No two portfolios will be the same but by following some simple guidelines you can decide which of the following suggestions will be appropriate in your case.

(a) **Your current CV**

   This should be at the front. It will give your personal details as well as brief descriptions of posts you have held with the most recent one shown first.

(b) **References and testimonials**

   References from previous employers may be included especially those of which you are particularly proud.

(c) **Your current job description**

   You should emphasise financial **responsibilities and duties**.

(d) **Your student record sheets**

   These should be supplied by AAT when you begin your studies, and your training provider should also have some if necessary.

(e) **Evidence from your current workplace**

   This could take many forms including **letters, memos, reports** you have written, **copies of accounts** or **reconciliations** you have prepared, **discrepancies** you have investigated etc. Remember to obtain permission to include the evidence from your line manager because some records may be sensitive. Discuss the performance criteria that are listed in your Student Record Sheets with your training provider and employer, and think of other evidence that could be appropriate to you.

(f) **Evidence from your social activities**

   For example you may be the treasurer of a club in which case examples of your cash and banking records could be appropriate.

(g) **Evidence from your studies**

   Few students are able to satisfy all the requirements of competence by workplace evidence alone. They therefore rely on simulations to provide the remaining evidence to complete a unit. If you are not working or not working in a relevant post, then you may need to rely more heavily on simulations as a source of evidence.

(h) **Additional work**

Your training provider may give you work that specifically targets one or a group of performance criteria in order to complete a unit. It could take the form of questions, presentations or demonstrations. Each training provider will approach this in a different way.

(i) **Evidence from a previous workplace**

This evidence may be difficult to obtain and should be used with caution because it must satisfy the 'rules' of evidence, that is it must be current. Only rely on this as evidence if you have changed jobs recently.

(j) **Prior achievements**

For example you may have already completed the health and safety unit during a previous course of study, and therefore there is no need to repeat this work. Advise your training provider who will check to ensure that it is the same unit and record it as complete if appropriate.

How should it be presented?

As you assemble the evidence remember to **make a note** of it on your Student Record Sheet in the space provided and **cross reference** it. In this way it is easy to check to see if your evidence is **appropriate**. Remember one piece of evidence may satisfy a number of performance criteria so remember to check this thoroughly and discuss it with your training provider if in doubt.

To keep all your evidence together a ring binder or lever arch file is a good means of storage.

When should evidence be assembled?

You should begin to assemble evidence **as soon as you have registered as a student**. **Don't leave it all** until the last few weeks of your studies, because you may miss vital deadlines and your resulting certificate sent by the AAT may not include all the units you have completed. Give yourself and your training provider time to examine your portfolio and report your results to AAT at regular intervals. In this way the task of assembling the portfolio will be spread out over a longer period of time and will be presented in a more professional manner.

What are the key criteria that the portfolio must fulfil?

As you assemble your evidence bear in mind that it must be:

- **Valid**. It must relate to the Standards.

- **Authentic**. It must be your own work.

- **Current**. It must refer to your current or most recent job.

- **Sufficient**. It must meet all the performance criteria by the time you have completed your portfolio.

What are the most important elements in a portfolio that covers Unit 6?

You should remember that the unit is about **recording cost information**. Therefore you need to produce evidence not only demonstrating that you can carry out certain tasks, but also you must show that you can record cost information correctly.

For Element 6.1 *Record and analyse information relating to direct costs*, you not only need to show that you can identify which costs in your organisation are direct, you also need to demonstrate that you can code them correctly and calculate any direct variances which have arisen.

The main evidence that you need for Element 6.2 *Record and analyse information relating to the allocation, apportionment and absorption of overhead costs* is detail of how overheads are correctly allocated, apportioned and absorbed in accordance with your organisation's procedures. You will also need to demonstrate that you have calculated overhead variances and analysed any which are significant.

To fulfil the requirements of Element 6.3 *Prepare and present standard cost reports* you need to demonstrate that you have calculated and analysed material, labour and overhead variances and presented them to management. You will also need to provide evidence of the methods of presentation that you have used in order to communicate this information (for example, written reports).

Finally

Remember that the portfolio is your property and your responsibility. Not only could it be presented to the external verifier before your award can be confirmed; it could be used when you are seeking promotion or applying for a more senior and better paid post elsewhere. How your portfolio is presented can say as much about you as the evidence inside.

Part A
Materials, labour and expenses

1 Cost information

This chapter contains

1 Introduction

2 What is cost accounting?

3 Cost units and cost centres

4 The analysis of cost

5 Product costing

6 Functional costs

7 Standard costs and variances

Learning objectives

On completion of this chapter you will be able to:

- Understand the objectives of a cost accounting system

- Recognise cost elements

- Distinguish between different types of cost

- Decide on appropriate costing methods

- Use costing terms

Knowledge and understanding

- Relationship between technical systems and costing systems – job, batch, unit systems

- Understanding of the ways the accounting systems of an organisation are affected by its organisational structure, its administrative systems and procedures and the nature of its business transactions

BPP PUBLISHING

1   INTRODUCTION

1.1   The aim of this chapter is to introduce you to some basic aspects of cost accounting.

- What are the objectives of a cost accounting system?
- What types of cost might be incurred in different kinds of organisation?

This chapter will provide you with the answers to questions such as these.

1.2   Later in this Interactive Text we will be returning to discuss in more detail many of the general principles and definitions that are introduced in this chapter. For now, you should try just to get a feel for what costing is all about, and the sort of terms that are used as the basic terminology of any cost accounting system.

2   WHAT IS COST ACCOUNTING?

2.1   Where can an organisation's managers find the answers to the following questions?

- What was the cost of goods produced or services provided last month?
- What was the cost of operating a department last period?

Yes, you've guessed it, from the **cost accounting system.**

2.2   That was quite easy. But where can managers find the answers to these questions?

- What are the future costs of goods and services likely to be?
- How do actual costs compare with planned costs?

Well, you may be surprised, but the answer again is the **cost accounting system.**

2.3   In this Interactive Text you will be seeing how a cost accounting system also provides information to managers to help them **budget and plan for the future of the organisation.**

2.4   The managers of an organisation have the responsibility of planning and controlling the resources used. To do this effectively they need **sufficiently accurate** and **detailed** information, and the cost accounting system should provide this. **A cost accounting system analyses past, present and future data to provide the basis for managerial action.**

2.5   A wide variety of organisations uses cost accounting systems, ranging from manufacturing and service industries to government departments and charities. Therefore a cost accounting system might answer the following types of question.

- What is the cost of cleaning a hotel bedroom?
- What does it cost to provide street lighting to a particular area?
- What is the cost of taking an X-ray?
- What does it cost to provide a mobile library service?

2.6   This chapter provides a brief introduction to recording cost information.

3   COST UNITS AND COST CENTRES

3.1   Before we can go on to look at costs in detail, you need to understand a bit about the organisation of the cost accounting system.

Cost units

> **KEY TERM**
>
> A **cost unit** is a unit of product which has a cost attached to it. The cost unit is the basic control unit for costing purposes.

3.2   A cost unit is not always a single item. It might be a batch of 1,000 if that is how the individual items are made. For example, a cost per 1,000 (or whatever) is often more meaningful information, especially if calculating a cost for a single item gives an amount that you cannot hold in your hand, like 0.003p. Examples of cost units are as follows.

- A batch of 1,000 pairs of shoes or 200 biros
- A passenger mile (for a bus company)
- A patient night (for a hospital)

3.3   Notice that the last two examples of cost units consisted of **two parts.** For instance a patient night is the cost of one patient staying for one night in a hospital. It would not be very meaningful to measure the 'cost per patient', because that would vary according to how long the patient stays. The 'cost per patient night', on the other hand, would not be affected by the length of stay of the individual patient.

Cost centres

> **KEY TERM**
>
> **Cost centres** are the essential 'building blocks' of a costing system. They act as a collecting place for certain costs before they are analysed further.

3.4   There are a number of different types of cost centre, which include the following.

- A **department,** for example in a factory making cakes there could be a mixing department and a baking department.

- A **person,** for example the company solicitor may incur costs on books and stationery that are unique to his or her function.

- A **group of people,** for example the laboratory staff.

- An **item of equipment** such as a machine which incurs running and maintenance costs.

3.5   The number and types of cost centres that an organisation uses will depend on the organisation structure and on the type of product or service it produces.

3.6   Cost centres may vary in nature, but what they have in common is that they **incur costs**. It is therefore logical to **collect costs** initially under the headings of the various different cost centres that there may be in an organisation. Then, when we want to know how much our products or services cost, we simply find out how many cost units have passed through the cost centre and share out the costs incurred by that cost centre amongst the cost units.

4 THE ANALYSIS OF COST

Production costs

4.1 Let us suppose that you are holding a red biro. Look at your biro and consider what it consists of. There is probably a red plastic cap and a little red thing that fits into the end, and perhaps a yellow plastic sheath. There is an opaque plastic ink holder with red ink inside it. At the tip there is a gold plastic part holding a metal nib with a roller ball. How much do all these separate **materials** cost?

4.2 Now think about how the biro was manufactured. The manufacturer probably has machines to mould the plastic and do some of the assembly. How much does it cost, per batch of biros, to run the machines: to set them up so that they produce the right shape of moulded plastic? How much are the production line workers' wages per batch of biros?

4.3 Any of these separate production costs are known as **direct costs** because they can be traced directly to specific units of production.

Overheads

4.4 **Overheads** (or indirect costs) include costs that go into the making of the biro that you do not see when you dismantle it. You can touch the materials and you can appreciate that a combination of man and machine put them together. It is not so obvious that the manufacturer also has to do other things including the following.

- Lubricate machines and employ people to supervise the assembly staff
- Pay rent for the factory and for somewhere to keep the stock of materials
- Pay someone to buy materials, recruit labour and run the payroll
- Deliver the finished biros to the wholesaler
- Employ staff at head office to take orders and collect payments

4.5 Overheads are the biggest problem for cost accountants because it is not easy to tell by either looking at or measuring the product, what overheads went into getting it into the hands of the buyer. Overheads, or indirect costs, unlike direct costs, will not be identified with any single cost unit because they are **incurred for the benefit of all units rather than for any one specific unit.**

4.6 In this Interactive Text you will see how the cost accounting system tries to **apportion overheads (indirect costs) to each cost unit as fairly as possible.**

4.7 To summarise so far, the cost of an item can be divided into the following cost elements.

(a) Materials
(b) Labour
(c) Expenses

Each element can be split into two, as follows.

Materials	=	Direct materials	+	Indirect materials
+		+		+
Labour	=	Direct labour	+	Indirect labour
+		+		+
Expenses	=	Direct expenses	+	Indirect expenses
Total cost	=	Direct cost	+	Overhead

Total direct cost is sometimes referred to as **prime cost.**

Activity 1.1   **Level: Pre-assessment**

List all of the different types of cost that a large supermarket might incur. Arrange them under headings of materials, labour and other expenses.

Fixed costs and variable costs

4.8   There is one other important way in which costs can be analysed and that is between fixed costs and variable costs.

    (a)   If you produce two identical biros you will use twice as many direct materials as you would if you only produced one biro. Direct materials are in this case a **variable cost**. They vary according to the volume of production.

    (b)   If you oil your machines after every 1,000 biros have been produced, the cost of oil is also a variable cost. It is an indirect material cost that varies according to the volume of production.

    (c)   If you rent the factory that houses your biro-making machines you will pay the same amount of rent per annum whether you produce one biro or 10,000 biros. Factory rental is an indirect expense and it is **fixed** no matter what the volume of activity is.

4.9   The examples in (b) and (c) are both indirect costs, or overheads, but (b) is a variable overhead and (c) is a fixed overhead. The example in (a) is a variable direct cost. Direct costs usually are variable although they do not have to be.

4.10   We are elaborating this point because it can be a source of great confusion. Variable cost is *not* just another name for a direct cost. The distinctions that can be made are as follows.

    (a)   **Costs are either direct or indirect, depending upon how easily they can be traced to a specific unit of production or service.**

    (b)   **Costs are either variable or fixed, depending upon whether they change when the volume of activity changes.**

Activity 1.2   **Level: Pre-assessment**

Do you think the following are likely to be fixed or variable costs?

(a)   Charges for telephone calls made
(b)   Charges for rental of telephone
(c)   Annual salary of the chief accountant
(d)   Managing director's subscription to the Institute of Directors
(e)   Cost of materials used to pack 20 units of product X into a box

---

5   PRODUCT COSTING

Job costing

5.1   There are several different ways of arriving at a value for the different cost elements (material, labour and expenses) which make up a unit cost of production. The most straightforward case is where the thing to be costed is a **one-off item**. For example, a furniture maker may make a table, say, to a customer's specific requirements. From start to finish the table is a separately identifiable unit. The costs incurred to make that table are relatively easily identifiable. It will cost so much for the table top, so much for the legs, and so on. This form of costing is known as **job costing**.

Batch costing

5.2 An item like a biro, however, will be produced as one of a **batch** of identical items, because it would clearly be uneconomical to set up the machinery, employ labour and incur overheads to produce each biro individually. There might be a production run of, say, 5,000 biros. The cost of producing 5,000 biros would be calculated and if we wanted to know the cost of one biro we would divide this total by 5,000. The answer would however be a fraction of a penny and this is not very meaningful information.

5.3 This method of costing is called **batch costing** and it applies to many everyday items. So far as costing techniques are concerned, job and batch costing are very similar.

Unit costing

5.4 With batch costing and job costing, each cost unit is separately identifiable. The costs incurred could be traced to each table or to each batch of biros.

5.5 Some organisations may produce goods or services as a continuous stream of identical units, neither of which is separately identifiable for costing purposes. For example:

- A sauce manufacturer produces a continuous stream of identical bottles of sauce.

- A fast food restaurant serves a continuous supply of packets of chips with meals.

5.6 In these types of environment the costing system averages the costs incurred over all the units of output in a period.

$$\text{Cost per unit} = \frac{\text{total cost for period}}{\text{number of units of output in the period}}$$

Activity 1.3   Level: Pre-assessment

Which method of costing (job, batch or unit costing) would be most appropriate for these businesses?

- A baker
- A transport company
- A plumber
- An accountancy firm
- A paint manufacturer

---

6 FUNCTIONAL COSTS

6.1 When we talk about functional costs we are not talking about a different **type** of cost to those we have met already, but about a way of grouping costs together according to what aspects of an organisation's operations (what **function**) causes them to be incurred.

6.2 A convenient set of functions is the following.

(a) **Production costs**. Materials and labour used and expenses incurred to make things and get them ready for sale.

(b) **Distribution and selling costs**. Costs incurred both to get the finished items to the point where people can buy them and to persuade people to buy them.

(c) **Administration costs**. These are the costs incurred in general office departments, such as accounting and personnel.

(d) **Financing costs**. The expenses incurred when a business has to borrow to purchase fixed assets, say, or simply to operate on a day to day basis.

6.3 These are not the only groupings of functional costs, nor are there rigid definitions of what is a production cost, what is an administration cost and so on.

7 STANDARD COSTS AND VARIANCES

7.1 When we were talking about the questions to be answered by a cost accounting system we saw that the system might involve not only recording what costs were, but also predicting what they ought to be.

7.2 Recognising the usefulness of cost information as a tool for controlling what goes on, many businesses adopt what are known as **standard costs**.

- They decide what the unit cost of each element **should** be in advance of the actual cost being incurred.

- Once the cost has been incurred it is **compared** with the estimated standard cost.

- If there is a difference (a **variance**) somebody is asked to explain why.

7.3 To set a standard cost it is necessary not only to know what the level of cost was in the past but also to have an idea of what it is likely to be in the future. In Chapter 9 we shall look at the various problems involved in setting standard costs.

7.4 **Standard costing** is not an alternative to job, batch or unit costing. It is an approach that **can be used in addition** to those costing methods.

Activity 1.4   **Level: Pre-assessment**

Explain the following terms in your own words.

(a) Cost unit   (f) Overhead
(b) Functional cost   (g) Cost centre
(c) Fixed cost   (h) Variable cost
(d) Standard cost   (i) Direct cost
(e) Indirect cost

Key learning points

- Costs can be divided into three elements, **materials, labour** and **expenses.**

- A **cost unit** is a unit of product or service which has costs attached to it.

- A **cost centre** is something that incurs costs. It may be a place, a person, a group of people or an item of equipment.

- Costs can be analysed in different ways. For example direct, indirect, fixed, variable.

- Costs can also be analysed according to their function. For example production, distribution and selling, administration and financing costs.

- The most appropriate costing method for an organisation will depend on the nature of its products and services.

- Costing using standards is a good way of keeping a business under control.

Quick quiz

1   What is a cost unit?

2   Which cost elements make up overheads?

3   Name the three main types of costing method mentioned in this chapter.

4   List four types of functional cost.

Answers to quick quiz

1   A unit of product or service which incurs cost.

2   Indirect materials, indirect labour and indirect expenses.

3   Job costing, batch costing, unit costing

4   •   Production costs
     •   Distribution and selling costs
     •   Administration costs
     •   Financing costs

2 Materials

This chapter contains

1 Introduction

2 Types of material

3 Buying materials

4 Valuing materials issues and stocks

5 Stock control

6 Computers and stock control

7 Reordering stock

Learning objectives

On completion of this chapter you will be able to:

- Identify and calculate direct material costs in accordance with organisational policies and procedures

- Establish indirect material costs in accordance with organisational procedures

- Ensure that information relating to direct material costs is clearly and correctly coded, analysed and recorded

- Ensure that data and information relating to indirect material costs is accurately and clearly coded, analysed and recorded

- Ensure that issues are in accordance with overall usage and stock control practices

- Deal with queries about direct and indirect materials

Performance criteria

6.1 (i)   Direct costs are identified in accordance with the organisation's costing procedures

6.1 (ii)   Information relating to direct costs is clearly and correctly coded, analysed and recorded

6.1 (iii) Direct costs are calculated in accordance with the organisation's policies and procedures

6.1 (v)   Information is systematically checked against the overall usage and stock control practices

6.1 (vi)   Queries are either resolved or referred to the appropriate person

6.2 (i)   Data are correctly coded, analysed and recorded

BPP PUBLISHING

6.2 (ii)   Overhead costs are established in accordance with the organisation's procedures

6.2 (iii) Information relating to overhead costs is accurately and clearly recorded

Range statement

6.1.1 Direct costs: standard and actual material costs

Materials: raw materials; part finished goods; materials issued from stores within the organisation; deliveries

6.2.1 Overhead costs: standard and actual indirect material costs

Knowledge and understanding

- Methods of stock control

- Relationships between the materials costing system and the stock control system

1   INTRODUCTION

1.1   In the last chapter you learned about the various cost elements that go to make up the total cost of a product or service. In this chapter you will be going on to learn about the first cost element in detail: **materials.**

1.2   You will learn about how material stocks are **valued,** and how to maintain an effective **stock control system.**

2   TYPES OF MATERIAL

Raw materials

KEY TERM

Raw materials are goods purchased for incorporation into products for sale.

2.1   **Raw materials** is a term which you are likely to come across often, both in your studies and your workplace. But what are raw materials?

2.2   Examples of raw materials are as follows.

- Clay for making terracotta garden pots.
- Timber for making dining room tables.
- Paper for making books.

Activity 2.1   **Level: Pre-assessment**

Without getting too technical, what are the main raw materials used in the manufacture of the following items?

(a)   A car
(b)   A box of breakfast cereal
(c)   A house (just the basic structure)
(d)   Your own organisation's products

Activity 2.2   Level: Pre-assessment

How would you distinguish direct materials from indirect materials?

Activity 2.3   Level: Pre-assessment

Classify the following as either direct or indirect materials.

(a)   The foil wrapping around Easter eggs
(b)   Paper used for the pages of a book
(c)   Lubricant used on sewing machines in a clothing factory
(d)   Plastic used to make audio cassette boxes
(e)   Shoe boxes

Work in progress

> **KEY TERM**
>
> **Work in progress** is a term used to represent an intermediate stage between the
> manufacturer purchasing the materials that go to make up the finished product
> and the finished product.

2.3   Work in progress is another term which you are likely to come across often, and
      valuing work in progress is one of **the most difficult tasks in costing.** Work in
      progress is another name for **part-finished goods**.

2.4   Work in progress means that some work has been done on the materials purchased
      as part of the process of producing the finished product, but **the production
      process is not complete.** Examples of work in progress are as follows.

      • Terracotta pots which have been shaped, but which have not yet been fired
      • Tables which have been assembled, but which have not yet been polished

2.5   Work in progress must be subjected to further processing before it becomes
      finished goods, which are completed and ready for sale.

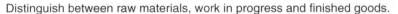

Activity 2.4   Level: Pre-assessment

Distinguish between raw materials, work in progress and finished goods.

3   BUYING MATERIALS

Purchasing procedures

3.1   All businesses have to buy materials of some sort, and this means that decisions
      have to be made and somebody has to be responsible for doing the **buying.** Large
      businesses have specialist **buying departments** managed by people who are very
      skilled at the job.

3.2   A buying transaction is not complicated. In fact, the process is familiar because
      most people buy things every week and go through the following process.

BPP
PUBLISHING

- You need something.

- You find out where you can buy it.

- If there is a choice you identify which item is most suitable, taking into account the cost and the quality, and from whom you will buy it.

- You order the item, or perhaps several if you will need more in the future.

- You receive the item.

- You pay for the item.

3.3 In a business this process will be more involved, but only because different people are responsible for each stage in the process. The following diagram illustrates who will be involved.

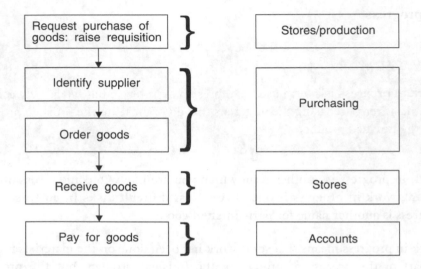

Purchasing documentation

3.4 Clearly there needs to be some means by which different departments can let each other know what they want and what is being done about it. Even the smallest business will need to keep records of some sort.

3.5 We shall describe a manual system that might be used in a fairly large organisation. In reality it is likely that much of the procedure would be computerised, but this does not alter the basic principles or information flows.

Purchase requisition

3.6 The first stage will be that the department requiring the goods will complete a **purchase requisition** asking the **purchasing department** to carry out the necessary transaction. An example is shown below.

PURCHASE REQUISITION Req. No.			
Department _____ Suggested Supplier:		Date Requested by: Latest date required:	
Quantity	Description	Estimated Cost	
		Unit	£
Authorised signature:			

3.7   Note that the purchase requisition will usually need some form of **authorisation**, probably that of a senior person in the department requiring the goods and possibly also that of a senior person in the finance department if substantial expense is involved.

Order form

3.8   Once a **purchase requisition** is received in the purchasing department, the first task is to identify the most suitable **supplier**. Often the business will use a regular source of supply. The purchasing department may be aware of special offers or have details of new suppliers: part of its job is to keep up to date with what is on the market.

3.9   An **order form** is then completed by the purchasing department and this is sent to the supplier. An order form is a legally binding document, therefore only authorised personnel should complete it.

3.10   The **purchase order** is important because it provides a means by which the business can later **check that the goods received are the same as those ordered.** Copies of the purchase order can be sent to the following people/departments.

- The person who requisitioned the goods
- The stores department
- The accounts department

3.11   A purchase order form will look like this. Take a bit of time to familiarise yourself with the details it contains.

Purchase Order/Confirmation				Fenchurch Garden Centre Pickle Lane Westbridge Kent	
Our Order Ref:		Date			
To					
⌐(Address)			⌐	Please deliver to the above address	
				Ordered by:	
				Passed and checked by:	
				Total Order Value £	
∟			∟		

Quantity	Code No	Description		Unit cost £	Total £
			Subtotal		
			VAT (@ 17.5%)		
			Total		

Despatch note

3.12 Certain other documents may arise before the goods are actually received. The supplier may acknowledge the order and perhaps indicate how long it is likely to take to be fulfilled. A **despatch note** may be sent to warn that the goods are on their way.

Delivery note

3.13 We now move to the stores department. When the goods are delivered, the goods inwards department will be presented with a **delivery note** or **advice note** (although bear in mind that smaller suppliers may not go to these lengths). This is the supplier's document and a copy is signed by the person receiving the goods and this copy is returned to the supplier. If the actual goods cannot be inspected immediately, the delivery note should be signed 'subject to inspection'.

Goods received note

3.14 Once the goods have been delivered they should be inspected and checked as soon as possible. A **goods received note (GRN)** will then be completed and a copy would be sent to the following departments.

(a) The **purchasing department**, so that it can be matched with the **purchase order**. If there are any discrepancies, these should be sorted out with the supplier.

(b) The **accounts department**, so that it can be matched with the **supplier's invoice**.

```
                                                    ACCOUNTS COPY
  ┌─────────────────────────────────────────────────────────┐
  │  GOODS RECEIVED NOTE  WAREHOUSE COPY                     │
  │  DATE: _7 March 20X1_ _ _  TIME: _ _2.00 pm_ _ _   NO 5565│
  │  ORDER NO: _ _ _ _ _ _ _ _ _ _ _ _ _ _ _ _ _ _ _.        │
  │  SUPPLIER'S ADVICE NOTE NO: _ _ _ _ _ _ _ _ _ _  WAREHOUSE A│
  ├────────────┬───────────┬──────────────────────────────────┤
  │  QUANTITY  │  CAT NO   │  DESCRIPTION                     │
  │            │           │                                  │
  │    20      │  TP 400   │  Terracotta pots, medium         │
  │            │           │                                  │
  ├────────────┴───────────┴──────────────────────────────────┤
  │ RECEIVED IN GOOD CONDITION:   L.W.          (INITIALS)    │
  └─────────────────────────────────────────────────────────┘
```

3.15 The transaction ends with payment of the invoice (once any discrepancies have been sorted out).

Activity 2.5 **Level: Pre-assessment**

Name four items that would be shown on a purchase order.

Helping hand. Thinking about the purpose of a purchase order will help you to reason through what details are required.

Activity 2.6 **Level: Pre-assessment**

Draw a flow diagram illustrating the main documents involved in a materials purchase, from its initiation up until the time of delivery.

---

4 VALUING MATERIALS ISSUES AND STOCKS

4.1 When a stock item is issued from the stores to be used, say, in production, the cost accountant will record the **value of stock to be charged to the relevant cost centre.** But how does the cost accountant work out the correct price to be charged? And how does the system record the **value of the remaining items in stock?**

4.2 EXAMPLE: STOCK VALUATION

(a) Suppose, for example, that you have 50 litres of a chemical in stock. You buy 2,000 litres to allow for the next batch of production. Both the opening stock and the newly-purchased stock cost £2 per litre.

	Litres	£
Opening stock	50	100
Purchases	2,000	4,000
	2,050	4,100

(b) You actually use 1,600 litres, leaving you with 450 litres in stock. You know that each of the 1,600 litres used cost £2, as did each of the 450 litres remaining. There is no costing problem here.

(c) Now suppose that in the following month you decide to buy another 1,300 litres, but have to pay £2.10 per litre because you lose a 10p discount if buying under 1,500 litres.

	Litres	Cost per litre £	Total cost £
Opening stock	450	2.00	900
Purchases	1,300	2.10	2,730
	1,750		3,630

(d) For the next batch of production you use 1,600 litres, as before. What did the 1,600 litres used cost, and what value should you give to the 150 litres remaining in stock?

4.3 SOLUTION

(a) If we could identify which litres were used there would be no problem. Some would cost £2 per litre but most would cost £2.10. It may not, however, be possible to identify litres used. For instance, the chemical may not be perishable, and new purchases may be simply mixed in with older stock in a central tank. There would thus be no way of knowing which delivery the 1,600 litres used belonged to. Even if the chemical were stored in tins with date stamps it would be a tedious and expensive chore to keep track of precisely which tins were used when.

(b) It may not therefore be possible or desirable to track the progress of each individual litre. However **we need to know the cost of the litres that we have used** so that we know how much to charge for the final product and so that we can compare this cost with the equivalent cost in earlier or future periods. We also **need to know the cost of closing stock** both because it will form part of the usage figure in the next period and for financial accounting purposes. Closing stock is often a significant figure in the financial statements and it appears in both the profit and loss account and the balance sheet.

(c) We therefore have to use a consistent method of pricing the litres which provides a reasonable approximation of the costs of the stock.

4.4 There are a number of different methods of valuing stock and the issues from stock.

(a) **FIFO - First in, first out**

This method values **issues at the prices of the oldest items in stock at the time the issues were made.** The remaining **stock will thus be valued at the price of the most recent purchases.** Say, for example ABC Ltd's stock consisted of four deliveries of raw material in the last month:

		Units		
1 September		1,000	at	£2.00
8 September		500	at	£2.50
15 September		500	at	£3.00
22 September		1,000	at	£3.50

If on 23 September 1,500 units were issued, 1,000 of these units would be priced at £2 (the cost of the 1,000 oldest units in stock), and 500 at £2.50 (the cost of the next oldest 500). 1,000 units of closing stock would be valued at £3.50 (the cost of the 1,000 most recent units received) and 500 units at £3.00 (the cost of the next most recent 500).

(b) **LIFO - Last in, first out**

This method is the opposite of FIFO. **Issues will be valued at the prices of the most recent purchases; hence stock remaining will be valued at the cost of the oldest items.** In the example in (a) it will be 1,000 units of **issues** which will be valued at £3.50, and the other 500 units issued will be valued at £3.00. 1,000 units of **closing stock** will be valued at £2.00, and 500 at £2.50.

(c) **Cumulative weighted average pricing**

With this method we calculate an **average cost of all the units in stock whenever a new delivery is received.** Thus the individual price of the units issued *and* of the units in closing stock will be (22 September being the date of the last delivery):

$$\frac{\text{Total cost of units in stock at 22 September}}{\text{Units in stock at 22 September}}$$

The average price per unit will be $\dfrac{£8,250}{3,000} = £2.75$.

(d) **Replacement cost**

This method values issues and stock **at the cost to the business of replacing that stock.** If replacement cost is used, managers can take recent cost trends into account when making decisions such as product pricing.

(e) **Standard cost**

Under the standard costing method, all issues are at a predetermined standard price. We shall look at standard costing in more detail in Chapter 9.

4.5 EXAMPLE: FIFO, LIFO AND CUMULATIVE WEIGHTED AVERAGE PRICING

Let's go back to the example in parts (c) and (d) of Paragraph 4.2.

(a) **FIFO**

	Litres	Cost £	£
Opening stock	450	2.00	900
Purchases	1,300	2.10	2,730
	1,750		3,630
Usage (oldest items first)	(450)	2.00	(900)
	1,300		2,730
Usage (1,600 – 450)	(1,150)	2.10	(2,415)
Closing stock	150		315

Total cost of usage is £900 + £2,415 = £3,315 and the value of closing stock is £315.

(b) **LIFO**

	Litres	Cost £	£
Opening stock	450	2.00	900
Purchases	1,300	2.10	2,730
	1,750		3,630
Usage (most recent items first)	(1,300)	2.10	(2,730)
	450		900
Usage (1,600 – 1,300)	(300)	2.00	(600)
	150		300

Total cost of usage is £2,730 + £600 = £3,330 and the value of closing stock is £300.

(c) **Cumulative weighted average pricing**

	Litres	Cost £	£
Opening stock	450	2.000	900
Purchases	1,300	2.100	2,730
Stock at (£3,630/1,750)	1,750	2.074	3,630
Usage (at average price)	(1,600)	2.074	(3,318)
	150		312

Usage costs £3,318 under this method and closing stock is valued at £312.

4.6 For FIFO, LIFO and cumulative weighted average pricing, note that the total of usage costs plus closing stock value is the same (£3,630) whichever method is used. In other words, **the total expenditure of £3,630 is simply split in different proportions between the usage cost for the period and the remaining stock value**. The total expense will eventually be charged as usage costs but, according to the method used, different amounts will be charged in different periods.

ASSESSMENT ALERT

Tasks in both the June and December 1999 Central Assessments included completing a stores ledger account using the **Last In First Out** (LIFO) method to cost issues and value stock of an item. In December 2001, there was a similar task that required students to calculate the FIFO value of stock.

Activity 2.7   **Level: Assessment**

The following transactions took place during May 20X1. You are required to calculate the value of all issues and of closing stock using each of the following methods of valuation.

(a) FIFO
(b) LIFO
(c) Cumulative weighted average pricing

TRANSACTIONS DURING MAY 20X1

	Quantity	*Unit cost*	*Total cost*
	Units	£	£
Opening balance, 1 May	100	2.00	200
Receipts, 3 May	400	2.10	840
Issues, 4 May	200		
Receipts, 9 May	300	2.12	636
Issues, 11 May	400		
Receipts, 18 May	100	2.40	240
Issues, 20 May	100		
Closing balance, 31 May	200		
			1,916

Which method is correct?

4.7 This is a trick question, because there is no single correct method. Each method has **advantages** and **disadvantages**.

4.8 **Advantages and disadvantages of the FIFO method**

Advantages	Disadvantages
It is a logical pricing method which probably represents what is physically happening: in practice the oldest stock is likely to be used first.	FIFO can be cumbersome to operate because of the need to identify each batch of material separately.
It is easy to understand and explain to managers.	Managers may find it difficult to compare costs and make decisions when they are charged with varying prices for the same materials.
The closing stock value can be near to a valuation based on the cost of replacing the stock.	

4.9 **Advantages and disadvantages of the LIFO method**

Advantages	Disadvantages
Stocks are issued at a price which is close to current market value. This is not the case with FIFO when there is a high rate of inflation.	The method can be cumbersome to operate because it sometimes results in several batches being only part-used in the stock records before another batch is received.
Managers are continually aware of recent costs when making decisions, because the costs being charged to their department or products will be current costs.	LIFO is often the opposite to what is physically happening and can therefore be difficult to explain to managers.
	As with FIFO, decision making can be difficult because of the variations in prices.

BPP PUBLISHING

4.10 Advantages and disadvantages of average pricing

Advantages	Disadvantages
Fluctuations in prices are smoothed out, making it easier to use the data for decision making.	The resulting issue price is rarely an actual price that has been paid, and can run to several decimal places.
It is easier to administer than FIFO and LIFO, because there is no need to identify each batch separately.	Prices tend to lag a little behind current market values when there is gradual inflation.

Activity 2.8   **Level: Assessment**

(a)   What is the main disadvantage of the FIFO method of stock valuation?

(b)   What is the main advantage of the LIFO method?

(c)   What is the main advantage and the main disadvantage of the cumulative weighted average method?

5   STOCK CONTROL

KEY TERM

Stock control is the regulation of stock levels, one aspect of which is putting a value to the amounts of stock issued and remaining. The stock control system can also be said to include ordering, purchasing and receiving goods and keeping track of them while they are in the warehouse.

Why hold stock?

5.1   The cost of purchasing stock is usually one of the largest costs faced by an organisation and, once obtained, stock has to be carefully controlled and checked.

5.2   Some organisations operate a **just-in-time (JIT)** stock system. With a JIT system, supplies are ordered and delivered just as they are needed for production, and goods are manufactured just as they are needed for sales. In this way **stocks are kept to a minimum,** but the system relies on **accurate forecasting** and **reliable suppliers.**

5.3   Most organisations keep a certain amount of stock in reserve to cope with **fluctuations in demand** and with possible **interruptions to** supply. This reserve of stock is known as **buffer stock.**

5.4 **The main reasons for holding stocks**

- To ensure sufficient goods are available to meet expected demand
- To provide a buffer between processes
- To meet any future shortages
- To take advantage of bulk purchasing discounts
- To absorb seasonal fluctuations and any variations in usage and demand
- To allow production processes to flow smoothly and efficiently
- As a necessary part of the production process (such as when maturing cheese)
- As a deliberate investment policy, especially in times of inflation or possible shortages

Holding costs

5.5 If stocks are too high, **holding costs** will be incurred unnecessarily. Such costs occur for a number of reasons.

(a) **Costs of storage and stores operations.** Larger stocks require more storage space and possibly extra staff and equipment to control and handle them.

(b) **Interest charges.** Holding stocks involves the tying up of capital (cash) on which interest must be paid.

(c) **Insurance costs.** The larger the value of stocks held, the greater the insurance premiums are likely to be.

(d) **Risk of obsolescence.** When materials or components become out-of-date and are no longer required, existing stocks must be thrown away and their cost written off to the profit and loss account.

(e) **Deterioration.** When materials in store deteriorate to the extent that they are unusable, they must be thrown away with the likelihood that disposal costs would be incurred. The value written off stock plus the disposal costs will be a charge to the profit and loss account.

(f) **Theft**.

Costs of obtaining stock

5.6 On the other hand, if stocks are kept low, small quantities of stock will have to be ordered more frequently. This increases the amount of **ordering costs.** The following costs are included in ordering costs.

(a) **Clerical and administrative costs** associated with purchasing, accounting for and receiving goods.

(b) **Transport costs**

(c) **Production run costs,** for stock which is manufactured internally rather than purchased from external sources.

Recording stock levels

5.7 One of the objectives of storekeeping is to **maintain accurate records of current stock levels.** This involves the recording of stock movements (issues from and receipts into stores). The most common system for recording stock movements is the use of **bin cards** and **stores record cards.**

5.8 A **bin card** shows the level of stock of an item at a particular stores location. It is kept with the actual stock and is updated by the storekeeper as stocks are received and issued. A typical bin card is shown below.

BIN CARD

Description .... Bin No: ....
Reorder Quantity .... Code No: ....
Maximum: ....
Minimum: ....
Re-order Level: ....

Receipts			Issues			Balance	Remarks
Date	G.R.N No.	Quantity	Date	Req. No.	Quantity	Quantity	

Note that the bin card does not need to show any information about the cost of materials.

5.9 Organisations will also maintain a **stores record card** for each stock item.

STORES RECORD CARD

Material: .... Maximum Quantity: ....
Code: .... Minimum Quantity: ....
Re-order Level: ....
Re-order Quantity: ....

Date	Receipts				Issues				Stock		
	G.R.N. No.	Quantity	Unit Price £	Amount £	Materials Req. No.	Quantity	Unit Price £	Amount £	Quantity	Unit Price £	Amount £

Details from **GRNs** and **materials requisition notes** (see later) are used to update **stores record cards,** which then provide a record of the quantity and value of each stock item in the stores. The stores record cards are normally kept in the cost department or in the stores office.

5.10 The use of bin cards and stores record cards provides a **control check.** The balances on the bin cards in the stores can be compared with the balances on the stores record cards in the office.

5.11 The use of bin cards and stores record cards ensures that every issue and receipt of stock is recorded as it occurs so that there is a continuous clerical record of the balance of each item of stock. This is known as a **perpetual inventory system.**

Coding of materials

5.12 Each item held in stores must be **unambiguously identified** and this can best be done by numbering them with stock codes. The advantages of this are as follows.

(a) **Ambiguity is avoided.** Different people may use different descriptions for materials. This is avoided if numbers are used.

(b) **Time is saved.** Descriptions can be lengthy and time-consuming, particularly when completing written forms.

(c) **Production efficiency is improved.** If the correct material can be accurately identified from a code number, production hold-ups caused by the issue of incorrect material can be avoided.

(d) **Computerised processing** is made easier.

(e) Numbered code systems can be designed to be **flexible**, and can be **expanded** to include more stock items as necessary.

5.13 The digits in a code can stand for the type of stock, supplier, location and so forth. For example stock item A234/1279 might refer to the item of stock kept in row A, bay 2, bin 3, shelf 4. The item might be identified by the digits 12 and its supplier might be identified by the digits 79.

ASSESSMENT ALERT

Candidates were asked to give two benefits to a company from coding materials in the June 1999 Central Assessment.

Issuing materials

5.14 The sole point of holding stocks is so that they can be used to make products. This means that they have to be issued from stores to production. This transaction will be initiated by production who will complete a **materials requisition note** and pass it to the warehouse.

BPP PUBLISHING

MATERIALS REQUISITION NOTE						
Material Required for: (Job or Overhead Account) Department:					No. Date:	
Quantity	Description	Code No.	Weight	Price	Value £	Notes
Supervisor signature:						

5.15 The stores department will locate the stock, withdraw the amount required and **update the bin card** as appropriate. The **stores record card** will also be updated.

5.16 The materials requisition note may also contain a space to show the **account code to be charged** with the cost of the materials issued.

(a) If the material is required for a specific job, the **job number** will be inserted to ensure that the correct job is charged with the cost of the materials.

(b) If the material is issued to a cost centre to be used as direct materials in producing a number of cost units, the **cost centre code** will be inserted, followed by the code for **direct materials.**

(c) If the material is to be used for indirect purposes, for example as maintenance or cleaning materials, the **cost centre code** will be inserted, followed by the code for **indirect materials.**

Activity 2.9   **Level: Assessment**

An extract from the accounts code list of A Limited is as follows.

Cost centre codes		*Expenditure codes*	
Machining cost centre	100	Direct materials	100
Finishing cost centre	200	Indirect materials	200
Packing cost centre	300		
Maintenance cost centre	400		

Insert the correct account codes for the following materials issues from stores.

	Cost centre code no.	Expenditure code no.
Issue of packing materials to production	....	....
Issue of raw materials to machining centre	....	....
Issue of lubricating oils to maintenance	....	....
Issue of cleaning materials to finishing centre	....	....

Helping hand. The expenditure code will be 100, ie direct materials, if the materials are to become part of the finished product. If the materials cannot be traced directly to the finished product they should be coded as indirect materials.

5.17 Remember that the cost of the material issues will be established using either the **FIFO, LIFO or average** pricing method, as described earlier.

5.18 If the amount of materials required is overestimated the excess should be put back into store accompanied by a **materials returned note**. The form in our illustration is almost identical to a requisition note. In practice it would be wise to colour code the two documents (one white, one yellow, say) to prevent confusion.

MATERIALS RETURNED NOTE						
Material not needed for: (Job or Overhead Account) Department:					No. Date:	
Quantity	Description	Code No.	Weight	Price	Value £	Notes
Supervisor signature:						

5.19 There may be occasions when materials already issued but not required for one job can be used for another job in progress. In this case there is no point in returning the materials to the warehouse. Instead a **materials transfer note** can be raised. This prevents one job being charged with too many materials and another with too little.

Stocktaking

5.20 Stocktaking involves **counting the physical stock on hand** at a certain date and then **checking this against the balance shown in the clerical records**. There are two methods of carrying out this process.

> **KEY TERMS**
>
> • **Periodic stocktaking.** This is usually carried out annually and the objective is to count all items of stock on a specific date.
>
> • **Continuous stocktaking.** This involves counting and checking a number of stock items on a regular basis so that each item is checked at least once a year, and valuable items can be checked more frequently. This has a number of advantages over periodic stocktaking. It is less disruptive, less prone to error, and achieves greater control.

Stock discrepancies

5.21 There will be occasions when stock checks disclose **discrepancies between the physical amount of an item in stock and the amount shown in the stock records**. When this occurs, the cause of the discrepancy should be investigated, and appropriate action taken to ensure that it does not happen again. Possible causes of discrepancies are as follows.

(a) **Suppliers deliver a different quantity of goods than is shown on the goods received note (GRN)**. Since this note is used to update stock records, a discrepancy will arise. This can be avoided by ensuring that all stock is counted as it is received, and a responsible person should sign the GRN to verify the quantity.

(b) **The quantity of stock issued to production is different from that shown on the materials requisition note**. Careful counting of all issues will prevent this.

(c) **Excess stock is returned from production without documentation**. This can be avoided by ensuring that all movements of stock are accurately documented - in this case, a **materials returned note** should be raised.

(d) **Clerical errors may occur in the stock records**. Regular checks by independent staff should detect and correct mistakes.

(e) **Breakages in stores may go unrecorded**. All breakages should be documented and noted on the stock records.

(f) **Stock may be stolen**. Regular checks or continuous stocktaking will help to minimise this, and only authorised personnel should be allowed into the stores.

Activity 2.10   **Level: Assessment**

Give five reasons why stocktaking may identify discrepancies between physical stock held and stock records.

6 COMPUTERS AND STOCK CONTROL

6.1 Although the basic principles of stock control are not difficult in themselves, you will appreciate by now that **an effective system requires a good deal of administrative effort,** even if only a few items of stock are involved. There is therefore a good deal to be gained from computerisation of this function.

6.2 A typical computerised stock system would contain a **stock file or record for each stock item,** recording similar information to that which is available from a manual stores record card.

6.3 A computerised stock control system is usually able to give **more up to date information** and **more flexible reporting** than a manual system. However you should remember that both manual and computer based stock control systems need the **same types of data** to function properly.

7 REORDERING STOCK

7.1 As noted earlier, the ideal is for businesses not to have any stocks on the premises **unless they are about to be used in production which can be sold immediately.** In practice many businesses would regard this approach as **too risky or impractical** because they are unable to predict either their own levels of demand or the reliability of their suppliers or both. They therefore set various **control levels**, the purpose of which is to ensure the following.

(a) The business **does not run out of stock** and **suffer disruption to production** as a result.

(b) The business **does not carry an excessive amount of stocks** which take up space, incur storage costs and possibly deteriorate with age.

7.2 To illustrate the problems involved in deciding when to reorder stock and how much to reorder, we shall consider an example.

7.3 EXAMPLE: STOCK CONTROL LEVELS

(a) A new manufacturing business is being set up to make a single product, by moulding plastic. Jonathan, the manager, expects to make 10 units per day and has found that each unit will require 5 kg of plastic. He decides to obtain enough materials to last a week (5 days). How much should he order?

(b) This is not difficult. Jonathan should order 5 days × 10 units × 5 kg = 250 kg.

The materials are placed in the stores ready for the commencement of production on the following Monday.

(c) The following week everything goes as planned. The following Monday however, Jonathan realises that he has no materials left. (This is called a **'stock-out'**). He contacts a number of suppliers but to his dismay none can deliver in less than 2 days. There is therefore no production for the whole of Monday and Tuesday.

(d) Jonathan doesn't want this to happen again so he orders four weeks' worth of materials, even though this means increasing his overdraft at the bank by £4,000.

(e) The materials duly arrive on Wednesday morning but of the 1,000 kg delivered (20 × 10 × 5 = 1,000) Jonathan finds he only has room to store 500 kg . To accommodate the remainder he has to rent space in the factory next door at a cost of £20.

(f) Twenty days go by and production goes as planned. Jonathan doesn't want to get caught out again, so two days before he is due to run out of materials he places a fresh order, this time for only 500 kg .

(g) Unfortunately, this time the suppliers are unable to deliver in 2 days as promised, but take 4 days. Another 2 days' production is lost.

(h) As Jonathan's product establishes itself in the market, demand starts to increase. He starts to produce 15 units a day but again he is caught out because, obviously, this means that the materials are used up more quickly. He often runs out before the next delivery has arrived.

(i) So it goes on for the whole of Jonathan's first year in business. By the end of this time he works out that he has lost nearly three weeks' production due to materials shortages. In despair he contacts a management consultant for advice.

7.4 SOLUTION

(a) Jonathan is told to calculate a number of figures from his records.

    (i)   The maximum daily usage

    (ii)   The maximum lead time. (**Lead time** is the time it takes between ordering stocks and having them delivered.)

    (iii)   The average daily usage and average lead time

    (iv)   The minimum daily usage and minimum lead time

    (v)   The cost of holding one unit of stock for one year (holding cost)

    (vi)   The cost of ordering a consignment of stock

    (vii)   The annual demand for materials

(b) Jonathan has kept careful records and can easily calculate some of these figures.

Maximum usage	100 kg per day
Average usage	75 kg per day
Minimum usage	50 kg per day
Annual demand	19,500 kg (52 weeks × 5 days × 75 kg)
Maximum lead time	4 days
Average lead time	3 days
Minimum lead time	2 days

(c) The calculation of the **holding cost** is quite complicated. Jonathan has to work out a number of figures.

    (i)   Materials can only be bought in 5 kg boxes and therefore 'one unit' of stock is 5 kg , not 1 kg .

    (ii)   The total cost of holding one box in stock is made up of a number of separate costs.

        •   Interest paid on the money borrowed to buy one box

        •   Rental of the floor space taken up by one box

        •   The warehouse keeper's wages

        •   Administrative costs of taking deliveries, issuing materials, and keeping track of them

        •   The cost of insuring the stock

Eventually Jonathan works out that the figure is £0.62 per 'unit' of 5 kg . He is shocked by this and wonders whether he should order smaller quantities more frequently. (Fortunately for Jonathan, there is little risk of obsolescence or deterioration of boxes. Many organisations have to include the cost of obsolescence or deterioration in holding costs, however.)

(d) To calculate the **ordering costs** Jonathan has to take into account:

    •   The cost of stationery and postage
    •   The cost of phoning round to suppliers
    •   The time taken up by doing this

He is surprised to find that the figure works out to £19.87 per order. He wonders whether he should make fewer larger orders to reduce these costs.

(e) Now that Jonathan has these figures the consultant tells him how to calculate four stock control levels. These will help him to avoid running out of stock and to keep down the costs of holding and ordering stock.

    (i)   **Reorder level**. Jonathan already realises that stocks have to be reordered before they run out completely. **This number tells him how low stocks can be allowed to fall before an order should be placed.** It assumes that maximum usage and maximum lead time, the two worst events from the point of view of stock control, coincide.

> **KEY TERM**
>
> **Reorder level** = maximum usage × maximum lead time

$$\text{Reorder level} = 100 \text{ kg} \times 4 \text{ days}$$
$$= 400 \text{ kg}$$

    (ii)   **Reorder quantity**

> **KEY TERM**
>
> The **reorder quantity** is the quantity of stock which is to be re-ordered when stock reaches the reorder level.

Jonathan has never known what the best amount to order would be. He is beginning to understand that there must be some way **of juggling the costs of holding stock, the costs of ordering stock and the amount of stock needed** but he does not know how to work it out. His consultant fortunately does and she gives him the following formula.

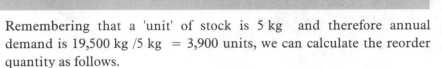

> **KEY TERM**
>
> The **economic order quantity (Q)**, or **EOQ** is the best amount to order and is calculated as follows.
>
> $$Q = \sqrt{\frac{2cd}{h}}$$
>
> where   h   is the cost of holding one unit of stock for one year
>   c   is the cost of ordering a consignment
>   d   is the annual demand
>   Q   is the 'economic order quantity' (EOQ), that is, the best amount to order

Remembering that a 'unit' of stock is 5 kg and therefore annual demand is 19,500 kg /5 kg = 3,900 units, we can calculate the reorder quantity as follows.

$$Q = \sqrt{\frac{2 \times 19.87 \times 3,900}{0.62}}$$

$$= 500 \text{ units (approximately)}$$
$$= 2,500 \text{ kg}$$

(f)   Jonathan is not entirely convinced by the EOQ calculation but promises to try it out since it seems like a reasonable amount to order. He then asks what the other two control levels are, since he seems to have all the information he needs already.

(g)   The consultant points out that the calculations done so far don't allow for other **uncertain factors** like a severe shortage of supply or unexpected rises or falls in demand.

(h)   As a precaution Jonathan needs a **minimum stock level** below which stocks should never be allowed to fall, and a **maximum stock level** above which stock should not be able to rise. There is a **risk of stock-outs** if stock falls below the minimum level and a **risk of stock being at a wasteful level** if above the maximum level.

> ### KEY TERM
>
> **Minimum stock level**   = reorder level – (average usage × average lead time)

Minimum stock level   =   400 kg – (75 kg × 3 days)
                                    =   175 kg

> ### KEY TERM
>
> **Maximum stock level**   = reorder level + reorder quantity –
>   (minimum usage × minimum lead time)

Maximum stock level   =   400 kg + 2,500 kg – (50 kg × 2 days)
                                     =   2,800 kg

(i)   The maximum stock level and minimum stock level act as **management warnings levels**. If stock regularly reaches either of these levels, Jonathan will need to **review his reorder level and reorder quantity**. It may be that the usage and delivery patterns are now different from those that were used to determine the various control levels.

7.5   The story has a happy ending. Jonathan finds that the EOQ and control levels work very well in practice. His costs are reduced and he suffers no stock-outs in the following year.

Buffer stock

7.6   Jonathan is delighted that his stock is now well controlled, but to be on the safe side, he decides to hold a **buffer stock** in future. The buffer stock is to be equal to two days' average usage.

Buffer stock = 2 × 75 kg = 150 kg

This buffer stock will remain as a **permanent 'buffer'** against unexpected circumstances.

7.7   This permanent buffer stock means that Jonathan will need to reorder at a higher stock level, to ensure that the buffer stock always remains untouched. The new formula for the reorder level, **when a buffer stock exists**, will be

Reorder level = Buffer stock + (maximum usage × maximum lead time)

= 150 kg + (100 kg × 4 days)

= 550 kg

ASSESSMENT ALERT

In the December 2000 Central Assessment the assessor used this formula to calculate the reorder level. It can be viewed as a **more cautious approach** to the calculation of the reorder level, ensuring that the buffer stock level is never reached.

Activity 2.11   Level: Assessment

Watkins Ltd uses 4,000 kg of a raw material in a year. It costs £10 to hold 1 kg for one year, and the costs of ordering each consignment of raw materials are £200.

Watkins Ltd uses between 100 kg and 600 kg a month, and the company's suppliers can take between 1 and 3 months to deliver materials that have been ordered.

Task

Calculate the following.

(a) The reorder quantity
(b) The reorder level
(c) The maximum level of stock the company should hold

Activity 2.12   Level: Assessment

You are given the following information about material Zenith which is used by Zeta Beta Ltd in the production of a number of their products.

(a) The maximum usage in any one week is 600 kilos and the minimum 400 kgs.

(b) On average the orders take anything from one to three weeks to be delivered.

(c) The cost accountant has calculated the optimum order quantity to be 1,732 kgs.

Task

Calculate the following.

(a) The reorder level for material Zenith
(b) The minimum level of stock that should be held
(c) The maximum level of stock that should be held

Activity 2.13   Level: Assessment

Complete the following stores record card to show the quantity and value of stock on 12 November.

Comment on any occasions when company stock control practices were not correctly observed.

BPP PUBLISHING

Part A: Materials, labour and expenses

STORES RECORD CARD

Material: A4 paper, white ....   Maximum Quantity: 140 boxes ....
Code: .....PWA4..............................   Minimum Quantity: 40 boxes ....
                                                Re-order Level: ....60 boxes ....
                                                Re-order Quantity: ....80 boxes ....

Date	Receipts				Issues				Stock balance		
	Document number	Qty	Price £ per box	Total £	Document number	Qty	Price £ per box	Total £	Qty	Price £ per box	Total £
1/11									60	2.30	138.00
									20	2.32	46.40
									80		184.40
3/11					389	30	2.30	69.00	30	2.30	69.00
									20	2.32	46.40
									50		115.40
5/11	123	100	2.33								
8/11					397	40					
9/11					401	30					
12/11	137	80	2.35								

Key learning points

- **Raw materials** are goods purchased **for incorporation into products for sale.**

- **Work in progress** represents an **intermediate stage** between the manufacturer purchasing the materials that go to make up the finished product, and the finished product. It is another name for **part-finished goods.**

- A **finished good** is a product **ready for sale** or despatch.

- **FIFO (first in, first out)** prices materials issues at the prices of the **oldest items in stock,** and values closing stock at the value of the **most recent purchases.**

- **LIFO (last in, last out)** prices materials issues at the prices of the **most recent purchases,** and values closing stock at the value of the **oldest items.**

- **Cumulative weighted average pricing** calculates an average cost of all stock items **whenever a new delivery is received.** The price for materials issues and for closing stock will be the same.

- Under the **standard costing method** all issues are at a predetermined standard price.

- **Stock control** is the regulation of stock levels, which includes **putting a value** to the amounts of stock issued and remaining. Stock control also includes **ordering, purchasing, receiving and storing goods.**

- Materials held in stock are generally **coded** in order that each item is clearly identified.

- **Periodic stocktaking** is usually carried out **annually,** when all items of stock are counted on a specific date.

- **Continuous stocktaking** involves counting and checking a number of stock items **on a regular basis** so that each item is checked at least once a year.

- **Stock control levels** can be calculated in order to maintain stocks at the optimum level. The four critical control levels are **reorder level, reorder quantity, minimum stock level** and **maximum stock level.**

- The **economic order quantity** is the ordering quantity which minimises stock costs (holding costs and ordering costs).

Quick quiz

1   What are raw materials?

2   What is work in progress?

3   Generally, are items which are ready for sale or despatch known as work in progress?

4   List the five documents which you are likely to use when buying materials.

5   The goods received note is matched with two other documents in the buying process. What are they?

6   How would you calculate the cost of a unit of material using cumulative weighted average pricing?

7   What are the advantages of FIFO?

8   Which purchasing documents are used to update the stores record card?

9   What does stocktaking involve?

10 What are the two methods of stocktaking that are commonly used?

11 What are the main reasons for setting control levels with regard to stock?

12 What is the formula for the economic order quantity?

13 How would you calculate the minimum and maximum stock levels?

Answers to quick quiz

1   Goods purchased for incorporation into products for sale.

2   An intermediate stage between the purchase of raw materials and the completion of the finished product.

3   No. Finished goods.

4   • Purchase requisition form
    • Order form
    • Despatch note
    • Delivery note
    • Goods received note (GRN)

5   The purchase order and the invoice.

6   $$\frac{\text{Total cost of units in stock}}{\text{Number of units in stock}}$$

7   • It is a logical pricing method
    • It is easy to understand
    • The closing stock can be near to a valuation based on the cost of replacing the stock

8   Goods received notes, materials requisition notes and materials returned notes.

9   Counting physical stock at a certain date, and checking this against the stock records.

10 Periodic stocktaking and continuous stocktaking.

11 To ensure that stock does not run out, and to ensure that stock levels are not too high.

12 $Q = \sqrt{\dfrac{2cd}{h}}$

13 Minimum stock level = reorder level – (average usage × average lead time)

    Maximum stock level = reorder level + reorder quantity – (minimum usage × minimum lead time)

3 Labour costs

This chapter contains

1   Introduction
2   Determining labour costs
3   Recording labour costs
4   Overtime, bonuses and absences
5   Labour turnover
6   Analysis of labour efficiency and utilisation rates

Learning objectives

On completion of this chapter you will be able to:

- Identify and calculate direct labour costs in accordance with organisational policies and procedures

- Establish indirect labour costs in accordance with organisational procedures

- Ensure that data and information relating to direct labour costs and indirect labour costs is clearly and correctly coded, analysed and recorded

- Deal with queries about direct and indirect labour

Performance criteria

6.1   (i)   Direct costs are identified in accordance with the organisation's costing procedures

6.1   (ii)   Information relating to direct costs is clearly and correctly coded, analysed and recorded

6.1   (iii)   Direct costs are calculated in accordance with the organisation's policies and procedures

6.1   (vi)   Queries are either resolved or referred to the appropriate person

6.2   (i)   Data are correctly coded, analysed and recorded

6.2   (ii)   Overhead costs are established in accordance with the organisation's procedures

6.2   (iii)   Information relating to overhead costs is accurately and clearly recorded

6.2   (viii)   Staff working in operational departments are consulted to resolve any queries in the data

Range statement

6.1.1 Direct costs: standard and actual labour costs

Labour: employees of the organisation on the payroll; sub-contractors; agency staff

6.2.1 Overhead costs: standard and actual indirect labour costs

Knowledge and understanding

- Methods of payment for labour: salaried labour; performance related pay; profit related pay

- Analysis of labour rate and efficiency: idle time; overtime levels; absenteeism; sickness rates

- Control ratios of efficiency, capacity and activity

- Relationships between the labour costing system and the payroll accounting system

1 INTRODUCTION

1.1 In this chapter you will be learning more about the second cost element we discussed in Chapter 1: labour.

1.2 You will be looking at a variety of aspects of **direct labour** and **indirect labour:** how labour costs are **calculated, analysed and recorded;** the various **methods of payment** for labour, and monitoring the **efficiency and productivity** of labour.

2 DETERMINING LABOUR COSTS

What are labour costs?

2.1 Labour costs include any or all of the following items.

- The gross amount of salary or wages due to an employee
- Employer's national insurance
- Amounts paid to recruit labour
- Amounts paid for staff welfare
- Training costs
- The costs of benefits like company cars

The list could be extended, but we shall not go any further because in this chapter we will be concentrating on the first item, the employee's gross salary.

2.2 The word **labour** is generally associated with strenuous physical effort but in the context of cost accounting it is not confined to manual work. **Labour costs** are the amounts paid to any employee, including supervisors, office staff, and tea ladies.

Determining labour costs

2.3 There are three ways in which labour costs can be determined.
- According to some prior agreement
- According to the amount of time worked
- According to the amount and/or quality of work done

2.4 Payment for most jobs is by a combination of the first two methods. There will be the following.

- A **basic wage** or **salary** which is agreed when the appointment is made.

- A **set number of hours per week** during which the employee is expected to be available for work.

- **Extra payments** for time worked over and above the set hours.

- **Deductions** for time when the employee is not available, beyond an agreed limit.

2.5 There may be periods when an organisation might wish to increase its activity, even though it does not have adequate resources to do so. In such situations, an organisation might wish to do the following.

- Use **sub-contractors** to carry out any additional work
- Hire **agency staff** for a fixed period

3 RECORDING LABOUR COSTS

3.1 You can see from the previous section that records of labour costs fall into three categories.

- Records of agreed basic wages and salaries
- Records of time spent working
- Records of work done

3.2 There are a number of ways in which this can be organised, but basically the information flow will be as follows.

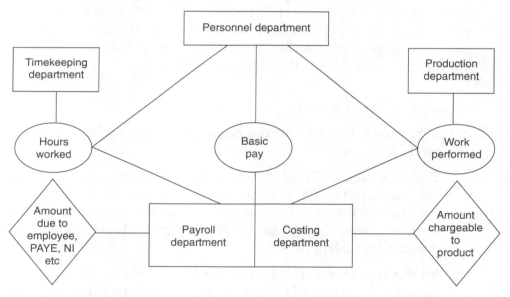

3.3 In practice, timekeeping would probably be a sub-function of production or of personnel. Alternatively, personnel may keep records of hours spent on the premises and available for work, while the production department keeps records of time spent doing different tasks. The totals of the two time records would be reconciled, so that all employee hours spent on the premises can be accounted for.

3.4 The actual time recording mechanisms in use will depend on:

- The nature of operations, eg a job costing environment or a continuous flow environment

- The bases selected for paying employees eg time based or output based

Time records and performance records

Attendance time

3.5 The bare minimum record of employees' time is a **simple attendance record** showing days absent because of holiday, sickness or other reason. Such a system is usually used when it is assumed that all of the employees' time is taken up doing one job and no further analysis is required.

3.6 The next step up is to have some **record of time of arrival, time of breaks and time of departure**. The simplest form is a **'signing-in' book** at the entrance to the building with, say, a page for each employee. Many employers use a **time recording clock** which stamps the time on a **clock card** inserted by the employee.

3.7 More modern systems involve the use of a plastic card like a credit card which is 'swiped' through a device which makes a **computer record** of the time of arrival and departure.

3.8 The next step is to analyse the hours spent at work according to what was done during those hours.

Detailed analysis of time: continuous production

3.9 Where **routine, repetitive work** is carried out it might not be practical to record the precise details. For example if a worker stands at a conveyor belt for seven hours his work can be measured by keeping a note of the number of units that pass through his part of the process during that time. If a group of employees all contribute to the same process, the total units processed per day (or week or whatever) can be divided by the number of employees.

Detailed analysis of time: job costing

3.10 When the work is not of a repetitive nature the records required might be one or more of the following.

(a) **Daily time sheets**. These are filled in by the employee to indicate the **time spent on each job**. The total time on the time sheet should correspond with the total time shown on the attendance record. **Times are recorded daily** and so there is less risk that they will be forgotten. This system does produce considerable paperwork.

(b) **Weekly time sheets**. These are similar to daily time sheets but are passed to the cost office at the end of the week. **Paperwork is reduced** and weekly time sheets are particularly suitable where there are few job changes in a week.

(c) **Job cards**. Cards are prepared for each job (or operation forming part of a complete job) unlike time sheets which are made out for each employee. When an employee works on a job he or she records on the job card the time spent on that job. Job cards may also carry instructions to the operator on how the job is to be carried out. Such records **reduce the amount of writing to be done by the employee and therefore the possibility of error.**

(d) **Route cards**. These are similar to job cards, except that they follow the product through the works and carry details of all operations to be carried out. They thus carry the cost of all operations involved in a job and are very useful for control purposes.

3.11 It is important to note the following.

- **Wages** are calculated on the basis of the hours noted on the **attendance card.**
- **Production costs** are obtained from the **time sheets/job cards/route cards.**

3.12 Time sheets and job or route cards can take many different forms, some of which involve computerised systems of time-recording. The following examples may help to indicate the basic principles of recording labour costs of production work.

Time Sheet No.							
Employee Name............... Clock Code............... Dept							
Date .... Week No.							
Job No.	Start Time	Finish Time	Qty	Checker	Hrs	Rate	Extension

JOB CARD			
Department _ _ _ _ _ _ _ _ _ _ _ _ _ _ _ _ _.		Job no _.	
Date _ _ _ _ _ _ _ _ _ _ _ _ _ _ _ _ _ _		Operation no _	
Time allowance _ _ _ _ _ _ _ _ _ _ _ _ _ _		Time started _.	
		Time finished _	
		Hours on job _ _ _ _ _ _ _ _ _ _ _ _ _ _ _ _ _ _ _.	
Description of job	Hours	Rate	Cost
Employee no _ _ _ _ _ _ _ _ _ _ _ _ _ _ _ _		Certified by _	
Signature _ _ _ _ _ _ _ _ _ _ _ _ _ _ _ _ _ _ _			

3.13 The **time sheet** will be filled in by the employee, for **hours worked** on each job (job code) or **area of work** (cost code). The cost of the hours worked will be entered at a later stage in the costing department.

3.14 A **job card** will be given to the employee, showing the work to be done and the expected time it should take. The employee will record the time started and time finished for each job. Breaks for tea and lunch may be noted on the card, as standard times. The hours actually taken and the cost of those hours will be calculated by the costing department.

Salaried labour

3.15 You might think there is little point in salaried staff filling in a detailed timesheet about what they do every hour of the day, as their basic pay is a flat rate every month. In fact, in many enterprises they are required to do so. There are a number of reasons for this.

(a) Such timesheets aid the creation of **management information** about product costs, and hence **profitability**.

(b) The timesheet information may have a direct impact on the **revenue the enterprise receives.** For example a consultancy firm might charge their employees' time to clients. This means that if an employee spends an hour with a particular client, the client will be invoiced for one hour of the employees' time.

(c) Timesheets are used to record hours spent and so **support salaried staffs' claims for overtime payments.**

3.16 Below is shown the type of time sheet which can be found in large service organisations, for example firms of solicitors and management consultants.

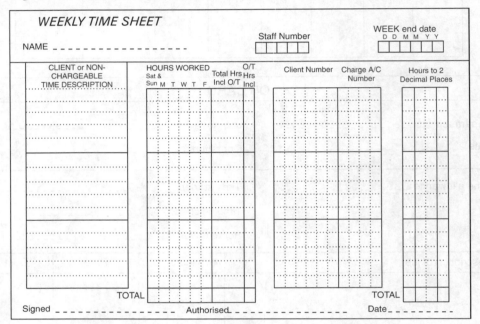

___

Activity 3.1   Level: Assessment

Below is shown Peter's payslip for April 20X1. Peter spent the whole of April working on Job 472 without assistance. What is the direct labour cost of Job 472?

Employee: TORK, P Staff No: 017 NI No: NA 123456C Tax Code: 344L Pay By: Cheque	Employer: SLEEPY JEANS LTD Date: 30/4/X1 Tax Period: 1		
DESCRIPTION		AMOUNT	THIS YEAR
BASIC BONUS		1,327.42 145.83	
TOTAL PAY >>>		1,473.25	1,473.25
OTHER DEDUCTIONS INCOME TAX NATIONAL INSURANCE		282.41 93.44	282.41 93.44
NET PAY >>>		1,097.40	
OTHER ITEMS ADD EXPENSES REIMBURSED		301.28	
(HOL PAY ACCRUED 0.00) TOTAL NET PAY >>>		1,398.68	

Idle time

3.17 There may be times when, through no fault of their own, employees cannot get on with their work. A machine may break down or there may simply be a temporary shortage of work.

3.18 **Idle time** has a cost because employees will still be paid their basic wage or salary for these unproductive hours. Therefore there must be a record of idle time. This may simply comprise an entry on time sheets coded to 'idle time' generally. Alternatively a supervisor might enter the following details on separate **idle time record cards.**

- The time and duration of a stoppage
- The cause of the stoppage
- The employees made idle.

Each stoppage should have a separate reference number which can be entered on time sheets or job cards as appropriate.

Measurement by output

3.19 (a) **Piecework** is a method of labour payment where workers are paid according to the amount of production completed.

(b) The labour cost of work done by pieceworkers is determined from what is known as a **piecework ticket** or an **operation card**. The card records the total number of items (or **pieces**) produced and the number of rejects. Payment is only made for 'good' production.

OPERATION CARD

Operator's Name ....   Total Batch Quantity ....

Clock No ....   Start Time ....

Pay week No .... Date ....   Stop Time ....

Part No ....   Works Order No ....

Operation ....   Special Instructions ....

Quantity Produced	No Rejected	Good Production	Rate	£

Inspector ....   Operative ....

Supervisor ....   Date ....

PRODUCTION CANNOT BE CLAIMED WITHOUT A PROPERLY SIGNED CARD

(c) A **disadvantage of the piecework method** is that workers may be so concerned with the volume of output that they produce, that the **quality** of the goods might suffer.

Activity 3.2   Level: Assessment

(a) Walter Wally is chief foreman in a medium-sized factory which is working on about thirty different jobs at any one time. He spends most of his day on his feet, dealing with personnel and technical problems as and when they arise.

 How might Walter's time be analysed?

(b) Peter Pratt is a bank clerk.

 How might Peter's time be analysed?

Activity 3.3   Level: Pre-assessment

Does the payroll department tell the costing department what the monthly labour costs should be or vice versa?

Coding of job costs

3.20 By now you will appreciate that to analyse labour costs effectively it is necessary to be able to link up different pieces of information in various ways. To facilitate analysis organisations therefore develop a series of codes for each of the following.

- **Employee number** and perhaps a team number

- **Pay rate**, for example 'A' for £6 per hour, 'B' for £7 per hour and so on

- **Department** and/or **location**

- **Job** or **batch type**, for example different codes for bodywork and mechanical repairs in a garage

- **Job** or **batch number**

- **Client number**

Activity 3.4   Level: Assessment

Below are shown some extracts from the files of Penny Lane Ltd. You are required to calculate the labour cost of jobs 249 and 250.

Personnel files

	George	Paul	Ringo	John
Grade	A	B	C	D

Payroll - Master file

Grade	Basic rate per hour
A	£8.20
B	£7.40
C	£6.50
D	£5.30

Production report - labour

Job	Employee	Hours
249	George	14
249	Paul	49
250	George	2
250	John	107
250	Ringo	74

Activity 3.5   Level: Assessment

The labour force of Limpsfield Ltd is divided into a team of six processing workers and four finishing workers. During a particular week 10,000 units were finished and 12,000 were processed. Processors work a 40 hour week, but finishers only work 35 hours. Their rates of pay are as follows.

	£ per hour
Processors	6.40
Finishers	9.00

Tasks

Calculate how many units each team processes or finishes per hour, how long each team takes to process one unit and the labour cost of one unit for each team. You should present the information in a form that would be generally understood and appreciated.

---

4 OVERTIME, BONUSES AND ABSENCES

4.1 This section is concerned with two things.

- What happens when more or less work is done than the basic amount agreed.
- The consequences of employees not coming to work.

Overtime

4.2 Before considering overtime payments, let us consider one of the most common forms of **time work**, namely a **day-rate system**, in which wages are calculated by the following formula.

Wages = Hours worked × rate of pay per hour

4.3 **Important points to note about day-rate systems**

(a) They are easy to understand.

(b) They do not lead to very complex negotiations when they are being revised.

(c) They are most appropriate when the quality of output is more important than the quantity, or where there is no basis for payment by performance.

(d) There is no incentive for employees who are paid on a day-rate basis to improve their performance.

4.4 If an employee works for more hours than the basic daily requirement many organisations pay an extra amount, known as an **overtime payment.**

4.5 The overtime payment may simply be at the **basic rate**. If an employee earns £6 an hour he will get an extra £6 for every hour worked in addition to the basic hours.

4.6 Usually, however, overtime is paid at a **premium rate**. You will hear expressions like 'time and a third', ' time and a half' and so on. This means that the hourly rate for overtime hours is $(1 + \frac{1}{3}) \times$ basic rate or $(1 + \frac{1}{2}) \times$ basic rate.

4.7 **EXAMPLE: OVERTIME PREMIUM**

Pootings Ltd pays overtime at time and a quarter. Jo's basic hours are 9 to 5 with an hour for lunch, but one particular Friday she worked until six o'clock. She is paid a basic wage of £6 per hour. How much did she earn on the Friday in question, and how much of this is overtime premium?

4.8 For costing purposes, the overtime premium must always be **identified separately** from the basic pay for the hours worked. Therefore the calculation is best presented as follows.

	£
Basic pay (8 × £6)	48.00
Overtime premium (¼ × £6)	1.50
	49.50

4.9 The **overtime premium** is thus £1.50. This is an important point because overtime premium is usually treated as an **indirect cost**. This is quite reasonable if you think about it. If you and your colleague use identical calculators it is reasonable to suppose that they cost the same amount to produce. It might be that one was assembled at 10 o'clock in the morning and the other at 10 o'clock at night but this doesn't make the calculators different from each other. They should therefore have the same cost and so **most organisations treat overtime premium as an indirect cost or overhead** and do not allocate it to the products manufactured outside basic hours.

4.10 There are two exceptions to this rule.

(a) If overtime is worked at the specific request of a customer to get his order completed, the premium is a **direct cost of the order.**

(b) If overtime is worked regularly by a production department in the normal course of operations, the overtime paid to direct workers could be incorporated into an **average direct labour hourly rate** (though it does not need to be).

Activity 3.6   Level: Assessment

What information would you need in order to be able to code the overtime premium paid during a period?

ASSESSMENT ALERT

If you have trouble remembering how to deal with overtime premiums, think how you would feel if you had to pay more for your new car radio than all of the others in the shop, simply because it was made after 5.30 pm.

Incentives and bonuses

4.11 **Overtime premiums** are paid to encourage staff to work longer hours than normal or to reward them for doing so. **Incentives and bonuses** are paid to encourage staff to work harder whatever the time of day.

4.12 Incentive schemes include the following.

- Piecework
- Time-saved bonus
- Group bonus scheme
- Profit-sharing scheme

Piecework

4.13 **Pieceworking** can be seen as an incentive scheme since the more output you produce the more you are paid. If you are paid 5p per unit produced and you want to earn £300 gross a week you know you have to produce 6,000 units that week.

4.14 The system can be further refined by paying a different rate for different levels of production (**differential piecework**). For example the employer could pay 3p per unit for output of up to 3,500 a week, 5p per unit for every unit over 3,500.

4.15 In practice, persons working on such schemes normally receive a **guaranteed minimum wage** because they may not be able to work due to problems outside their control.

4.16 EXAMPLE: PIECEWORK

An employee is paid £5 per piecework hour produced. In a 35 hour week he produces the following output.

	Piecework time allowed per unit
3 units of product A	2.5 hours
5 units of product B	8.0 hours

Task

Calculate the employee's pay for the week.

4.17 SOLUTION

Piecework hours produced are calculated as follows.

Product A	3 × 2.5 hours	7.5 hours
Product B	5 × 8 hours	40.0 hours
Total piecework hours		47.5 hours

Therefore employee's pay = 47.5 × £5 = £237.50 for the week.

Activity 3.7 **Level: Assessment**

Using the information on piecework rates, complete the operation card shown below and calculate Mr Shah's gross wages for pay week number 17.

Piecework rates
Up to 100 units a day	20p per unit on all units produced
101 to 120 units a day	30p per unit on all units produced
121 to 140 units a day	40p per unit on all units produced
Over 140 units a day	50p per unit on all units produced

OPERATION CARD

Operator's Name ... Shah, L .... Total Batch Quantity ... - ....

Clock No ...... 7142 .... Start Time ... - ....

Pay week No .... 17 .... Date W/E XX/XX/XX Stop Time ...... - ....

Part No .... 713/V .... Works Order No .... 14 A.B ....

Operation .... Drilling .... Special Instructions ..... - ....

Quantity Produced	No Rejected	Good Production	Rate	£
Monday 173	14			
Tuesday 131	2			
Wednesday 92	-			
Thursday 120	7			
Friday 145	5			

Inspector .... ND ...... Operative .... LS ....

Supervisor .... AN .... Date .... XX/XX/XX ....

PRODUCTION CANNOT BE CLAIMED WITHOUT A PROPERLY SIGNED CARD

Time-saved bonus

4.18 Suppose that a garage has calculated that it takes an average of 45 minutes for an engineer to perform an MOT test, but the job could be done competently in 30 minutes. It could encourage its engineers to do such work at the faster rate by paying **a bonus for every minute saved** on the job up to a maximum of 15 minutes.

4.19 There are problems with this approach.

• It may be difficult to establish a standard time for all types of work

- An engineer may be tempted to rush the job and not do it properly.

Activity 3.8   **Level: Assessment**

Chris Steele is paid an hourly rate of £8 per hour. She is paid a bonus of 40% of any time saved against a standard allowance for work done. Last week she worked 35 hours and completed 90 units. The standard time allowed for one unit is 30 minutes.

What were Chris's gross wages for last week?

Group bonus schemes

4.20 Sometimes it is not possible to measure individual effort because overall performance is not within any one person's control, for example a team of railway workers. In such cases, however, it is possible to measure overall performance of the team and **a bonus can therefore be paid to all those who contributed.**

Profit-sharing schemes

4.21 In a **profit-sharing scheme** employees receive **a certain proportion of their company's year-end profits.** The size of their bonus might also be related to level of responsibility and length of service.

Activity 3.9   **Level: Pre-assessment**

List five ways in which a company might reward extra effort by its employees.

Absence from work

4.22 An employee may be absent from work for a variety of reasons, the most common are as follows.

- Holidays
- Sickness
- Maternity leave
- Training

4.23 The costs relating to absence through sickness, maternity and training are usually **treated as an overhead or indirect labour cost** rather than a direct cost of production.

4.24 Although some organisations treat holiday pay as an overhead, the normal treatment is to regard it as a direct cost by charging an **inflated hourly rate.**

(a) Suppose an employee is normally paid £8 an hour for a 35 hour week and is entitled to four weeks' annual holiday. He will therefore receive £1,120 (£8 × 35 × 4) holiday pay.

(b) Assuming that the employee works the remaining 48 weeks, his attendance time will total 1,680 (48 × 35) hours.

(c) Dividing £1,120 by 1,680 hours gives an addition of approximately 67p per hour to the employee's hourly rate to ensure that holiday pay is recovered.

4.25 Time absent because of holidays is paid at the normal basic rate, as is absence on training courses as a rule. There are statutory minimum levels for maternity pay and sickness pay, but above these employers can be as generous (or otherwise) as they wish.

Activity 3.10   Level: Assessment

J. Wain's latest time sheet is shown below. You are required to use the following information to complete the time sheet and the accounts code boxes.

- J Wain is paid an hourly rate of £11 per hour.
- The first two digits of the code represent the cost centre to be charged.

  10   Finishing cost centre
  20   Packing cost centre
  30   Administration department
  40   Personnel department

- The last three digits of the code represent the expenditure code to be charged.

  100   Direct wages
  200   Indirect wages

- Administration, training and holiday time are classified as indirect time.
- Time spent on training courses is charged to the personnel department.
- Holiday pay is charged to the administration department.

WEEKLY TIME SHEET

Name .... J. Wain ....   Staff number 1 7 2 5 4   Week ending 0 9 1 2 0 1

	M	T	W	T	F	TOTAL Hours	TOTAL £	CODE
Direct time								
Finishing	5	4		1	3			
Packing				6	3			
Direct total	5	4		7	6			
Administration								
Budget meeting	2				1			
Total admin	2				1			
Training and courses								
First Aid course			3					
Total training			3					
Holidays, sickness								
Holiday			7					
Total leave			7					
TOTAL	7	7	7	7	7	35		

Signed .... RS ....   Authorised .... LW ....

Activity 3.11   Level: Pre-assessment

(a)   What is differential piecework?
(b)   Why might a company operate a group bonus scheme?

5   LABOUR TURNOVER

5.1   Labour turnover is a measure of the rate at which employees are leaving an organisation and are replaced.

The reasons for labour turnover

5.2   There are many reasons why employees will leave their job. It may be because they wish to go to work for another organisation. Alternatively it may be for one of the following unavoidable reasons.

- Illness or accidents
- A family move away from the locality
- Marriage, pregnancy or difficulties with child care provision
- Retirement or death

5.3   Other causes of labour turnover are as follows.

- Paying a lower wage rate than is available elsewhere
- Requiring employees to work unsociable hours in stressful conditions
- Poor relationships between management and staff
- Lack of opportunity for career enhancement
- Requiring employees to work in inaccessible places (eg no public transport)
- Discharging employees for misconduct, bad timekeeping or unsuitability

Measuring labour turnover

> **KEY TERMS**
>
> - **Labour turnover** is a measure of the number of employees leaving/being recruited in a period of time (say one year) expressed as a percentage of the total labour force.
>
> - **Labour turnover rate** $= \dfrac{\text{Replacements}}{\text{Average number of employees in period}} \times 100\%$

5.4   **EXAMPLE: LABOUR TURNOVER**

Florence plc had a staff numbering 800 at the beginning of 20X1 and 1,200 at the end of that year. Four hundred employees resigned on 30 June, and were immediately replaced by 400 new employees on 1 July. 400 extra employees were also recruited at that time.

What is the labour turnover rate?

$$\text{Rate} = \frac{400}{(800+1,200) \div 2} \times 100\% = 40\%$$

ASSESSMENT ALERT

One of the tasks in the June 1999 Central Assessment required candidates to give a ratio that would express labour turnover.

BPP PUBLISHING

The costs of labour turnover

5.5 The costs of labour turnover can be large and management should attempt to keep labour turnover as low as possible so as to minimise these costs. The **cost of labour turnover** may be divided into the following.

- Preventative costs
- Replacement costs

5.6 **Replacement costs** are the costs incurred as a result of **hiring new employees** and they include the following.

- Cost of **selection** and **placement**.
- **Inefficiency** of new labour; **productivity will be lower**.
- Costs of **training**.
- Loss of output due to **delay in new labour becoming available**.
- **Increased wastage** and spoilage due to **lack of expertise** among new staff.

5.7 **Preventative costs** are costs incurred in order to **prevent employees leaving** and they include the following.

- Cost of **personnel administration** incurred in **maintaining good relationships**
- Cost of **medical services** including check-ups, nursing staff and so on
- Cost of **welfare services**, including sports facilities and canteen meals
- **Pension schemes** providing security to employees

The prevention of high labour turnover

5.8 Labour turnover will be reduced by the following actions.

- Paying satisfactory wages, and offering satisfactory hours and conditions of work
- Creating a good relationship between fellow workers and supervisors
- Offering good training schemes and clear career prospects
- Improving the content of jobs to create job satisfaction
- Investigating the cause of high labour turnover rates

6 ANALYSIS OF LABOUR EFFICIENCY AND UTILISATION RATES

Labour efficiency

6.1 Labour costs are a **large proportion of the total costs** incurred by many organisations. It is important therefore that the performance of the labour force is **continually monitored**.

Efficiency, capacity and activity ratios

6.2 Three ways of measuring labour activity include the following control ratios.

- Efficiency ratio (or productivity ratio)

- Capacity ratio
- Activity ratio, or production volume ratio

These ratios are usually expressed as percentages.

> **KEY TERMS**
>
> - **Efficiency ratio** $= \dfrac{\text{Expected hours to make output}}{\text{Actual hours worked}} \times 100\%$
>
> - **Capacity ratio** $= \dfrac{\text{Actual hours worked}}{\text{Hours budgeted}} \times 100\%$
>
> - **Activity ratio** $= \dfrac{\text{Output measured in expected or standard hours}}{\text{Hours budgeted}} \times 100\%$

6.3 EXAMPLE: CONTROL RATIOS

Barney Rubble Ltd budgets to make 25,000 standard units of output (in four hours each) during a budget period of 100,000 hours.

Actual output during the period was 27,000 units which took 120,000 hours to make.

Task

Calculate the efficiency, capacity and activity ratios.

6.4 SOLUTION

(a) Efficiency ratio $\quad \dfrac{(27,000 \times 4)\ \text{hours}}{120,000} \times 100\% = \quad 90\%$

(b) Capacity ratio $\quad \dfrac{120,000\ \text{hours}}{100,000\ \text{hours}} \times 100\% = \quad 120\%$

(c) Activity ratio $\quad \dfrac{(27,000 \times 4)\ \text{hours}}{100,000} \times 100\% = \quad 108\%$

The labour force was working at only 90 per cent efficiency, but more hours were worked than budgeted (capacity ratio = 120%), with the result that the activity achieved was 108 per cent of that budgeted.

6.5 These ratios may be used, therefore, to measure the performance of the labour force. At a later stage in your studies you will come across **variances**, in particular **labour variances** which are another means of measuring labour efficiency.

Labour utilisation

6.6 It is possible to monitor the efficient use of labour by calculating **labour utilisation rates** or ratios. These ratios consider how actual working time is utilised, that is to say whether the time is **productive** or **non-productive.** We shall now consider some of the ways in which labour utilisation can be measured.

Idle time

6.7 We considered idle time earlier in this chapter. A useful ratio for the control of idle time is the **idle time ratio.**

> **KEY TERM**
>
> **Idle time ratio** $= \dfrac{\text{Idle hours}}{\text{Total hours}} \times 100\%$

This ratio is useful because it shows the proportion of available hours which were lost as a result of idle time.

Absenteeism

6.8 When staff are absent from work, this is another reason why **productive time may be reduced.** We can also calculate ratios which might provide useful measures of absenteeism. These ratios include the following.

(a) $\dfrac{\text{Number of hours / days absent from work (in a given period)}}{\text{Total number of hours / days paid (in a given period)}}$

(b) $\dfrac{\text{Number of hours / days absent from work (in a given period)}}{\text{Total number of hours / days worked (in a given period)}}$

6.9 It is important to keep a check on absenteeism and management should be aware of any **patterns** which may begin to emerge within an organisation. For example if the absenteeism is high in one particular department this may signal labour relations problems in that department.

Sickness

6.10 As with absenteeism, it is important that sickness rates are monitored by management. Levels of sickness may be measured by means of ratios which are similar to those used for measuring absenteeism.

6.11 Ratios which might provide a useful measure of sickness include the following.

(a) $\dfrac{\text{Number of days off work due to sickness (in a given period)}}{\text{Total number of days paid (in a given period)}}$

(b) $\dfrac{\text{Number of days off work due to sickness (in a given period)}}{\text{Total number of days worked (in a given period)}}$

Overtime levels

6.12 The amount of overtime worked, and the costs of overtime, may also be monitored by calculating ratios.

6.13 Management may be interested to know whether the amount of overtime worked **increases at any particular time of the year.** If this is the case they may be justified in hiring extra staff during these periods.

6.14 The following ratios may be used to monitor overtime levels.

(a) $\dfrac{\text{Hours of overtime worked}}{\text{Total hours worked}}$

(b) $\dfrac{\text{Overtime labour costs}}{\text{Total labour costs}}$

ASSESSMENT ALERT

In the December 2001 Central Assessment, candidates were required to calculate an efficiency ratio and a capacity ratio. Make sure that you can remember the correct formulae in order to calculate these ratios.

BPP PUBLISHING

Key learning points

- **Labour costs** can be determined according to some prior agreement, the amount of time worked or the quantity/quality of work done.

- **Labour attendance time** is recorded on an **attendance record** or a **clockcard**. The analysis of time worked may be recorded on daily time sheets, weekly time sheets, job cards or route cards depending on the circumstances.

- **Idle time** may occur when employees are not able to get on with their work through no fault of their own. Idle time has a cost and must therefore be recorded.

- The labour cost of work done by **pieceworkers** is recorded on a **piecework ticket/operation card**.

- There are four main types of **incentive scheme**: piecework, time-saved bonus, group bonus scheme and profit-sharing scheme.

- **Labour turnover** is the rate at which employees leave a company and are replaced. Labour turnover should be kept as low as possible. The cost of labour turnover can be divided into **preventative costs** and **replacement** costs.

Quick quiz

1   What are the three basic ways of determining labour costs?

2   Which two documents can be used to record attendance time?

3   Which four documents may be used to record the amount of time spent on a job?

4   Give three reasons why salaried staff may be required to fill in detailed timesheets.

5   What is idle time? Give two examples of why it may occur.

6   What is overtime premium?

7   List four types of incentive scheme.

8   What is the formula used to calculate the labour turnover rate?

9   List four methods used to reduce labour turnover.

10   What is another name for the activity ratio, and how is it calculated?

Answers to quick quiz

1   Agreed basic wages and salaries, time spent, work done.

2   A record of attendance and a clockcard.

3   Daily time sheets, weekly time sheets, job cards and route cards.

4   (a)   Timesheets assist in the creation of management information about product costs and profitability.

         (b)   Timesheet information may have a direct impact on the revenue an organisation receives.

         (c)   Timesheet information may support overtime claims made by salaried staff.

5   Time during which employees cannot get on with their work (though it is not their fault). It may occur when a machine breaks down or when there is a temporary shortage of work.

6   The extra amount paid, above the base rate, for working overtime.

7   Piecework, time-saved bonus, group bonus scheme, profit-sharing scheme.

8      $\text{Labour turnover rate} = \dfrac{\text{Replacements}}{\text{Average number of employees in period}} \times 100\%$

9
- Paying satisfactory wages
- Offering satisfactory hours and conditions of work
- Offering good training schemes
- Improving job content to create job satisfaction

10   Activity ratio   =   production volume ratio

                = $\dfrac{\text{output measured in standard or expected hours}}{\text{hours budgeted}} \times 100\%$

4 Expenses

This chapter contains

1   Introduction
2   Revenue and capital expenditure
3   Types of expense
4   Depreciation and obsolescence
5   Recording and coding expenses

Learning objectives

On completion of this chapter you will be able to:

- Identify and calculate direct revenue expenditure in accordance with organisational policies and procedures

- Establish indirect expenses in accordance with organisational procedures

- Ensure that data and information relating to direct expenses and indirect expenses is clearly and correctly coded, analysed and recorded

- Deal with queries about direct and indirect expenses

Performance criteria

6.1   (i)   Direct costs are identified in accordance with the organisation's costing procedures

6.1   (ii)   Information relating to direct costs is clearly and correctly coded, analysed and recorded

6.1   (vi)   Queries are either resolved or referred to the appropriate person

6.2   (i)   Data are correctly coded, analysed and recorded

6.2   (ii)   Overhead costs are established in accordance with the organisation's procedures

6.2   (iii)   Information relating to overhead costs is accurately and clearly recorded

6.2   (viii) Staff working in operational departments are consulted to resolve any queries in the data

Range statement

6.1.1 Direct costs: actual expenses

Expenses; direct revenue expenditure

6.2.1 Overhead costs: actual indirect expenses; depreciation charges

Knowledge and understanding

- Main types of expenses: expenses directly charged to cost units; indirect expenses; depreciation charges
- Procedures and documentation relating to expenses
- Allocation of expenses to cost centres
- Relationships between the expenses costing system and the accounting system
- Objectives of depreciation accounting

1   INTRODUCTION

1.1   We have now looked at materials costs and labour costs in some detail in Chapters 2 and 3. Any other costs that might be incurred by an organisation are generally known as **expenses**. In this chapter we will be going on to look at a variety of **direct expenses** and **indirect expenses**.

2   REVENUE AND CAPITAL EXPENDITURE

2.1   Like materials and labour costs, expenses can also be divided into different categories. One such classification of expenses is as either **revenue expenditure** or as **capital expenditure.**

KEY TERMS

- **Capital expenditure** is expenditure which results in the acquisition of fixed assets.
- **Fixed assets** are assets which are acquired to provide benefits in more than one accounting period and are not intended to be resold in the normal course of trade.

2.2   Capital expenditure is not charged to the profit and loss account as an expense. Instead a **depreciation charge** is charged to the profit and loss account in order to write off the capital expenditure over a period of time. The depreciation charge is therefore an expense in the profit and loss account, so that the cost of the asset is spread over the years which benefit from its use.

2.3   EXAMPLE: DEPRECIATION CHARGES

If an asset is bought for £20,000 and it is expected to last for 5 years and have no value at the end of that time, then for five years, £4,000 (£20,000 ÷ 5 years) will be charged as a **depreciation expense** to the profit and loss account.

> **KEY TERM**
>
> **Revenue expenditure** is expenditure which is incurred for one of the following reasons.
>
> - For the purpose of the trade of the business, including administration expenses, selling and distribution expenses and finance charges.
>
> - In order to maintain the existing earning capacity of fixed assets.

2.4 **Revenue expenditure** is charged to the profit and loss account in the period to which it relates.

Revenue and capital expenditure compared

2.5 Let us look at an example which should help you to distinguish between **revenue expenses** and **capital expenses**.

2.6 EXAMPLE: REVENUE ITEMS AND CAPITAL ITEMS

Suppose that Bevan Ltd purchases a building for £30,000. A few years later it adds an extension to the building at a cost of £10,000. The building needs to have a few broken windows mended, its floors polished, and some missing roof tiles replaced. These cleaning and maintenance jobs cost £900.

Which items of expenditure are revenue expenditure and which are capital expenditure?

2.7 SOLUTION

The original purchase cost (£30,000) and the cost of the extension (£10,000) are **capital expenditure** because they are incurred to acquire and then improve a fixed asset. The other costs of £900 are **revenue expenditure** because they are maintaining the existing earning capacity of the building.

2.8 The capital expenditure would be shared over several years' profit and loss accounts via a **depreciation expense.** The revenue expenditure would be charged as an **expense in the year it is incurred.**

Revenue and capital expenditure and costing

2.9 Revenue expenditure is of more relevance to the costing of products than capital expenditure. Capital expenditure is only of relevance when it is turned into revenue expenditure in the form of a **depreciation expense**.

Activity 4.1   **Level: Pre-assessment**

Distinguish between capital expenditure and revenue expenditure and give an example of each.

Direct expenses and indirect expenses

2.10 A second major distinction that must be made is between **direct** and **indirect** expenses.

> **KEY TERMS**
>
> - A **direct cost** is a cost that can be traced in full to the product, service, or department that is being costed.
>
> - **Direct material** is all material becoming part of the product (unless used in negligible amounts and/or having negligible cost).
>
> - **Direct wages** are all wages paid for labour (either as basic hours or as overtime) expended on work on the product itself.
>
> - **Direct expenses** are any expenses which are incurred on a specific product or service other than direct material cost and direct wages.

2.11 **Direct expenses** are charged to the product or service as part of the **prime cost** or **total direct cost**. Examples of direct expenses are as follows.

- The cost of **special** designs, drawings or layouts for a particular job
- The **hire of tools** or equipment for a particular job
- **Royalties** payable for each unit produced, for use of a copyright design

Direct expenses are also referred to as **chargeable expenses.**

2.12 **Indirect expenses** are expenses which cannot be identified in full with a specific item that is being costed. They are also known as overheads and are studied in detail in the next chapter.

Activity 4.2   Level: Assessment

State whether each of the following items should be classified as 'capital' or 'revenue' expenditure.

(a)   Purchase of leasehold premises

(b)   Annual depreciation of leasehold premises

(c)   Solicitors' fees in connection with the purchase of leasehold premises

(d)   Costs of adding extra storage capacity to a mainframe computer used by the business

(e)   Computer repairs and maintenance costs

(f)   Cost of new machinery

(g)   Customs duty charged on the machinery when imported into the country

(h)   'Carriage' costs of transporting the new machinery from the supplier's factory to the premises of the business purchasing the machinery

(i)   Cost of installing the new machinery in the premises of the business

(j)   Wages of the machine operators

3 TYPES OF EXPENSE

3.1 Revenue expenditure other than materials and labour costs can arise for a number of different reasons include the following.

(a) **Buildings costs**. The main types are rent, business rates and buildings insurance.

(b) **The costs of making buildings habitable**. Gas and electricity bills and water rates, repairs and maintenance costs and cleaning costs.

(c) **People-related costs**. These include expenditure on health and safety, and the cost of staff welfare provisions like canteen costs and staff training.

(d) **Machine operating costs**. For example cleaning, maintenance and insurance costs. A proportion of the capital cost of the machines becomes revenue expenditure in the form of depreciation. Some machines are hired.

(e) **Information processing costs**. For example the cost of computer disks and stationery, and subscriptions to information sources, like trade journals.

(f) **Finance costs**. If there is a bank loan there will be interest and bank charges to pay, and if equipment is leased there will be lease interest.

(g) **Selling and distribution costs**. Selling expenses include advertising, the salaries and commissions of sales people, and the costs of providing after sales service. Distribution expenses include warehouse charges and running costs of delivery vehicles.

(h) Finally there are the **costs of dealing with the outside world**. Fees paid to professionals like external auditors or solicitors would be collected under this heading.

3.2 Before we go on to consider the way in which expenses are recorded and coded, we are going to look in a bit more detail at the expense of depreciation.

4 DEPRECIATION AND OBSOLESCENCE

Depreciation

4.1 We have already described depreciation as a method of writing off capital expenditure.

There are two principal methods of depreciating a fixed asset, the **straight line method** and the **reducing balance method**.

(a) The **straight line method** charges an equal amount of depreciation each period.

(b) The **reducing balance method** charges the largest amount of depreciation at the beginning of an asset's life. As the asset grows older the amount charged each period gets steadily smaller.

ASSESSMENT ALERT

Methods of depreciating an asset has been a common Unit 6 Central Assessment topic. Make sure you understand how the two main methods differ

4.2 EXAMPLE: DEPRECIATION METHODS

Two fixed assets are purchased for £8,000 each. They will have no value after four years. One is depreciated over four years using the straight line method and the other is depreciated at the rate of 25% per annum on the reducing balance. What is the book value of each asset after four years and how much per year is charged to the profit and loss account as depreciation expense?

4.3 SOLUTION

| | Asset A | | Asset B | |
	Balance sheet	Profit and loss account	Balance sheet	Profit and loss account
	£	£	£	£
Capital cost	8,000		8,000	
Year 1 depreciation charge	(2,000)	2,000	(2,000)	2,000
c/f	6,000		6,000	
Year 2 depreciation charge	(2,000)	2,000	1,500	1,500
c/f	4,000		4,500	
Year 3 depreciation charge	(2,000)	2,000	(1,125)	1,125
c/f	2,000		3,375	
Year 4 depreciation charge	(2,000)	2,000	(844)	844
c/f	-		2,531	

4.4 The profit and loss account charge for asset A is calculated by dividing the £8,000 capital cost by four. For asset B it is calculated by taking 25% of the opening balance each year.

4.5 In order to decide which method is most appropriate we need to think a little more about why we are depreciating the asset at all.

The objectives of depreciation accounting

4.6 If an asset is purchased for £8,000 at the beginning of the year and sold for £6,000 at the end of the year then it is reasonable to conclude that the cost of owning the asset for a year is £2,000. This £2,000 is in addition to the costs of using the asset, like fuel and repairs costs.

4.7 If the business had not owned the asset it would not have been able to make its product or provide its service. It is therefore reasonable that the £2,000 cost should be recorded and charged as a cost of the product or service.

4.8 One of the objectives of depreciation accounting is therefore **to find some way of calculating this cost of ownership.**

4.9 Consider, however, the use of a machine that is constructed to do a specific job for a specific firm. It may last 20 years and yet be of no use to anybody else at any time in which case its resale value would be nil on the same day that it was bought. It is, however, hardly fair to charge the whole cost of the machine to the first product that it makes, or even to the first year's production. Very probably the products it is making in year 19 will be just as well made as the products made in year 1.

4.10 Thus a second objective of depreciation accounting is **to spread out the capital cost of the asset over as long a period as the asset is used.** In the example given there is a good case for spreading this cost in equal proportions over the whole 20 years.

4.11 The answer to the question 'which method is best?' therefore depends upon the following.

- The asset in question

- The way it is used

- The length of time it is used

- The length of time it is useful in the light of changes in products, production methods and technology

Depreciation in practice

4.12 This sounds as if there are a lot of things to take into account, but in practice you may find that the method most often used is the **straight line method** because it is simple and gives a reasonable approximation (given that depreciation is at best an estimate).

4.13 Typical depreciation rates under the **straight line method** are as follows.

Freehold land	Not depreciated
Freehold buildings	2% per annum (50 years)
Leasehold buildings	Over the period of the lease
Plant and machinery	10% per annum (10 years)
Motor vehicles	25% per annum (4 years)

Note that these are not rules. Businesses can choose whatever method or rate they think is most appropriate. Motor vehicles, for example, are often depreciated using the **reducing balance method** since it is well known that in reality they lose the largest proportion of their value in their first few years.

4.14 Sometimes you may encounter depreciation methods that try to measure the fall in value/cost of use more accurately. A typical example is the machine-hour method which is illustrated below.

4.15 EXAMPLE: THE MACHINE-HOUR METHOD

A machine costs £100,000 and it is estimated that it will be sold for £5,000 at the end of its useful life. Experience has shown that such machines can run for approximately 10,000 hours before they wear out. What is the depreciation charge for the first year if the machine was used for 1,500 hours during the year?

4.16 SOLUTION

The machine hour rate is calculated as follows.

$$\text{Depreciation per machine hour} = \frac{\text{Cost} - \text{residual value}}{\text{Useful life}}$$

$$\frac{\pounds(100,000 - 5,000)}{10,000 \text{ hours}} = \pounds9.50 \text{ per machine hour}$$

The depreciation charge for the first year is therefore

$$1,500 \text{ hours} \times \pounds9.50 = \pounds14,250$$

This method is all very well if there are only a few such assets and **careful records are kept of operating times**. However this method would cause quite an administrative burden if there were many such machines with different values, different lives and different usage rates.

Obsolescence

KEY TERM

Obsolescence is the loss in value of an asset because it has been superseded, for example due to the development of a technically superior asset or changes in market conditions.

4.17 As the loss in value is due to quite another reason than the **wear and tear** associated with depreciation and because obsolescence may be rapid and difficult to forecast, it is not normal practice to make regular charges relating to obsolescence. Instead, **the loss resulting from the obsolescence should be charged as an expense direct to the costing profit and loss account when it arises.**

Activity 4.3   Level: Assessment

(a)   It has been calculated that a fork-lift truck is used 65% of the time in the warehouse and the rest of the time in the production department.

      Does this have any significance for costing purposes?

(b)   At the end of its first year of use the meter on a leather stamping machine read 9728. It cost £4,000 and the suppliers are willing to buy it back for 20% of its cost at any time so that it can be used for parts. The sales literature claimed that it was capable of producing at least 100,000 stampings. The machine is used exclusively on one product, which will be discontinued in three years' time.

      (i)   Is the depreciation charge for the machine a direct expense or an indirect expense?

      (ii)   What is the depreciation charge for the first year?

Activity 4.4   Level: Assessment

A machine was purchased three years ago for £75,000. Due to a change in government regulations, the component the machine produces can only be used for a further two years. At the end of two years, however, the machine can be sold for scrap for £5,000.

Task

Calculate the depreciation charge for the five years the machine is owned using both the straight line method and a rate of 42% per annum on the reducing balance.

5 RECORDING AND CODING EXPENSES

5.1 In this chapter we are going to deal only with the initial stages of recording expenses. Much more detail will be found in the next chapter which explains how overhead costs are attributed to the total costs of individual units of product.

Direct expenses

5.2 **Direct expenses** (such as plant hire for a specific job or a solicitor's fees for drawing up a contract to provide a specific service) can simply be **coded to the appropriate job or client** when the invoice arrives. The expense would be recorded together with other direct costs against the relevant job or client numbers.

Indirect expenses

5.3 Indirect expenses **cannot be charged directly** to a **specific** cost unit. Instead a process of **allocation and apportionment** is necessary.

KEY TERM

Allocation is the process by which whole cost items are charged direct to a cost unit or cost centre.

5.4 **Indirect expenses** are initially allocated to the appropriate **cost centres**. We met cost centres briefly in Chapter 1 but in case you have forgotten, a cost centre is something (location, function, activity or item of equipment, say) which incurs costs that can be attributed to units of production (cost units). That something may be any of the following.

	Examples	
Cost centre type	**Production**	**Service**
Location	Finishing department	Hotel restaurant
Function	Sales department	Accounts department
Activity	Painting	Invoicing
Item of equipment	Spray-gun	Computer

5.5 The decision as to which cost centre is the appropriate one for an expense depends upon the type of expense. Some expenses will be **solely related to production** or to **administration** or to **selling and distribution** and can easily be **allocated** to the appropriate cost centre.

5.6 Other costs, however, will be shared between these various functions and so such costs cannot be allocated directly to one particular cost centre. Cost centres therefore have to be established for the **initial allocation** of such shared expenses.

Examples of shared expenses include: rent, rates, heating and lighting, buildings maintenance and so on.

5.7 EXAMPLE: OVERHEAD ALLOCATION

The coding, analysis and recording of indirect expenses and other overheads at the initial stage may be demonstrated by the following example.

The weekly costs of Medlycott Ltd include the following.

Wages of supervisor of Department A	£1,000
Wages of supervisor of Department B	£1,200
Indirect materials consumed in Department A	£400
Rent of premises shared by Departments A and B	£1,500

Medlycott Ltd's cost accounting system includes the following cost centres.

Code	
101	Department A
102	Department B
201	Rent

Show the cost centres to which the costs will be initially coded.

5.8 SOLUTION

(a)

	£	*Code*
Wages of supervisor of Department A	1,000	101
Wages of supervisor of Department B	1,200	102
Indirect materials consumed in Department A	400	101
Rent of premises shared by Departments A and B	1,500	201

(b)   You may think that this is so obvious as not to be worth explaining. You will certainly not be surprised to be told that the next stage is to **share the rent paid between the two departments.** Why, you might ask, do we not split the cost of rent straightaway and not bother with cost centre 201?

(c)   To answer this question consider the following extract from the cost accounts of Medlycott Ltd, several months after the previous example. Cost centre 201 is no longer used because nobody could see the point of it.

	Cost centre	
	101	*102*
	£	£
Wages	1,172.36	1,415.00
Materials	73.92	169.75
Rent	638.25	1,086.75

You have just received a memo telling you that starting from this month (to which the above figures relate), Department A is to pay 25% of the total rent for the premises shared with Department B and Department B is to be split into two departments, with the new department (C) paying 37% of the remaining rent charge. The manager of Department B is standing over you asking you how much the department's new monthly rent charge will be.

(d)   The answer is £815.06. More importantly the first thing you have to do to calculate the answer is to recreate the total cost information that used to be allocated to cost centre 201. This is not very difficult in the present example, but imagine that there were ten cost centres sharing premises and the cost information was recorded in a bulky ledger. Do you think it would have been easy to spot that the monthly rent had increased to £1,725?

Documentation

5.9 There are several ways in which this initial allocation could be documented. A common method is to put a stamp on the invoice itself with boxes to fill in, as appropriate. Suppose that Department C is given the code number 103. The rent invoice would be coded as follows.

%	Account codes no.	£	p
25.00	101	431	25
47.25	102	815	06
27.75	103	478	69
TOTAL	201	1725	00
Approved		Date	
Authorised		Date	
Posted		Date	

5.10 The dividing up of the total cost into portions to share it over the relevant cost centres is called **apportionment**. This process will be described in more detail in the next chapter.

Apportionment and responsibility accounting

5.11 The apportionment of costs raises another important question. It is unlikely that the managers of departments A, B and C have any **control** over the amount of rent that is paid for the building. They need to be **made aware that their part of the building is not free** but they are not **responsible** for the cost. The person responsible for controlling the amount of a cost such as this is more likely to be a separate manager, who looks after the interests of all of the company's buildings.

5.12 If cost centre 201 is maintained it can therefore be used to collect all the costs that are the **responsibility of the premises manager.** This approach is known as **responsibility accounting** and such cost centres can be called **responsibility centres.**

Activity 4.5   Level: Assessment

Listed below are fifteen entries in the cash book of Beancounters, a small firm of accountants. You are required to code the invoices according to the sort of expense you think has been incurred.

Nominal codes	Nominal account
0010	Advertising
0020	Bank charges
0030	Books and publications
0040	Cleaning
0050	Computer supplies

Nominal codes	Nominal account
0060	Heat and light
0070	Motor expenses
0080	Motor vehicles
0090	Office equipment
0100	Printing, postage and stationery
0110	Rates
0120	Rent
0130	Repairs and maintenance
0140	Staff training
0150	Staff welfare
0160	Subscriptions
0170	Telephone
0180	Temporary staff
0190	Travel

Invoice received from	£	Code
Strange (Properties) Ltd	4,000.00	
Yorkshire Electricity plc	1,598.27	
Dudley Stationery Ltd	275.24	
Dora David (cleaner)	125.00	
BPP Publishing Ltd	358.00	
AAT	1,580.00	
British Telecom	1,431.89	
Kall Kwik (Stationers)	312.50	
Interest to 31.3.X3	2,649.33	
L & W Office Equipment	24.66	
Avis	153.72	
Federal Express	32.00	
Starriers Garage Ltd	79.80	

Activity 4.6   Level: Assessment

Beancounters is divided up into three departments: audit, business services and tax. Which of the expenses listed in Activity 4.5 do you think are chargeable in total directly to individual clients, which are chargeable in total directly to departments and which cannot be split except by some method of apportionment?

Helping hand. There is no definitive answer to this activity, but take a few minutes to give it some thought. If you consider that you need more information, think about the queries that you would raise and who you would ask for the information.

ASSESSMENT ALERT

The following notes have been extracted from the guidance for element 6.1.

'*Expenses*

- Procedures and documentation relating to expenses
- Allocation of expenses to cost centres
- Objectives of depreciation accounting'

Make sure that you are happy with all of the above since assessments are likely to include tasks relating to these areas.

Key learning points

- **Capital expenditure** is expenditure which results in the acquisition of fixed assets. Fixed assets are assets acquired to provide benefits in more than one accounting period. Capital expenditure is charged as an **expense** to the profit and loss account via a depreciation charge over a period of time.

- **Revenue expenditure** is expenditure which is incurred for the purpose of the trade of the business, or in order to maintain the existing earning capacity of fixed assets. It is charged as an **expense** to the profit and loss account in the period to which it relates.

- There are two principal methods of depreciating an asset, the **straight-line** method and the **reducing balance** method.

- **Obsolescence** is the loss in value of an asset because it has been superseded.

- **Direct expenses** are recorded by coding them to the appropriate job or client.

- **Indirect expenses** are initially **allocated** to appropriate cost centres and then spread out or **apportioned** to the cost centres that have benefited from the expense.

- In **responsibility accounting,** cost centres collect the costs that are the responsibility of the cost centre manager, and hence may be known as **responsibility centres.**

Quick quiz

1 What is capital expenditure?

2 What is revenue expenditure?

3 What are the two main methods of depreciating an asset?

4 Which method of depreciation would be best for a machine that is used most in its early years? Why?

5 What are the two main objectives of depreciation accounting?

6 What is obsolescence?

7 What is responsibility accounting?

Answers to quick quiz

1 Expenditure resulting in the acquisition of fixed assets. It is not classified as an expense. Instead a depreciation charge is calculated which writes off the capital expenditure over a period of time.

2 Revenue expenditure is expenditure incurred for the purpose of the trade of the business, or in order to maintain the existing earning capacity of fixed assets. It is charged as an expense in the period to which it relates.

3 Straight line method and reducing balance method.

4 Reducing balance depreciation would be best because it charges higher amounts of depreciation in the earlier years of an asset's life.

5 To find a way of calculating the cost of ownership of fixed assets and to spread out the capital cost of the asset over its lifetime.

6 The loss in value of an asset because it has been superseded.

7 When cost centre managers have responsibility for controlling the amount of the cost collected within certain cost centres, such cost centres are called responsibility centres.

Part B
Overheads and absorption costing

5 Overheads and absorption costing

This chapter contains

Learning objectives

On completion of this chapter you will be able to:

- Attribute actual overhead costs to cost centres in accordance with agreed methods of allocation, apportionment and absorption

- Adjust for under or over recovered overhead costs in accordance with established procedures

- Use different methods of apportionment

- Follow procedures for establishing absorption rates

- Review methods of allocation, apportionment and absorption

Performance criteria

6.2   (iv)   Overhead costs are correctly attributed to producing and service cost centres in accordance with agreed methods of allocation, apportionment and absorption

6.2   (v)   Adjustments for under or over recovered overhead costs are made in accordance with established procedures

BPP
PUBLISHING

6.2 (vii) Methods of allocation, apportionment and absorption are reviewed at regular intervals in discussions with senior staff, and agreed changes to methods are implemented

Range statement

6.2.1 Overhead costs: standard and actual indirect material costs; standard and actual indirect labour costs; indirect expenses; depreciation charges

6.2.2 Methods of allocation and apportionment: direct; reciprocal allocation; step down method

Knowledge and understanding

- Analysis of the effect of changing activity levels on unit costs

- Procedures for establishing standard absorption rates

- Bases of allocating and apportioning indirect costs to responsibility centres: direct; reciprocal allocation; step down method

- Activity based systems of allocating costs: cost drivers; cost pools

- Bases of absorption

- Effect of changes in capacity levels

- Arbitrary nature of overhead apportionments

1 INTRODUCTION

1.1 Now that we have completed our detailed study of direct materials, direct labour and direct expenses, we can move on to look in more depth at **indirect costs,** or **overheads.**

2 WHAT ARE OVERHEADS?

KEY TERM

An **overhead** is the cost incurred in the course of making a product, providing a service or running a department, but which cannot be traced directly and in full to the product, service or department.

2.1 **Overheads** are the total of the following.

- Indirect materials
- Indirect labour
- Indirect expenses

(Note that in the previous chapter we were looking at **expenses,** and whether they were direct or indirect.)

2.2 Before we go any further let us look at one common way of categorising overheads.

- Production overhead
- Administration overhead
- Selling overhead
- Distribution overhead

> **KEY TERMS**
>
> - **Production (or factory) overhead** includes all indirect material costs, indirect wages and indirect expenses incurred in the factory.
>
> - **Administration overead** is all indirect material costs, wages and expenses incurred in the direction, control and administration of an organisation.
>
> - **Selling overhead** is all indirect material costs, wages and expenses incurred in promoting sales and retaining customers.
>
> - **Distribution overhead** is all indirect material costs, wages and expenses incurred in making the packed product ready for despatch and delivering it to the customer.

2.3 Examples of production overhead which cannot be traced directly to the finished product include the following.

- **Indirect materials** eg cleaning materials and maintenance materials
- **Indirect wages**, eg salaries of supervisors
- **Indirect expenses** eg rent of the factory and depreciation of machinery

2.4 **Examples of administration overhead**

- **Depreciation** of office equipment
- **Office salaries**, including salaries of secretaries and accountant
- Rent, rates, insurance, lighting, cleaning and heating of **general offices**

2.5 **Examples of selling overhead**

- **Printing** and **stationery**, such as catalogues and price lists
- **Salaries** and **commission** of sales representatives and sales department staff
- **Advertising** and **sales promotion**, market research
- Rent and insurance of **sales offices**, bad debts and collection charges

2.6 **Examples of distribution overhead**

- Cost of **packing cases.**
- **Wages** of packers, drivers and despatch clerks.
- **Freight** and **insurance** charges, **depreciation** of delivery vehicles.

2.7 Overheads may be dealt with in a number of different ways.

- Traditional absorption costing
- Activity based costing
- Marginal costing

We will be looking at traditional absorption costing in detail, and we will also consider activity based costing briefly in Section 11 of this chapter. Marginal costing is beyond the scope of Unit 6.

3 WHAT IS ABSORPTION COSTING?

3.1 **The objective of absorption costing is to include in the total cost of a product or service an appropriate share of the organisation's total overhead.** By an appropriate share we mean an amount that reflects the amount of time and effort that has gone into producing the unit of product or service.

3.2 If an organisation had only one production department and produced identical units then the total overheads would be divided among the total units produced. Life is, of course, never that simple. **Absorption costing is a method of sharing overheads between a number of different products or services on a fair basis.**

The effect of absorption costing

3.3 Before describing the procedures by which overhead costs are shared out among products or services, it may be useful to consider the reasons why absorption costing is commonly used.

3.4 Suppose that a company makes and sells 100 units of a product each week. The direct cost per unit is £6 and the unit sales price is £10. Production overhead costs £200 per week and administration, selling and distribution overhead costs £150 per week. The weekly profit could be calculated as follows.

	£	£
Sales (100 units × £10)		1,000
Direct costs (100 × £6)	600	
Production overheads	200	
Administration, selling, distribution costs	150	
		950
Profit		50

3.5 **In absorption costing, production overhead costs will be added to each unit of product manufactured and sold.**

	£ per unit
Direct cost per unit	6
Production overhead (£200 per week for 100 units)	2
Full production cost	8

The weekly profit would be calculated as follows.

	£
Sales	1,000
Less production cost of sales (100 × £8)	800
Gross profit	200
Less administration, selling, distribution costs	150
Net profit	50

3.6 It may already be apparent that the weekly profit is £50 no matter how the figures have been presented. This being so, how does absorption costing serve any useful purpose in accounting? Is it necessary?

Is absorption costing necessary?

3.7 The reasons for using absorption costing have traditionally been identified as follows.

(a) **Stock valuations**. Stock in hand must be valued for two reasons.

   (i) For the **closing stock figure** in the balance sheet

(ii) For the **cost of sales figure** in the profit and loss account. The valuation of stocks will actually affect profitability during a period because of the way in which cost of sales is calculated.

The cost of goods produced
+ the value of opening stocks
− the value of closing stocks
= the cost of goods sold.

In our example above, any closing stocks could be valued at direct cost (£6). However, in absorption costing they would be valued at a fully absorbed production cost of £8 per unit.

(b) **Pricing decisions.** Many companies attempt to fix selling prices by calculating the full cost of production or sales of each product, and then adding a margin for profit. In our example, the company might have fixed a gross profit margin at 25% on production cost, or 20% of the sales price, in order to establish the unit sales price of £10. '**Full cost plus pricing**' can be particularly useful for companies which do jobbing or contract work, where **each job or contract is different**, so that a standard unit sales price cannot be fixed. Without using absorption costing, a full cost is difficult to ascertain.

(c) **Establishing the profitability of different products.** This argument in favour of absorption costing is more contentious, but is worthy of mention here. If a company sells **more than one product**, it will be difficult to judge how profitable each individual product is, unless overhead costs are **shared on a fair basis** and charged to the cost of sales of each product.

Costing procedures

3.8 The three stages of calculating the costs of overheads to be charged to cost units are **allocation**, **apportionment** and **absorption**.

3.9 **Allocation** is the process of assigning whole items of cost to cost centres. We studied the process of allocation in the previous chapter.

3.10 We shall now begin our study of absorption costing by looking at the process of **overhead apportionment.**

Activity 5.1   **Level: Assessment**

(a) What is absorption costing?
(b) Identify three reasons for using absorption costing.
(c) What are the three stages of absorption costing?

---

4   OVERHEAD APPORTIONMENT

KEY TERM

Apportionment is a procedure whereby indirect costs (overheads) are spread fairly between cost centres.

Stage one: sharing out common costs

4.1 Overhead apportionment follows on from overhead allocation. The first stage of overhead apportionment is to **identify all overhead costs** as production, administration, selling and distribution overhead. This means that the shared costs (such as rent and rates, heat and light and so on) initially allocated to a single cost centre must now be **shared out** between the other (functional) cost centres.

Bases of apportionment

4.2 It is important that overhead costs are shared out on a **fair basis** but this is much more easily said than done. It is rarely possible to use only one method of apportioning costs to the various cost centres of an organisation. The bases of apportionment for the most usual cases are given below.

Overhead to which the basis applies	Basis
Rent, rates, heating and light, repairs and depreciation of buildings	Floor area occupied by each cost centre
Depreciation, insurance of equipment	Cost or book value of equipment
Personnel office, canteen, welfare, wages and cost office, first aid	Number of employees, or labour hours worked in each cost centre
Heating, lighting (see above)	Volume of space occupied by each cost centre

4.3 Don't forget that some overhead costs can be **allocated directly** to the user cost centre without having to be apportioned. For example indirect wages and consumable supplies can be directly allocated because they relate solely to that cost centre.

4.4 EXAMPLE: OVERHEAD APPORTIONMENT

Kettle Ltd incurred the following overhead costs.

	£
Depreciation of factory	1,000
Factory repairs and maintenance	600
Factory office costs (treat as production overhead)	1,500
Depreciation of equipment	800
Insurance of equipment	200
Heating	390
Lighting	100
Canteen	900
	5,490

Information relating to the production and service departments in the factory is as follows.

	Department			
	Production	*Production*	*Service*	*Service*
	A	*B*	*X*	*Y*
Floor space (sq. metres)	1,200	1,600	800	400
Volume (cubic metres)	3,000	6,000	2,400	1,600
Number of employees	30	30	15	15
Book value of equipment	£30,000	£20,000	£10,000	£20,000

How should the overhead costs be apportioned between the four departments?

4.5 SOLUTION

Item of cost	Basis of apportionment	Total cost £	To Department A £	B £	X £	Y £
Factory depreciation	floor area	1,000	300	400	200	100
Factory repairs	floor area	600	180	240	120	60
Factory office	no. of employees	1,500	500	500	250	250
Equipment depn	book value	800	300	200	100	200
Equipment insurance	book value	200	75	50	25	50
Heating	volume	390	90	180	72	48
Lighting	floor area	100	30	40	20	10
Canteen	no. of employees	900	300	300	150	150
Total		5,490	1,775	1,910	937	868

ASSESSMENT ALERT

Would you be able to explain the difference between allocated overheads and apportioned overheads if you were asked to do so in an assessment? This is exactly what candidates in the December 1999 Central Assessment had to do.

4.6 EXAMPLE: MORE OVERHEAD APPORTIONMENT

Friar Tuck Ltd is preparing its production overhead budgets. Cost centre expenses and related information have been budgeted as follows.

	Total £	Machine shop A £	Machine shop B £	Assembly £	Canteen £	Mainten- ance £
Indirect wages	78,560	8,586	9,190	15,674	29,650	15,460
Consumable materials (inc. maintenance)	16,900	6,400	8,700	1,200	600	-
Rent and rates	16,700					
Buildings insurance	2,400					
Power	8,600					
Heat and light	3,400					
Depreciation of machinery	40,200					
Value of machinery	402,000	201,000	179,000	22,000	-	-
Other information:						
Power usage - technical estimates (%)	100	55	40	3	-	2
Direct labour (hours)	35,000	8,000	6,200	20,800	-	-
Machine usage (hours)	25,200	7,200	18,000	-	-	-
Area (square metres)	45,000	10,000	12,000	15,000	6,000	2,000

How should the overheads be apportioned to the five cost centres?

BPP PUBLISHING

4.7 SOLUTION

	Total £	A £	B £	Assembly £	Canteen £	Maintenance £	Basis of apportionment
Indirect wages	78,560	8,586	9,190	15,674	29,650	15,460	Actual
Consumable materials	16,900	6,400	8,700	1,200	600	-	Actual
Rent and rates	16,700	3,711	4,453	5,567	2,227	742	Area
Insurance	2,400	533	640	800	320	107	Area
Power	8,600	4,730	3,440	258	-	172	Usage
Heat and light	3,400	756	907	1,133	453	151	Area
Depreciation	40,200	20,100	17,900	2,200	-	-	Value
	166,760	44,816	45,230	26,832	33,250	16,632	

Workings

1   *Rent and rates, insurance, heat and light*

Floor area is a sensible measure to use as the basis for apportionment.

	Area Sq metres	Proportion total area	Share of rent & rates £	Share of insurance £	Share of heat & light £
Machine shop A	10,000	10/45	3,711	533	756
Machine shop B	12,000	12/45	4,453	640	907
Assembly	15,000	15/45	5,567	800	1,133
Canteen	6,000	6/45	2,227	320	453
Maintenance	2,000	2/45	742	107	151
	45,000		16,700	2,400	3,400

2   *Power*

	Percentage %	Share of cost £
Machine shop A	55	4,730
Machine shop B	40	3,440
Assembly	3	258
Maintenance	2	172
		8,600

3   *Depreciation*

In the absence of specific information about the fixed assets in use in each department and the depreciation rates that are applied, this cost is shared out on the basis of the **relative value of each department's machinery** to the total. In practice more specific information would (or should) be available.

ASSESSMENT ALERT

In an assessment, you may be asked to comment on the information that you would require to carry out a more accurate apportionment. In the example of depreciation here, we would have preferred to know the fixed assets in use in each department, and what depreciation rates were applied.

Stage two: apportioning service cost centre costs to production cost centres

4.8 The second stage of overhead apportionment concerns **the treatment of service cost centres**. A factory is divided into several production cost centres and also many service cost centres. Service cost centres might include the stores or the canteen.

4.9 **Only the production cost centres are directly involved in the manufacture of the units.** In order to be able to add production overheads to unit costs, it is necessary to have all the overheads charged to (or located in) the production cost centres.

4.10 The next stage in absorption costing is therefore to **apportion the costs of service cost centres to the production cost centres.**

4.11 There are three methods by which the apportionment of service cost centre costs can be done.

(a) Apportion the costs of each service cost centre to production cost centres only (the **direct** method).

(b) Apportion the costs of each service cost centre not only to production cost centres, but also to other service cost centres which make use of its services. Eventually apportion all costs to the production cost centres alone by a gradual process of **repeated distribution**.

(c) Apportion the costs of each service cost centre, not only to production cost centres, but also to some (but not all) of the service cost centres that make use of its services. This is known as the **step-down** method.

We shall look at each of these methods in more detail below.

4.12 Whichever method is used, **the basis of apportionment must be fair**. A different apportionment basis may be applied for each service cost centre. This is demonstrated in the following table.

Service cost centre	Possible basis of apportionment
Stores	Number or cost value of material requisitions
Maintenance	Hours of maintenance work done for each cost centre
Production planning	Direct labour hours worked in each production cost centre

4.13 EXAMPLE: DIRECT APPORTIONMENT

Maid Marion Ltd incurred the following overhead costs.

	Production departments		*Stores*	*Maintenance*
	P	*Q*	*department*	*department*
	£	£	£	£
Allocated costs	6,000	4,000	1,000	2,000
Apportioned costs	2,000	1,000	1,000	500
	8,000	5,000	2,000	2,500

Production department P requisitioned materials to the value of £12,000. Department Q requisitioned £8,000 of materials. The maintenance department provided 500 hours of work for department P and 750 hours for department Q. What are the total production overhead costs of Departments P and Q?

4.14 SOLUTION

Service department	Basis of apportionment	Total cost	Dept P	Dept Q
		£	£	£
Stores	Value of requisitions	2,000	1,200	800
Maintenance	Direct labour hours	2,500	1,000	1,500
		4,500	2,200	2,300
Previously allocated and apportioned costs		13,000	8,000	5,000
Total overhead		17,500	10,200	7,300

The total overhead has now been shared, on a fair basis, between the two production departments.

4.15 EXAMPLE: DIRECT APPORTIONMENT AGAIN

Look back to the example solution in Paragraph 4.7. Using the bases of apportionment which you consider most appropriate from the information provided in Paragraph 4.6, calculate overhead totals for Friar Tuck Ltd's three production departments, Machine Shop A, Machine Shop B and Assembly.

4.16 SOLUTION

	Total	A	B	Assembly	Canteen	Mainten-ance	Basis of apportionment
	£	£	£	£	£	£	
Total overheads	166,760	44,816	45,230	26,832	33,250	16,632	
Re-apportion	-	7,600	5,890	19,760	(33,250)	-	Dir labour
Re-apportion	-	4,752	11,880	-	-	(16,632)	Mac usage
Totals	166,760	57,168	63,000	46,592	-	-	

The total overhead has now been shared, on a fair basis, between the three production departments.

The repeated distribution/reciprocal allocation method of apportionment

4.17 **Apportionment** is a procedure whereby indirect costs are spread fairly between cost centres. It could therefore be argued that a fair sharing of service cost centre costs is not possible **unless consideration is given to the work done by each service cost centre for other service cost centres.**

4.18 For example, suppose a company has two production departments and two service departments (stores and maintenance). The following information about activity in a recent costing period is available.

	Production departments		Stores department	Maintenance department
	1	2		
Overhead costs	£10,030	£8,970	£10,000	£8,000
Value of material requisitions	£30,000	£50,000	-	£20,000
Maintenance hours used	8,000	1,000	1,000	-

The problem is that the stores department uses the maintenance department, and the maintenance department uses the stores. This is known as **reciprocal servicing.**

(a) If service department overheads were apportioned directly to production departments, ignoring the reciprocal servicing, the apportionment would be as follows.

Service department	Basis of apportionment	Total cost £	1 £	2 £
Stores	Material requisitions	10,000	3,750	6,250
Maintenance	Maintenance hours	8,000	7,111	889
		18,000	10,861	7,139
Overheads of departments 1 and 2		19,000	10,030	8,970
		37,000	20,891	16,109

(b) If, however, recognition is made of the fact that **the stores and maintenance department do work for each other,** and the basis of apportionment remains the same, we ought to apportion service department costs as follows. The percentages are based on the value of material requisitions and the maintenance hours.

	Production departments		Stores	Maintenance
	1	2	department	department
Stores (100%)	30%	50%	-	20%
Maintenance (100%)	80%	10%	10%	-

This may be done using the **repeated distribution method of apportionment** as follows.

4.19 EXAMPLE: REPEATED DISTRIBUTION (RECIPROCAL ALLOCATION) METHOD OF APPORTIONMENT

	Production departments		Stores	Maintenance
	1 £	2 £	department £	department £
Overhead costs	10,030	8,970	10,000	8,000
Apportion stores (see note (a))	3,000	5,000	(10,000)	2,000
			0	10,000
Apportion maintenance	8,000	1,000	1,000	(10,000)
			1,000	0
Repeat: Apportion stores	300	500	(1,000)	200
Repeat: Apportion maintenance	160	20	20	(200)
Repeat: Apportion stores	6	10	(20)	4
Repeat: Apportion maintenance (b)	4	-	-	(4)
	21,500	15,500	0	0

Notes

(a) The first apportionment could have been the costs of maintenance, rather than stores; there is no difference to the final results. The apportionments are based on the percentages calculated in paragraph 4.18.

(b) When the repeated distributions bring service department costs down to small numbers (here £4), the final apportionment to production departments is an approximate rounding.

BPP PUBLISHING

4.20 The total overhead of £37,000 has now been apportioned to the service departments. Have a look at the difference in the final overhead apportionments to each production department using the different apportionment methods. Unless the difference is substantial, the first method, ignoring the reciprocal servicing, might be preferred because it is **clerically simpler to use.**

Step-down method

4.21 The **step-down** method is very similar to the repeated distribution method. The main difference is that the final results will depend upon which apportionment was made first.

4.22 The method works by first apportioning one of the service cost centres **to all of the other centres which make use of its services.** When the remaining service cost centre is re-apportioned, **the work done for the other service cost centre is ignored.**

4.23 EXAMPLE: STEP-DOWN METHOD OF APPORTIONMENT

Using the information in the example in paragraph 4.19, apportion the overhead costs using the step-down method of apportionment, starting with the stores department.

| | Production departments | | Stores | Maintenance |
	1	2	department	department
	£	£	£	£
Overhead costs	10,030	8,970	10,000	8,000
Apportion stores (30%/50%/20%)	3,000	5,000	(10,000)	2,000
Apportion maintenance ($^8/_9$/$^1/_9$)	8,889	1,111	-	10,000
				(10,000)
	21,919	15,081	-	-

If the first apportionment had been the maintenance department, then the overheads of £8,000 would have been apportioned as follows.

| | Production departments | | Stores | Maintenance |
	1	2	department	department
	£	£	£	£
Overhead costs	10,030	8,970	10,000	8,000
Apportion maintenance (80%/10%/10%)	6,400	800	800	(8,000)
			10,800	-
Apportion stores ($^3/_8$/$^5/_8$)	4,050	6,750	(10,800)	
	20,480	16,520	-	-

Note

Notice how the final results differ, depending upon whether stores or maintenance are apportioned first.

Activity 5.2   **Level: Assessment**

Sandstorm Ltd is a jobbing engineering concern which has three production departments (forming, machines and assembly) and two service departments (maintenance and general).

The following analysis of overhead costs has been made from the year just ended.

	£	£
Rent and rates		8,000
Power		750
Light, heat		5,000
Repairs, maintenance:		
Forming	800	
Machines	1,800	
Assembly	300	
Maintenance	200	
General	100	
		3,200
Departmental expenses:		
Forming	1,500	
Machines	2,300	
Assembly	1,100	
Maintenance	900	
General	1,500	
		7,300
Depreciation:		
Plant		10,000
Fixtures		250
Insurance:		
Plant		2,000
Buildings		500
Indirect labour:		
Forming	3,000	
Machines	5,000	
Assembly	1,500	
Maintenance	4,000	
General	2,000	
		15,500
		52,500

Other available data are as follows.

	Floor area sq.metres	Plant value £	Fixtures value £	Effective horse-power	Direct cost for year £	Labour hours worked	Machine hours worked
Forming	2,000	25,000	1,000	40	20,500	14,400	12,000
Machines	4,000	60,000	500	90	30,300	20,500	21,600
Assembly	3,000	7,500	2,000	15	24,200	20,200	2,000
Maintenance	500	7,500	1,000	5	-	-	-
General	500	-	500	-	-	-	-
	10,000	100,000	5,000	150	75,000	55,100	35,600

Service department costs are apportioned as follows.

	Maintenance %	General %
Forming	20	20
Machines	50	60
Assembly	20	10
General	10	–
Maintenance	–	10
	100	100

Task

Using the data provided prepare an analysis showing the apportionment of overhead costs to departments.

5 OVERHEAD ABSORPTION

KEY TERM

Overhead absorption is the process whereby overhead costs allocated and apportioned to production cost centres are added to unit, job or batch costs. Overhead absorption is sometimes called **overhead recovery.**

5.1 Having allocated and/or apportioned all overheads, the next stage in the costing treatment of overheads is to add them to, or **absorb them into, cost units.**

5.2 Overheads are usually added to cost units using a **predetermined overhead absorption rate,** which is calculated using figures from the budget.

5.3 An overhead absorption rate for the forthcoming accounting period is calculated and used as follows.

Step 1	**Estimate the overhead** likely to be incurred during the coming period.
Step 2	**Estimate the activity level for the period.** This could be **total hours, units, or direct costs** or whatever measure of activity upon which the overhead absorption rates are to be based.
Step 3	**Divide the estimated overhead by the budgeted activity level.** This produces the overhead absorption rate.
Step 4	**Absorb** or **recover** the overhead into the cost unit by **applying** the calculated absorption rate.

5.4 EXAMPLE: THE BASICS OF ABSORPTION COSTING

Athena Ltd makes two products, the Greek and the Roman. Greeks take 2 labour hours each to make and Romans take 5 labour hours. What is the overhead cost per unit for Greeks and Romans respectively if overheads are absorbed on the basis of labour hours?

5.5 SOLUTION

Step 1	Estimate the overhead likely to be incurred during the coming period

Athena Ltd estimates that the total overhead will be £50,000

Step 2	Estimate the activity level for the period

Athena Ltd estimates that a total of 100,000 direct labour hours will be worked

Step 3	Divide the estimated overhead by the budgeted activity level

$$\text{Absorption rate} = \frac{£50,000}{100,000 \text{ hrs}} = £0.50 \text{ per direct labour hour}$$

Step 4	Absorb the overhead into the cost unit by applying the calculated absorption rate

	Greek	*Roman*
Labour hours per unit	2	5
Absorption rate per labour hour	£0.50	£0.50
Overhead absorbed per unit	£1	£2.50

Possible bases of absorption

5.6 The most common absorption bases (or **'overhead recovery rates'**) are as follows.

- A rate per machine hour
- A rate per direct labour hour
- A percentage of direct labour cost
- A percentage of direct materials cost
- A percentage of total direct cost (prime cost)
- A rate per unit
- A percentage of factory cost (for administration overhead)
- A percentage of sales or factory cost (for selling and distribution overhead)

5.7 The most appropriate basis for production overhead depends largely on the organisation concerned. As with apportionment it is a matter of being fair.

5.8 Many factories tend to use the **direct labour hour rate** or **machine hour rate** in preference to a rate based on a percentage of direct materials cost, wages or prime cost. It is argued that a time-based method is fairer because overhead costs tend to increase with time. For example rents, rates and supervisory salaries are time-based costs.

5.9 A **machine hour rate** would be used in departments where production is controlled or dictated by machines. In such a situation, where a small number of workers supervise a process that is performed almost entirely by machine, the distinction between direct and indirect labour may be difficult to identify, and labour costs may not be the principal costs of production. A **direct labour hour basis** is more appropriate in a labour intensive environment.

5.10 EXAMPLE: OVERHEAD ABSORPTION RATES

The budgeted production overheads and other budget data of Eiffel Ltd are as follows.

Budget	*Production dept X*	*Production dept Y*
Production overhead cost	£36,000	£5,000
Direct materials cost	£32,000	
Direct labour cost	£40,000	
Machine hours	10,000	
Direct labour hours	18,000	
Units of production		1,000

What would the absorption rate be for each department using the various bases of apportionment?

5.11 SOLUTION

(a) Department X

    (i)   Rate per machine hour $\dfrac{£36,000}{10,000 \text{ hrs}} = £3.60$ per machine hour

    (ii)   Rate per direct labour hour $\dfrac{£36,000}{18,000 \text{ hrs}} = £2$ per direct labour hour

    (iii)   % of direct labour cost $\dfrac{£36,000}{£40,000} \times 100\% = 90\%$

    (iv)   % of direct materials cost $\dfrac{£36,000}{£32,000} \times 100\% = 112.5\%$

    (v)   % of total direct cost $\dfrac{£36,000}{£72,000} \times 100\% = 50\%$

(b) For department Y the absorption rate will be based on units of output.

$$\frac{£5,000}{1,000 \text{ units}} = £5 \text{ per unit produced}$$

Activity 5.3   Level: Assessment

Using the information in Paragraph 4.6 and the example solution in Paragraph 4.16, determine budgeted overhead absorption rates for each of Friar Tuck Ltd's production departments using bases of absorption which you consider most appropriate from the information provided.

Helping hand. A time-based method is usually the most appropriate. For a machine intensive department use a machine hour rate. For a labour intensive department use a labour hour rate.

Activity 5.4   Level: Assessment

(a) List six possible bases of overhead absorption.

(b) If production overheads in total are expected to be £108,000 and direct labour hours are planned to be 90,000 hours costing £5 per hour, what is the overhead absorption rate:

    (i)   per direct labour hour
    (ii)   as a percentage of direct labour cost?

The effect on total cost of applying different bases

5.12   The choice of the basis of absorption is significant in determining the cost of individual units, or jobs, produced. Using the Eiffel Ltd example in Paragraphs 5.10 and 5.11, suppose that in department X an individual product has the following data.

- a materials cost of £80
- a labour cost of £85
- 36 labour hours required to complete
- 23 machine hours required to complete.

The overhead cost of the product would vary, depending on the basis of overhead absorption used by the company.

(a)   Using a machine hour basis: 23 hrs × £3.60 = £82.80

(b)   Using a labour hour basis: 36 hrs × £2 = £72.00

(c)   As a percentage of direct labour cost: 90% × £85 = £76.50

(d)   As a percentage of direct material cost: 112.5% × £80 = £90.00

(e)   As a percentage of total direct cost: 50% × £165 = £82.50

5.13   In theory, each basis of absorption would be possible, but the company should choose the basis which seems to be **'fairest'**. In our example, this choice will be significant in determining the cost of individual products, as the following summary shows. However **the total cost of production overheads is the estimated overhead expenditure, no matter what basis of absorption is selected.** It is the relative share of overhead costs **borne by individual products and jobs** which is affected by the choice of overhead absorption basis.

5.14   A summary of the various costs of the product in the example beginning in Paragraph 5.12 is shown as follows.

	Basis of overhead recovery				
	Percentage of materials cost	*Percentage of labour cost*	*Percentage of prime cost*	*Machine hours*	*Direct labour hours*
	£	£	£	£	£
Direct material	80	80.0	80.0	80.0	80
Direct labour	85	85.0	85.0	85.0	85
Production overhead	90	76.5	82.5	82.8	72
Full production cost	255	241.5	247.5	247.8	237

5.15   Notice that **the direct cost of the product is not affected by the absorption basis chosen.** This will be determined from the costing records, perhaps via **material requisition notes** and completed **time sheets**.

The arbitrary nature of absorption costing

5.16   It should be obvious to you that, even if a company is trying to be 'fair', there is a great lack of precision about the way an absorption base is chosen.

5.17   This arbitrariness is one of the main criticisms of absorption costing, and if absorption costing is to be used (because of its other virtues) then it is important that **the methods used are kept under regular review.** Changes in working conditions should, if necessary, lead to changes in the way in which work is accounted for.

5.18   For example, a labour intensive department may become mechanised. If a direct labour hour rate of absorption had been used previous to the mechanisation, it would probably now be more appropriate to change to the use of a machine hour rate.

6 BLANKET ABSORPTION RATES AND SEPARATE DEPARTMENTAL ABSORPTION RATES

KEY TERM

A **blanket overhead absorption rate** is an absorption rate used throughout a factory for all jobs and units of output irrespective of the department in which they were produced.

6.1 Consider a factory in which total overheads were £500,000 and there were 250,000 machine hours, during the period under consideration. We could calculate a **blanket overhead absorption rate** of £2 per machine hour (£500,000 ÷ 250,000). This would mean that all jobs passing through the factory would be **charged at the same rate** of £2 per machine hour.

6.2 The factory may have a number of departments undertaking different activities and jobs may not spend an equal amount of time in each department. In this situation the use of a blanket overhead absorption rate is not really appropriate.

6.3 The main argument against the use of blanket overhead absorption rates is the fact that **some products will absorb a higher overhead charge than is fair**. Likewise, **other products will absorb less overhead cost than is fair**.

6.4 If different departments use separate absorption rates **appropriate to the department's activity**, overheads should be charged to products on a **fairer basis** than when blanket overhead absorption rates are used. The overhead charged to products should then be **representative of the costs of the efforts and resources put into making them**.

6.5 EXAMPLE: SEPARATE ABSORPTION RATES

(a) Gibson Ltd has two production departments, for which the following budgeted information is available.

	Department Alpha	Department Beta	Total
Estimated overheads	£360,000	£200,000	£560,000
Estimated direct labour hours	200,000	40,000	240,000

If a single factory overhead absorption rate per direct labour hour is applied, the factory-wide rate of overhead recovery would be:

$$\frac{£560,000}{240,000 \text{ hrs}} = £2.33 \text{ per direct labour hour}$$

(b) If separate departmental rates are applied, these would be:

$$Department\ Alpha = \frac{£360,000}{200,000 \text{ hours}} \qquad Department\ Beta = \frac{£200,000}{40,000 \text{ hours}}$$

$$= £1.80 \text{ per direct labour hour} \qquad\qquad = £5 \text{ per direct labour hour}$$

Department Beta has a higher overhead rate per hour worked.

Now let us consider two separate jobs.

- Job Xen has a total direct cost of £100, takes 30 hours in department Beta and does not involve any work in department Alpha.

- Job Yen has a total direct cost of £100, takes 28 hours in department Alpha and 2 hours in department Beta.

What would be the production cost of each job, using the following rates of overhead recovery based on direct labour hours?

- A single factory-wide rate of overhead recovery
- Separate departmental rates of overhead recovery

6.6 SOLUTION

	Job Xen		*Job Yen*
Single factory rate	£		£
Direct cost	100		100
Production overhead (30 × £2.33)	70		70
Production cost	170		170
Separate departmental rates	£		£
Direct cost	100		100.0
Production overhead			
department Alpha	0	(28 × 1.8)	50.4
department Beta (30 × 5)	150	(2 × 5)	10.0
Production cost	250		160.4

6.7 Using a single factory overhead absorption rate, both jobs would cost the same. However, job Xen is done entirely within department Beta where overhead costs are relatively higher per hour, whereas job Yen is done mostly within department Alpha, where overhead costs are relatively lower per hour.

6.8 Therefore it is arguable that job Xen should cost more in terms of overheads than job Yen. This will only occur if **separate departmental overhead recovery rates** are used to reflect the work done on each job in each department separately.

6.9 If all jobs do not spend approximately the same time in each department then, **to ensure that all jobs are charged with their fair share of overheads,** it is necessary to establish separate overhead rates for each department.

Activity 5.5   Level: Assessment

Pippin Ltd make two types of fruit juicer. One model is for domestic use selling for £400 and the other for industrial applications selling for £500. Unit costs are as follows.

	Domestic	Industrial
	£	£
Direct materials	28	40
Direct labour	180	80
Direct expenses	40	200

Direct labour is paid at the rate of £10 per hour. Direct expenses comprise machine running costs and these are incurred at the rate of £8 per hour.

Production overheads in the coming year are expected to be £1,040,000. Planned production volume is 20,000 units of each product.

Task

Calculate the production overhead absorption rate and the total (direct and indirect) production cost per unit of each product if a single factory overhead absorption rate per direct labour hour is used.

Helping hand. Use the information about labour cost per unit to derive the number of labour hours per unit, and hence the total forecast labour hours.

Activity 5.6   Level: Assessment

Cott and Wool Ltd has two service departments serving two production departments. Overhead costs apportioned to each department are as follows.

Production 1	Production 2	Service 1	Service 2
£	£	£	£
97,428	84,947	9,384	15,823

Service 1 department is expected to work a total of 40,000 hours, divided as follows.

	Hours
Production 1	20,000
Production 2	15,000
Service 2	5,000

Service 2 department is expected to work a total of 12,000 hours divided as follows.

	Hours
Production 1	3,000
Production 2	8,000
Service 1	1,000

Task

Reapportion the costs of the two service departments using the direct apportionment method.

Activity 5.7   Level: Assessment

The finance director of Cott and Wool Ltd has just seen your attempt to reapportion the service department costs. He commented 'Actually we use the repeated distribution method here' and walked away.

Task

Prove to the finance director that you know how to use the repeated distribution method.

Activity 5.8   Level: Assessment

When you show the finance director how you have reapportioned the costs of the two service departments, he says 'Did I say that we used the repeated distribution method? Well, I meant to say the step-down method.'

Task

Prove to the finance director that you know how to use the step-down method. (*Note.* Apportion the overheads of service department 1 first.)

7   OVER AND UNDER ABSORPTION

7.1   It was stated earlier that the usual method of accounting for overheads is to add overhead costs on the basis of a **predetermined recovery rate**. This rate is a sort of **standard cost** since it is based on figures representing what is supposed to happen (that is, figures from the budget). Using the predetermined absorption rate, the actual cost of production can be established as follows.

Direct materials
plus: direct labour
plus: direct expenses
plus: production overheads (based on the predetermined overhead absorption rate)
equals: actual cost of production

7.2   Many students become seriously confused about what can appear a very unusual method of costing (**actual cost** of production including a figure based on the **budget**). Study the following example. It will help clarify this tricky point.

7.3   EXAMPLE: USING THE PREDETERMINED RECOVERY RATE

Patrick Ltd budgeted to make 100 units of product called Jasmine at a cost of £3 per unit in direct materials and £4 per unit in direct labour. The sales price would be £12 per unit, and production overheads were budgeted to amount to £200. A unit basis of overhead recovery is in operation. During the period 120 units were actually produced and sold (for £12 each) and the actual cost of direct materials was £380 and of direct labour, £450. Overheads incurred came to £210.

What was the cost of sales of product Jasmine, and what was the profit? Ignore administration, selling and distribution overheads.

7.4   SOLUTION

The cost of production is the actual direct cost plus the cost of overheads, absorbed at a predetermined rate as established in the budget. In our example, the overhead recovery rate would be £2 per unit produced (£200 ÷ 100 units).

The actual cost of sales of product Jasmine is calculated as follows.

	£
Direct materials (actual)	380
Direct labour (actual)	450
Overheads absorbed (120 units × £2)	240
Full cost of sales	1,070
Sales value (120 units × £12)	1,440
Profit	370

7.5   You may already have noticed that **the actual overheads incurred**, £210, **are not the same as the overheads absorbed** (that is, included) into the cost of production and hence charged against profit, £240. Nevertheless, in normal absorption costing £240 is the 'correct' cost.

7.6   The discrepancy between actual overheads incurred, and the overheads absorbed, which is an inevitable feature of absorption costing, is the **under absorption** or **over absorption** of overhead.

Why does under or over absorption occur?

7.7   The rate of overhead absorption is **based on two estimates** and so it is quite likely that either one or both of the estimates will not agree with what actually occurs. Overheads incurred will, therefore, probably be different from the overheads absorbed into the cost of production. Let's consider an example.

7.8   Suppose that the estimated overhead in a production department is £80,000 and the estimated activity is 40,000 direct labour hours. The overhead recovery rate (using a direct labour hour basis) would be £2 per direct labour hour.

Actual overheads in the period are, say £84,000 and 45,000 direct labour hours are worked.

	£
Overhead incurred (actual)	84,000
Overhead absorbed (45,000 × £2)	90,000
Over absorption of overhead	6,000

In this example, the cost of produced units or jobs has been charged with £6,000 more than was actually spent. An adjustment to reconcile the overheads charged to the actual overhead is necessary and the over-absorbed overhead will be **written off as an adjustment to the profit and loss account** at the end of the accounting period.

7.9   **The overhead absorption rate is predetermined from estimates of overhead cost and the expected volume of activity**. Under or over recovery of overhead will therefore occur in the following circumstances, which can both occur together.

- Actual overhead costs are different from the estimates.
- The actual activity volume is different from the estimated activity volume.

7.10 EXAMPLE: UNDER/OVER ABSORPTION

Watkins Ltd has a budgeted production overhead of £50,000 and a budgeted activity of 25,000 direct labour hours and therefore a recovery rate of £2 per direct labour hour. Calculate the under-/over-absorbed overhead, and explain the reasons for the under/over absorption, in the following circumstances.

(a)   Actual overheads cost £47,000 and 25,000 direct labour hours are worked.
(b)   Actual overheads cost £50,000 and 21,500 direct labour hours are worked.
(c)   Actual overheads cost £47,000 and 21,500 direct labour hours are worked.

7.11 SOLUTION

(a)

	£
Actual overhead	47,000
Absorbed overhead (25,000 × £2)	50,000
Over-absorbed overhead	3,000

Here there is over absorption because although the actual and estimated direct labour hours are the same, actual overheads cost *less* than expected and so too much overhead has been charged against profit.

(b)

	£
Actual overhead	50,000
Absorbed overhead (21,500 × £2)	43,000
Under-absorbed overhead	7,000

Here there is under absorption because although estimated and actual overhead costs were the same, fewer direct labour hours were worked than expected and hence insufficient overheads have been charged against profit.

(c)

	£
Actual overhead	47,000
Absorbed overhead (21,500 × £2)	43,000
Under-absorbed overhead	4,000

The reason for the net under absorption is a combination of the reasons in (a) and (b).

7.12 EXAMPLE: ABSORPTION OF OVERHEADS

The actual total production overhead expenditure of Friar Tuck Ltd, the company we encountered earlier in the chapter, was £176,533. Its actual activity, and the predetermined overhead absorption rates we calculated earlier were as follows.

	Machine shop A	Machine shop B	Assembly
Direct labour hours	8,200	6,500	21,900
Machine usage hours	7,300	18,700	-
Predetermined overhead absorption rates	£7.94 per machine hr	£3.50 per machine hr	£2.24 per direct labour hr

Calculate the under or over absorption of overheads.

7.13 SOLUTION

		£	£
Actual expenditure			176,533
Overhead absorbed			
Machine shop A	7,300 hrs × £7.94	57,962	
Machine shop B	18,700 hrs × £3.50	65,450	
Assembly	21,900 hrs × £2.24	49,056	
			172,468
Under-absorbed overhead			4,065

ASSESSMENT ALERT

The following equation should help you to calculate the under/over recovery of overheads quickly and easily.

ACTUAL OVERHEADS – ABSORBED OVERHEADS = POSITIVE / NEGATIVE VALUE

- If the result is **NEGATIVE (N)**, there is **OVER ABSORPTION (O)**   Profit

- If the result is **POSITIVE (P)**, there is **UNDER ABSORPTION (U)**   Loss.

Remember **NOPU!**

Activity 5.9   Level: Assessment

Why does over or under absorption of overheads occur?

Activity 5.10 | **Level: Assessment**

Brave & Hart Ltd has a budgeted production overhead of £214,981 and a budgeted activity of 35,950 hours of direct labour. Before settling on these estimates the company's accountant had a number of other possibilities for each figure, as shown below. Determine (preferably by inspection rather than full calculation) whether overheads will be over or under absorbed in each case if the alternatives turn out to be the actual figures.

Over or under absorption

(a) $\dfrac{£215,892}{35,950}$

(b) $\dfrac{£214,981}{36,005}$

(c) $\dfrac{£213,894}{36,271}$

(d) $\dfrac{£215,602}{35,440}$

8 PREDETERMINED RATES AND ACTUAL COSTS

8.1 Using a **predetermined overhead absorption rate** usually leads to under or over absorption of overheads because actual output and overhead expenditure will turn out to be different from estimated output and expenditure. You might well wonder why the complications of under or over absorption are necessary. Surely it would be better to use actual costs and outputs, both to avoid under or over absorption entirely and to obtain more 'accurate' costs of production?

8.2 Suppose that a company draws up a budget (a plan based on estimates) to make 1,200 units of a product in the first half of 20X1. Budgeted production overhead costs, all fixed costs, are £12,000. Due to seasonal demand for the company's product, the volume of production varies from month to month. Actual overhead costs are £2,000 per month. Actual monthly production in the first half of 20X1 is listed below, and total actual production in the period is 1,080 units.

The table below shows the production overhead cost per unit using the following.

(a) A predetermined absorption rate of $\dfrac{£12,000}{1,200}$ = £10 per unit

(b) An actual overhead cost per unit each month

(c) An actual overhead cost per unit based on actual six-monthly expenditure of £12,000 and actual six-monthly output of 1,080 units = £11.11 per unit

			(a)	(b)	(c)
				Overhead cost per unit	
			Predetermined unit rate	Actual cost each month	Average actual cost in the six months
Month	*Expenditure* (A)	*Output* (B)		(A) ÷ (B)	
	£	Units	£	£	£
January	2,000	100	10	20.00	11.11
February	2,000	120	10	16.67	11.11
March	2,000	140	10	14.29	11.11
April	2,000	160	10	12.50	11.11
May	2,000	320	10	6.25	11.11
June	2,000	240	10	8.33	11.11
	12,000	1,080			

8.3 Methods (a) and (c) give a **constant overhead cost per unit each month,** regardless of seasonal variations in output. Method (b) gives **variable unit overhead costs,** depending on the time of the year. For this reason, it is argued that method (a) or (c) would provide **more useful (long-term) costing information.**

8.4 In addition, if prices are based on full cost with a percentage mark-up for profit, method (b) would give **seasonal variations in selling prices,** with high prices in low-season and low prices in high-season. Methods (a) and (c) would give a constant price based on this 'cost plus' method.

8.5 With method (a), overhead costs per unit are known throughout the period, and cost statements can be prepared at any time. This is because **predetermined overhead rates are known in advance.** With method (c), overhead costs cannot be established until after the end of the accounting period. For example, overhead costs of output in January 20X1 cannot be established until actual costs and output for the period are known, which will not be until after the end of June 20X1.

8.6 For all of these reasons, **predetermined overhead rates are preferable to actual overhead rates.**

Activity 5.11   **Level: Assessment**

Give three reasons why the use of predetermined overhead absorption rates is seen as being preferable to using actual overheads in costing.

---

9 FIXED AND VARIABLE OVERHEADS AND CAPACITY

9.1 We saw in Chapter 1 that costs can be analysed according to whether they are **fixed or variable** in nature.

- A **fixed overhead** remains unaltered, regardless of the level of activity, eg rent

- A **variable overhead** varies with the level of activity, eg machine running costs

9.2 When an organisation has estimated fixed and variable production overheads, it may calculate a separate absorption rate for each.

9.3 For example, suppose that a company expects its fixed overhead costs in period 9 to be £12,000 and its variable overhead costs to be £1 per direct labour hour.

(a) If the budget is for 4,000 direct labour hours, the absorption rate per hour would be as follows.

	£ per hour
Fixed overhead (£12,000 ÷ 4,000)	3
Variable overhead	1
Total	4

(b) If the budget is for 5,000 direct labour hours, the absorption rate per hour would be as follows.

	£ per hour
Fixed overhead (£12,000 ÷ 5,000)	2.4
Variable overhead	1.0
Total	3.4

The absorption rate, and so the fully absorbed cost of production, reduces as the budgeted volume of activity rises, but only for fixed overheads, not variable overheads. This is because **the (constant) fixed overheads are being shared between a greater number of hours.** The total amount of variable overhead continues to rise with the volume of activity and the hourly rate remains at £1 per hour.

Overhead absorption rates, costs and capacity

9.4 **The importance of the volume of activity in absorption costing cannot be overstated,** not only because large differences between budgeted and actual volume create large amounts of under- or over-absorbed overheads, but also because higher budgeted output reduces fixed overhead absorption rates and unit costs.

9.5 A major criticism of absorption costing derives from this point. Using absorption costing, managers are tempted to produce, not for the market, but **to absorb allocated overheads and reduce unit costs**. Production in excess of demand, however, really only increases the overheads (for example warehousing costs) that the organisation has to bear.

Full capacity, practical capacity and budgeted capacity

9.6 In connection with capacity you may come across a number of terms, as follows.

KEY TERMS

- **Full capacity** is the maximum number of hours that could be worked in ideal conditions.

- **Practical capacity** is full capacity less an allowance for hours lost unavoidably because conditions are not ideal.

- **Budgeted capacity** is the number of hours that a business plans to work.

As a simple example, budgeted capacity would be 60% of practical capacity if a business planned to work a 3 day week rather than a 5 day week. Full capacity would be a 7 day week.

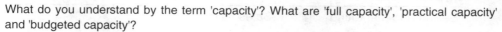

Activity 5.12   **Level: Assessment**

What do you understand by the term 'capacity'? What are 'full capacity', 'practical capacity' and 'budgeted capacity'?

---

10   NON-PRODUCTION OVERHEADS

10.1   For **external reporting** (eg statutory accounts) it is not necessary to allocate non-production overheads to products.

10.2   For **internal reporting** purposes and for a number of industries which base the selling price of their product on estimates of *total* cost or even actual cost (such industries usually use a job costing system), a **total cost per unit** of output may be required. Builders, law firms and garages often charge for their services by adding a percentage profit margin to actual cost. For product pricing purposes and for internal management reports it may therefore be appropriate to allocate non-production overheads to units of output.

Bases for allocating non-production overheads

10.3   A number of non-production expenses such as delivery costs or salespersons' salaries are clearly identified with particular products and can therefore be classified as direct costs. The majority of non-production overheads, however, cannot be directly allocated to particular units of output.

10.4   Two possible methods of allocating such non-production overheads are as follows.

Method 1

10.5   **Choose a basis for the overhead absorption rate** which most closely matches the non-production overhead such as direct labour hours, direct machine hours and so on.

The problem with such a method is that most non-production overheads are unaffected in the short term by changes in the level of output and tend to be fixed costs.

Method 2

10.6   **Allocate non-production overheads on the ability of the products to bear such costs.** One possible approach is to use the production cost as the basis for allocating non-production costs to products.

The **overhead absorption rate** is calculated as follows.

$$\text{Overhead absorption rate} = \frac{\text{Estimated non-production overheads}}{\text{Estimated production costs}}$$

10.7 If, for example, budgeted distribution overheads are £200,000 and budgeted production costs are £800,000, the predetermined distribution overhead absorption rate will be 25% of production cost.

10.8 Other bases for absorbing non-production overheads are as follows.

Types of overhead	Possible absorption base
Selling and marketing	Sales value
Research and development	Consumer cost (= production cost minus cost of direct materials) or added value (= sales value of product minus cost of bought in materials and services)
Distribution	Sales value, weight of products
Administration	Consumer cost or added value

Activity 5.13   Level: Pre-assessment

P Ltd manufactures product M. Data concerning product M for next period are as follows.

Direct material cost per unit	£21
Direct labour cost per unit (£5 per hour)	£50
Production overhead absorption rate	£2 per direct labour hour

Non-production overhead is to be absorbed on the basis of 10 per cent of total production cost.

What is the total cost of product M?

11 ACTIVITY BASED COSTING

11.1 Traditional **absorption costing** appears to be a relatively straightforward way of adding overhead costs to units of production using, more often than not, a volume-related absorption basis (such as direct labour hours or direct machine hours). **Absorption costing assumes that all overheads are related primarily to production volume**.

11.2 This system was developed in a time when most organisations produced only a narrow range of products and when **overhead costs were only a very small fraction of total costs**. Errors made in adding overheads to products were therefore not too significant.

11.3 Nowadays, however, with the advent of **advanced manufacturing technology**, overheads are likely to be far more important and in fact direct labour may account for as little as 5% of a product's cost. Moreover, there has been an **increase in the costs of service support functions,** such as setting-up, production scheduling, and data processing, which assist the efficient manufacture of a wide range of products. These overheads are not, in general, affected by changes in production volume. They tend to vary in the long term according to the **range and complexity of the products manufactured** rather than the volume of output.

11.4 Absorption costing tends to allocate too great a proportion of overheads to high volume products (which cause relatively little diversity), and too small a proportion of overheads to low volume products (which cause greater diversity and therefore use more support services). Therefore alternative methods of costing have been developed. **Activity based costing (ABC)** is one such development.

11.5   The major ideas behind **activity based costing** are as follows.

(a) **Activities cause costs**. Activities include ordering, materials handling, machining, assembly, production scheduling and despatching.

(b) **Producing products creates demand for the activities.**

(c) **Costs** are **assigned** to products **on the basis of a product's consumption of the activities.**

Outline of an ABC system

11.6   An ABC system operates as follows.

Step 1   **Identify an organisation's major activities.**

Step 2   **Identify the factors which determine the size of the costs of an activity/cause the costs of an activity.**

These factors are known as **cost drivers**.

Activity	Possible cost driver
Ordering	Number of orders
Materials handling	Number of production runs
Production scheduling	Number of production runs
Despatching	Number of despatches

Step 3   **Collect the costs of each activity into cost pools**. Cost pools are equivalent to the cost centres used under more traditional costing methods.

Step 4   **Charge overheads to products on the basis of their usage of the activity.**

A product's usage of an activity is measured by the number of the activity's cost driver it generates.

Suppose, for example, that the cost pool for the ordering activity totalled £100,000 and that there were 10,000 orders (the cost driver). Each product would therefore be charged with £10 for each order it required. A batch requiring five orders would therefore be charged with £50 as its fair share of the ordering costs.

Cost drivers

11.7   A **cost driver** is a factor which causes the costs of an activity to change. Examples of cost drivers include the following.

•   Sales levels as these **drive** the costs of invoice processing
•   Miles travelled as these **drive** the costs of customer deliveries
•   Hours worked as these **drive** the costs of production labour

11.8   **The principal idea of ABC is to identify cost drivers**. There are no clear-cut rules for selecting cost drivers, just as there are no rules for what to use as the basis for absorbing costs in traditional absorption costing.

11.9   (a)   **Overheads which vary with output** should be traced to products using volume-related cost drivers eg **direct labour hours** or **direct machine hours**.

        (b)   **Overheads which do not vary with output** should be traced to products using **transaction based cost drivers** eg number of production runs, or number of orders received.

11.10 EXAMPLE: ACTIVITY BASED COSTING

C Ltd makes a number of products, one of which is product W. Data for next period are as follows.

	Product W	All products
Direct cost	£250 per unit	
Short-run variable overheads		£3,080
Machine set up costs		£10,920
Materials handling costs		£7,700
Machine hours	2 per unit	440 hours
Production runs in the period	2	14
Material deliveries in the period	3	28
Production output	10 units	

Using suitable cost drivers, calculate the estimated total production cost per unit for product W for next period.

11.11 SOLUTION

First we need to calculate suitable cost driver rates.

Short-run overheads

The cost driver selected is machine hours.

Overhead rate per machine hour $= \dfrac{£3,080}{440} = £7$ per machine hour

Machine set up costs

The cost driver selected is the number of production runs.

Overhead rate per production run $= \dfrac{£10,920}{14} = £780$ per production run

Materials handling costs

The cost driver selected is the number of material deliveries.

Overhead rate per delivery $= \dfrac{£7,700}{28} = £275$ per delivery

We can now calculate the cost per unit of product W. First we need to calculate the total cost allocated to product W.

	Product W
	£
Direct cost (10 units × £250)	2,500
Short-run variable overheads (2 hrs × £7 × 10 units)	140
Machine set up costs (2 runs × £780)	1,560
Materials handling costs (3 deliveries × £275)	825
Total cost for all units produced	5,025

∴ Cost per unit of product W next period £5,025 ÷ 10 = £502.50

ABC versus traditional costing methods

11.12 **Traditional absorption costing** and **ABC** have many similarities. In both systems, **direct costs go straight to the product and overheads are allocated to production cost centres/cost pools.** The main difference is as follows.

(a) **Traditional absorption costing** usually uses volume-based **absorption bases** (labour hours and/or machine hours) to charge overheads to products.

(b) **ABC** uses many **cost drivers** as absorption bases (number of orders, number of despatches and so on) to charge overheads to products.

11.13 In summary, ABC has absorption rates which are more closely linked to the cause of the overheads.

Activity 5.14   Level: Assessment

What is the difference between traditional absorption costing and activity based costing? Which do you think is preferable?

Activity 5.15   Level: Assessment

D Vower & Co manufacture an assimilator with unit costs as follows.

	£
Direct labour (12 hours @ £7.50)	90
Direct materials	428
Direct expenses (22 machine hours @ £6)	132

Planned production for the coming year is 20,000 units and production overheads are expected to be £859,329. Total labour hours are expected to be 318,500 and total machine hours 637,000.

Task

Making any assumptions you think are appropriate, answer the following questions.

(a) Why are total labour hours different from total machine hours?

(b) What is the total production overhead absorbed by products other than the assimilator, if labour hours are used as an absorption base?

(c) What absorption base do you think would be most appropriate for the assimilator? Explain why.

(d) How much overhead is absorbed per unit of the assimilator using machine hours as the absorption base?

BPP PUBLISHING

Activity 5.16

Level: Assessment

Blott Ltd have cornered the market in hi-tech mopping up machines. Two models are available, one for domestic use selling for £200 and the other for industrial applications selling for £250. Unit costs are as follows.

	Squeegess £	Imbibulator £
Direct materials	14	20
Direct labour	90	40
Direct expenses	20	100

Direct labour is paid at the rate of £5 per hour. Direct expenses comprise machine running costs and these are incurred at the rate of £4 per hour.

Production overheads in the coming year are expected to be £1,000,000. Planned production volume is 10,000 units of each product.

Tasks

(a) Calculate the overhead absorption rate and the total (direct and indirect) production cost per unit of each product if a single factory overhead absorption rate per direct labour hour is used.

(b) State whether you think the unit costs you have calculated for (a) are fair. If not, describe a fairer approach to overhead absorption at Blott Ltd. Assume that any other information you might need could be made available.

Key learning points

- **Overhead** is the cost incurred in the course of making a product, providing a service or running a department, but which cannot be traced directly and in full to the product, service or department.

- The four main types of overhead are **production, administration, selling** and **distribution.**

- Overheads may be dealt with by **traditional absorption** costing, **activity based** costing or **marginal** costing.

- The main reasons for using absorption costing are for **stock valuations, pricing decisions** and **establishing the profitability of different products.**

- **Allocation, apportionment** and **absorption** are the three stages of calculating the costs of overheads to be charged to manufactured output.

- **Apportionment** is a procedure whereby indirect costs (overheads) are spread fairly between cost centres.

- Service cost centre costs may be apportioned to production cost centres by the **repeated distribution method,** or the **step-down method.**

- Overhead absorption is the process whereby costs of cost centres are added to unit, job or batch costs. Overhead absorption is sometimes called **overhead recovery.**

- **Predetermined overhead absorption** rates are calculated using budgeted figures.

- The actual cost of production is made up of the following.

    ° Direct materials
    ° Direct labour
    ° Direct expenses
    ° Overheads (based on the predetermined overhead absorption rate)

- **Under** or **over absorption** of overheads occurs because the predetermined overhead absorption rates are based on forecasts (estimates).

- If an organisation has estimated fixed and variable production overheads, it may calculate a **separate absorption rate** for each.

- The three main types of capacity levels are **full** capacity, **practical** capacity and **budgeted** capacity.

- **Non-production overheads** may be allocated by choosing a basis for the overhead absorption rate which most closely matches the non-production overhead, or on the basis of a product's ability to bear costs.

- **Activity based costing** is an alternative to traditional absorption costing. It involves the identification of the factors (**cost drivers**) which cause the costs of an organisation's major **activities**.

Quick quiz

1   What is the main objective of absorption costing?

2   What are the three stages in charging overheads to units of output?

3   What is overhead apportionment?

4   What are the two stages of overhead apportionment?

5   What is meant by reciprocal servicing?

6   What are the three methods by which the costs of service cost centres can be apportioned?

7   What is overhead absorption?

8   What is the main argument against the use of blanket overhead absorption rates?

9   What makes up the actual cost of production?

10   In which circumstances will under or over absorption of overheads occur?

11   What are the three types of capacity levels that you are likely to encounter and how would you define them?

12   Suggest two possible methods for allocating non-production overheads to products.

13   What are the major ideas behind activity based costing (ABC)?

14   In the context of ABC, what is a cost pool?

Answers to quick quiz

1   To include an appropriate share of the organisation's total overhead in the total cost of a product.

2   Allocation, apportionment and absorption.

3   A procedure whereby indirect costs (overheads) are spread fairly between cost centres.

4   Sharing out common costs and apportioning service cost centre costs to production cost centres.

5   Where the service cost centres make use of each other's services.

6   Direct, repeated distribution or reciprocal allocation and step-down method.

7   The process whereby costs of cost centres are added to the cost of cost units.

8   The fact that some products will absorb a higher or lower overhead charge than is fair.

9   Direct materials, direct labour, direct expenses and overheads (based on the predetermined overhead absorption rate).

10   • If actual overhead costs are different from estimates.

       • If actual activity volume is different from estimated activity volume.

       • If both actual overhead costs and actual activity are different from estimated costs and activity.

11   • Full capacity. The maximum number of hours that could be worked in ideal conditions.

       • Practical capacity. Full capacity less hours lost unavoidably because conditions are not ideal.

       • Budgeted capacity. The number of hours that a business plans to work.

12   By choosing a basis for the overhead absorption rate which most closely matches the non-production overhead or by allocating the non-production overheads on the product's ability to bear such costs.

13   •   Activities cause costs.
- Producing products creates demand for the activities.
- Costs are assigned to products on the basis of a product's consumption of the activities.

14   A cost pool is a 'collecting place' for the costs relating to a particular activity. It is similar to a cost centre in a traditional absorption costing system.

Part C
Cost accounting principles

6 Cost behaviour

This chapter contains

Learning objectives

On completion of this chapter you will be able to:

- Understand cost behaviour patterns

- Describe how cost behaviour is affected by levels of activity

- Use the high-low technique in order to determine fixed and variable elements of costs

Knowledge and understanding

- Analysis of the effect of changing activity levels on unit costs

- The distinction between fixed, semi-fixed and variable costs

BPP
PUBLISHING

1 INTRODUCTION

1.1 In Chapter 1 of this Interactive Text you saw that costs could be analysed according to whether they were **fixed** or **variable.** In this chapter we will be looking further at this sort of analysis of costs: the analysis according to the way costs behave in relation to the **level of activity.**

1.2 We can demonstrate the ways in which costs behave by drawing graphs. This chapter aims to examine the different ways in which costs behave (this is known as **cost behaviour** analysis) and to demonstrate this behaviour graphically.

2 GENERAL PRINCIPLES OF COST BEHAVIOUR

2.1 The general rule is that **variable costs vary directly with changes in activity levels,** whereas **fixed costs do not vary directly with changes in activity levels.**

> **KEY TERM**
>
> **Cost behaviour** is the way in which costs are affected by changes in the volume of output (level of activity).

Level of activity

> **KEY TERM**
>
> The **level of activity** refers to the amount of work done, or the number of events that have occurred.

2.2 Depending on circumstances, the level of activity may be measured in a number of different ways including the following.

- The volume of production
- The number or value of items sold
- The number of invoices issued
- The number of units of electricity consumed

For our purposes in this chapter, the level of activity for measuring cost will generally be taken to be the volume of production.

Basic principles of cost behaviour

2.3 The basic principle of cost behaviour is that **as the level of activity rises, costs will usually rise**. It will cost more to produce 2,000 units of output than it will cost to produce 1,000 units; it will usually cost more to make five telephone calls than to make one call and so on.

2.4 This principle is common sense. The problem for the cost accountant, however, is to determine for each item of cost the way in which costs rise and by how much as the level of activity increases.

3 COST BEHAVIOUR PATTERNS

Fixed costs

3.1 As you already know, a fixed cost is a cost which tends to be unaffected by increases or decreases in the volume of output. Fixed costs are a period charge, in that they relate to a span of time; as the time span increases, so too will the fixed costs (which are sometimes referred to as **period costs** for this reason).

3.2 A sketch graph of a fixed cost would look like this.

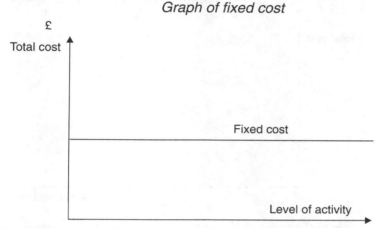

Graph of fixed cost

The following are fixed costs.

- The salary of the managing director (per month or per annum)
- The rent of a single factory building (per month or per annum)
- Straight line depreciation of a single machine (per month or per annum)

Step costs

3.3 Many items of cost are a **fixed cost in nature within certain levels of activity.** For example the depreciation of a machine may be fixed if production remains below 1,000 units per month, but if production exceeds 1,000 units, a second machine may be required, and the cost of depreciation (on two machines) would go up a step. A sketch graph of a step cost would look like this.

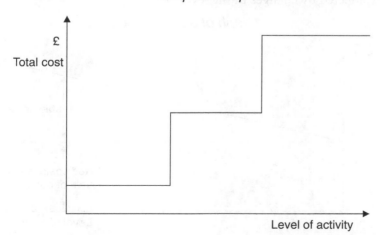

Graph of step cost

A step cost is sometimes called a **stepped-fixed cost.**

Other examples of step costs are as follows.

- **Rent**, where accommodation needs increase as output levels increase.

117

- **Basic wages**. As output rises, more employees with a fixed wage (direct workers, supervisors) are required.

Variable costs

3.4 A variable cost is a cost which tends to **vary directly with the volume of output.** The variable cost per unit is the **same amount for each unit produced** whereas *total* variable cost increases as volume of output increases. A sketch graph of a variable cost would look like this.

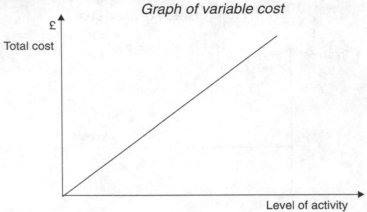

Graph of variable cost

3.5 A constant variable cost per unit implies that the purchase price per unit of material purchased or cost per labour hour worked and so on is constant, and that the rate of material usage/labour productivity is also constant. In other words, **constant rate and efficiency levels are implied in variable costs.**

(a) The most important variable cost is the cost of **raw materials** (where there is no discount for bulk purchasing. Bulk purchase discounts reduce the cost of purchases).

(b) Sales commission is variable in relation to the volume or value of sales.

Mixed costs (or semi-variable costs or semi-fixed costs)

3.6 These are cost items which are **part fixed** and **part variable**, and are therefore partly affected by changes in the level of activity.

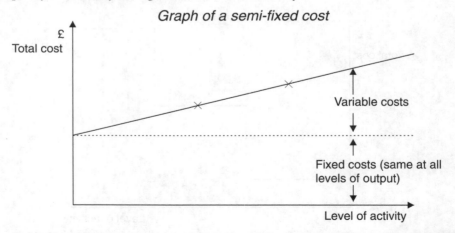

Graph of a semi-fixed cost

Examples of these costs include electricity and gas bills. Both of these costs usually include a standing basic charge plus a variable charge per unit of consumption.

Activity 6.1   Level: Pre-assessment

Are the following likely to be fixed, variable or mixed (semi-fixed) costs?

(a) Telephone bill
(b) Annual salary of the chief accountant
(c) The accounting technician's annual membership fee to AAT (paid by the company)
(d) Cost of materials used to pack 20 units of product X into a box
(e) Wages of warehousemen, paid on an hourly basis

Other cost behaviour patterns

3.7 Other cost behaviour patterns may be appropriate to certain cost items. Graphs (a) and (b) show the behaviour of the cost of materials after the deduction of a bulk purchase discount.

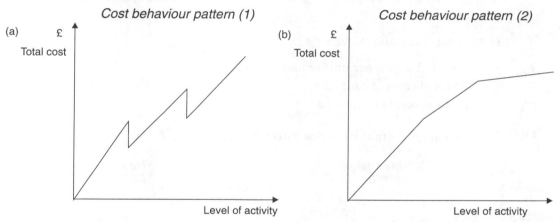

In graph (a) the bulk purchase discount applies **retrospectively** to all units purchased whereas in graph (b) the discount applies **only to units purchased in excess of a certain quantity**, the earlier units being paid for at a higher unit cost.

Graph (c) represents an item of cost which is variable with output up to a certain maximum level of cost; graph (d) represents a cost which is variable with output, subject to a minimum (fixed) charge.

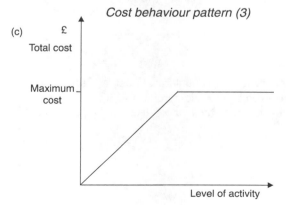

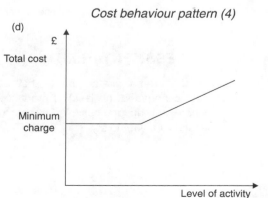

Activity 6.2   **Level: Assessment**

Can you think of a cost whose behaviour might be represented by each of graphs (c) and (d)?

Cost behaviour and total and unit costs

3.8 The following table relates to different levels of production of the Randolph. The variable cost of producing a Randolph is £5 per unit. Fixed costs are £5,000 per period.

	1 Randolph £	10 Randolphs £	50 Randolphs £
Total variable cost	5	50	250
Variable cost per unit	5	5	5
Total fixed cost	5,000	5,000	5,000
Fixed cost per unit	5,000	500	100
Total cost (fixed and variable)	5,005	5,050	5,250
Total cost per unit	5,005	505	105

By studying the table above, you should be able to see how different activity levels affect the variable cost per unit, fixed cost per unit and the total cost per unit of a Randolph.

In summary, as activity levels rise:

- the variable cost per unit remains constant;
- the fixed cost per unit falls;
- the total cost per unit falls.

3.9 In sketch graph form this may be illustrated as follows.

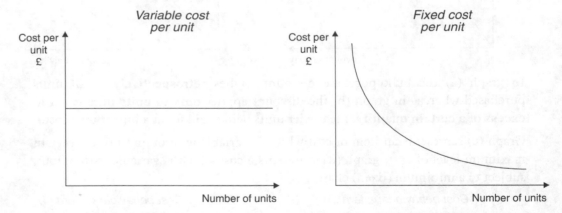

ASSESSMENT ALERT

Be prepared to sketch graphs showing how fixed and variable costs behave in general with changes in the level of production. Remember to use a ruler and a sharp pencil when drawing graphs in an assessment - you are much more likely to impress the assessor if you do so!

Activity 6.3　　　　　　　　　　　　　**Level: Pre-assessment**

Draw graphs to illustrate the following cost behaviour patterns.

(a)　Variable costs
(b)　Fixed costs
(c)　Step costs

4　COST BEHAVIOUR AND LEVELS OF ACTIVITY

4.1　The following example highlights how and why costs may be analysed into fixed, variable and step cost items. Make sure that you study it carefully and that you have a clear understanding of the cost behaviour principles involved.

4.2　EXAMPLE: COST BEHAVIOUR AND LEVELS OF ACTIVITY

Brandy Snap Ltd has a fleet of company cars for sales representatives. Running costs have been estimated as follows.

(a)　Cars cost £12,000 when new, and have a guaranteed trade-in value of £6,000 at the end of two years. Depreciation is charged on a straight-line basis.

(b)　Petrol and oil cost 15 pence per mile.

(c)　Tyres cost £300 per set to replace; replacement occurs after 30,000 miles.

(d)　Routine maintenance costs £200 per car (on average) in the first year and £450 in the second year.

(e)　Repairs average £400 per car over two years and are thought to vary with mileage. The average car travels 25,000 miles per annum.

(f)　Tax, insurance, membership of motoring organisations and so on cost £400 per annum per car.

Task

Calculate the average cost per annum of cars which travel 20,000 miles per annum and 30,000 miles per annum.

4.3　SOLUTION

Costs may be analysed into fixed, variable and step cost items, a step cost being a cost which is fixed in nature but only within certain levels of activity.

(a)　*Fixed costs*

	£ per annum
Depreciation £(12,000 − 6,000) ÷ 2	3,000
Routine maintenance £(200 + 450) ÷ 2	325
Tax, insurance etc	400
	3,725

(b)　*Variable costs*

	Pence per mile
Petrol and oil	15.0
Repairs (£400 ÷ 50,000 miles)	0.8
	15.8

(c)　Step costs are tyre replacement costs, which are £300 at the end of every 30,000 miles.

　　(i)　If the car travels less than or exactly 30,000 miles in two years, the tyres will not be changed. Average cost of tyres per annum　=　£0.

(ii)   If a car travels more than 30,000 miles and up to (and including) 60,000 miles in two years, there will be one change of tyres in the period. Average cost of tyres per annum = £150 (£300 ÷ 2).

(iii)   If a car exceeds 60,000 miles in two years (up to 90,000 miles) there will be two tyre changes. Average cost of tyres per annum = £300. (£600 ÷ 2).

The estimated costs per annum of cars travelling 20,000 miles per annum and 30,000 miles per annum would therefore be as follows.

	20,000 miles per annum £	30,000 miles per annum £
Fixed costs	3,725	3,725
Variable costs (15.8p per mile)	3,160	4,740
Tyres	150	150
Cost per annum	7,035	8,615
Cost per mile	£0.35	£0.29

4.4   Notice that the cost per mile is lower if more miles are travelled in a year. This is because the **fixed element** of the various costs is **spread over a greater number of miles.**

5   DETERMINATION OF FIXED AND VARIABLE ELEMENTS: THE HIGH-LOW TECHNIQUE

5.1   We have seen that a semi-fixed or semi-variable cost has a **basic fixed cost element,** and a variable cost element which **depends on the level of activity.** But how can we identify how much of the cost is fixed, and how much is variable?

5.2   There are several methods for identifying the fixed and variable elements of semi-variable costs. Each method is only an estimate, and each will produce different results. One of the principal methods is the **high-low technique.**

High-low technique

5.3

Step 1   **Select the highest and lowest activity level**

Review records of costs in previous periods. Select the following.

- The period with the **highest** activity level
- The period with the **lowest** activity level

Step 2   **Determine the costs and units at each activity level**

- Total cost at high activity level
- Total cost at low activity level
- Total units at high activity level
- Total units at low activity level

Step 3	**Calculate the variable cost per unit**

$$\frac{\text{Total cost at high activity level} - \text{total cost at low activity level}}{\text{Total units at high activity level} - \text{total units at low activity level}}$$

This will be the variable cost per unit, since the change in costs at the two activity levels must be due to a change in variable costs.

Step 4	**Determine the fixed cost**

Fixed cost =   (Total cost at high activity level) – (total units at high activity level × variable cost per unit)

5.4   EXAMPLE: THE HIGH-LOW TECHNIQUE

G Ltd has recorded the following total costs during the last five years.

Year	Output volume	Total cost
	Units	£
20X3	65,000	145,000
20X4	80,000	160,000
20X5	90,000	170,000
20X6	60,000	140,000
20X7	75,000	155,000

Task

Calculate the total cost that should be expected in 20X8 if output is 85,000 units.

5.5   SOLUTION

Step 1	Select the highest and lowest activity level

- Period with highest activity = 20X5
- Period with lowest activity = 20X6

Step 2	Determine the costs and units at each activity level

- Total cost at high activity level   = 170,000
- Total cost at low activity level   = 140,000
- Total units at high activity level = 90,000
- Total units at low activity level = 60,000

Step 3	Calculate the variable cost per unit

Variable cost per unit (V) is calculated as follows.

$$\frac{\text{Total cost at high activity level} - \text{total cost at low activity level}}{\text{Total units at high activity level} - \text{total units at low activity level}}$$

$$= \frac{£170,000 - £140,000}{90,000 - 60,000} = \frac{£30,000}{30,000} = £1 \text{ per unit}$$

Step 4	Determine the fixed cost

Fixed costs (F) are calculated as follows.

F   =   (Total cost at high activity level) – (total units at high activity level × variable cost per unit)

=   170,000 – (90,000 × 1)

=   170,000 – 90,000

=   £80,000

Therefore the expected costs in 20X8 for output of 85,000 units are as follows.

		£
Variable costs (V) =	85,000 × £1 =	85,000
Fixed costs (F) =		80,000
		165,000

Activity 6.4   Level: Assessment

The costs of operating the Maintenance department of a computer manufacturer, Port and Lemon Ltd, for the last four months have been as follows.

Month	Output volume units	Total cost £
1	7,000	110,000
2	8,000	115,000
3	7,700	111,000
4	6,000	97,000

Task

What costs should be expected in month 5 when output is expected to be 7,500 units?

Key learning points

- **Cost behaviour patterns** demonstrate the way in which costs are affected by changes in the level of activity.

- Costs which are affected by the level of activity are **variable costs.**

- Costs which are not affected by the level of activity are **fixed costs** or **period costs.**

- **Step costs** are costs which are fixed in nature within certain levels of activity.

- **Mixed costs** (semi-variable/semi-fixed costs) are partly fixed and partly variable, and therefore only partly affected by changes in activity levels.

- The level of activity is the amount of work done or the number of events that have occurred.

- In general as activity levels rise, the variable cost per unit remains constant, the fixed cost per unit falls and the total cost per unit falls.

- The **high-low technique** is used to estimate the fixed and variable elements of semi-variable costs.

BPP PUBLISHING

Quick quiz

1   How do variable costs differ from fixed costs?

2   How would you describe cost behaviour?

3   What does the level of activity refer to?

4   What is a step cost?

5   How do mixed costs behave?

6   What is the formula used for estimating the variable cost per unit of a product using the high-low technique?

Answers to quick quiz

1   Variable costs vary directly with changes in activity levels, whereas fixed costs do not.

2   The way in which costs vary with the level of activity.

3   The amount of work done or the number of events that have occurred.

4   A cost which is fixed in nature within certain levels of activity.

5   They are only partly affected by changes in the level of activity (as they are part-fixed and part-variable costs).

6   $$\frac{\text{Total cost at high activity level } - \text{ total cost at low activity level}}{\text{Total units at high activity level } - \text{ total units at low activity level}}$$

7 Bookkeeping entries for cost information

This chapter contains

1   Introduction

2   Cost information and ledger accounting

3   Getting costs into finished units

4   Control accounts

5   Cost bookkeeping systems

Learning objectives

On completion of this chapter you will be able to:

- Code and record cost information

- Resolve queries or refer them to others as appropriate

Performance criteria

6.1   (ii)   Information relating to direct costs is clearly and correctly coded, analysed and recorded

6.1   (vi)   Queries are either resolved or referred to the appropriate person

6.2   (i)   Data are correctly coded, analysed and recorded

6.2   (viii)   Staff working in operational departments are consulted to resolve any queries in the data

Range statement

6.1.1 Direct costs: standard and actual material costs; standard and actual labour costs; standard and actual expenses

- Materials: raw materials; part finished goods; materials issued from stores within the organisation; deliveries

- Labour: employees of the organisation on the payroll; sub-contractors; agency staff

1 INTRODUCTION

1.1 You should now have a good idea of the way that the materials, labour and overhead costs of an item are determined. Now it is time to see how the costs and revenues are recorded **in total** in the cost accounting **bookkeeping system.**

2 COST INFORMATION AND LEDGER ACCOUNTING

2.1 In previous chapters we have scrupulously avoided T accounts, debits and credits, ledgers and bookkeeping. The cost records we have described so far are quite adequate for individual products or jobs, and it is not essential to go beyond this.

2.2 However, unless records of **totals** are maintained and checks of these records are made, there is no way of knowing whether all the costs that should have been recorded really have been recorded. The solution to this problem is **to link the cost records to the cash and credit transactions that are summarised in the nominal ledger**. If you like you can think of recording cost information as dealing with debits. Let us look at an example to illustrate what we mean.

2.3 EXAMPLE: COST INFORMATION AND LEDGER ACCOUNTING

(a) Suppose you buy £100 of materials for cash and £100 on credit. What entries will you make in the ledgers?

(b) From the knowledge you have already acquired elsewhere you should have no difficulty in answering this question. The cash transaction will be recorded in the cash book, analysed as appropriate. It will also be recorded in the nominal ledger as follows.

		£	£
DEBIT	Purchases	100	
CREDIT	Cash		100

(c) The credit transaction will be recorded in the purchase ledger under the name of the supplier in question. It will also be recorded in the nominal ledger as follows.

		£	£
DEBIT	Purchases	100	
CREDIT	Creditors ledger control account		100

(d) Now consider this transaction from the point of view of what you have learnt in this Interactive Text. The appropriate **stores record card** and **bin card** will have been updated to show the acquisition of £200 worth of stock but the cash and credit side of the transactions have not entered any cost records. In other words, the cost records are only interested in the entry made in the nominal ledger under purchases.

2.4 We could go further and explain that just as the analysed cash book is a very detailed breakdown of the entries in the cash control account in the nominal ledger, and just as the creditors ledger shows the detailed information behind the creditors ledger control account, **the cost records are a detailed breakdown of the information contained in the purchases account, the wages and salaries account, and all the expense accounts in the nominal ledger.**

2.5 It is tempting to go no further than this. So long as you understand the basic principles of double entry bookkeeping, the cost accounting aspects of it should cause you no more difficulty than any other aspects.

2.6 All you really need to know, however, is the following.

- How to turn purchases, wages and so on into finished units of production
- How to deal with under- or over-absorbed overheads

3 GETTING COSTS INTO FINISHED UNITS

3.1 First, let's look at how a single purchase of materials works through into the final accounts. The relevant double entries are as follows.

			£	£
(a)	DEBIT	Materials	X	
	CREDIT	Cash		X

Being the buying of materials which are put into raw materials stock

			£	£
(b)	DEBIT	Work in progress	X	
	CREDIT	Materials stock		X

Being the issue of materials to production for use in work in progress

(c)	DEBIT	Finished goods	X	
	CREDIT	Work in progress		X

Being the issue of units that are now finished to finished goods stock

(d)	DEBIT	Cost of sales	X	
	CREDIT	Finished goods		X

Being the taking of units out of finished goods stock and selling them

(e)	DEBIT	Profit and loss account	X	
	CREDIT	Cost of sales		X

Being the closing off of ledger accounts and the drawing up of financial statements. This entry would only be made at the end of a period.

3.2 EXAMPLE: BASIC COST ACCOUNTING ENTRIES FOR MATERIALS

Fred Flintstone Ltd begins trading with £200 cash. £200 is initially spent on timber to make garden furniture. £100 worth of timber is left in store, while the other £100 is worked on to make garden chairs and tables. Before long, £50 worth of timber has been converted into garden furniture and this furniture is sold for £150. How will these events and transactions be reflected in the accounts?

3.3 SOLUTION

CASH ACCOUNT

	£		£
Cash - opening balance	200	Purchase of materials	200
Sale of finished goods-sales	150	Closing balance	150
	350		350

MATERIALS ACCOUNT

	£		£
Cash purchase	200	Transfer to WIP	100
		Closing balance	100
	200		200

WORK IN PROGRESS ACCOUNT

	£		£
Transfer from materials	100	Transfer to finished goods	50
		Closing balance	50
	100		100

FINISHED GOODS ACCOUNT

	£		£
Transfer from WIP	50	Transfer to cost of sales	50
	50		50

COST OF SALES ACCOUNT

	£		£
Transfer from finished goods	50	Shown in profit and loss account	50
	50		50

SALES ACCOUNT

	£		£
Shown in profit and loss account	150	Cash	150
	150		150

FRED FLINTSTONE LTD
PROFIT AND LOSS ACCOUNT

	£
Sales	150
Cost of sales	50
Profit	100

Accounting for labour costs

3.4 We will use an example to review briefly the principal bookkeeping entries for wages.

3.5 EXAMPLE: THE WAGES CONTROL ACCOUNT

The following details were extracted from a weekly payroll for 750 employees at a factory in Trinidad.

Analysis of gross wages

	Direct workers £	Indirect workers £	Total £
Ordinary time	36,000	22,000	58,000
Overtime: basic wage	8,700	5,430	14,130
premium	4,350	2,715	7,065
Shift allowance	3,465	1,830	5,295
Sick pay	950	500	1,450
Idle time	3,200	-	3,200
Total gross wages	56,665	32,475	89,140
Net wages paid to employees	£45,605	£24,220	£69,825

Task

Prepare the wages control account for the week.

3.6   SOLUTION

(a)   **The wages control account** acts as a sort of **collecting place** for net wages paid and deductions made from gross pay. The gross pay is then analysed between **direct** and **indirect wages**.

(b)   The first step is to determine which wage costs are **direct** and which are **indirect**. The direct wages will be debited to the **work in progress account** and the indirect wages will be debited to the **production overhead account**.

(c)   There are in fact only two items of direct wages cost in this example, the ordinary time (£36,000) and the basic overtime wage (£8,700) paid to direct workers. All other payments (including the overtime premium) are indirect wages.

(d)   The net wages paid are debited to the control account, and the balance then represents the deductions which have been made for income tax, national insurance, and so on.

WAGES CONTROL ACCOUNT

	£		£
Bank: net wages paid	69,825	Work in progress: direct labour	44,700
Deductions control accounts* (£89,140 – £69,825)	19,315	Production overhead control: indirect labour	27,430
		Overtime premium	7,065
		Shift allowance	5,295
		Sick pay	1,450
		Idle time	3,200
	89,140		89,140

* In practice there would be a separate deductions control account for each type of deduction made (for example, PAYE and National Insurance).

Activity 7.1   **Level: Pre-assessment**

What items are included in a wages control account?

---

4   CONTROL ACCOUNTS

Control accounts

KEY TERM

A **control account** is an account which records total cost. In contrast, individual ledger accounts record individual debits and credits.

4.1   Obviously the previous section is highly simplified. This is to avoid obscuring the basic principles. For example, we have until now assumed that if £200 of materials are purchased the only entries made will be Dr Materials, Cr Cash. In practice, of course, this £200 might be made up of 20 different types of material, each costing £10, and if so each type of material is likely to have its own sub-account.

4.2   These sub-accounts would be exactly like individual personal accounts in the creditors' ledger or the debtors' ledger. You have probably guessed that we need to use **control accounts** to summarise the detailed transactions (such as how the £200 of materials is made up) and to maintain the double entry in the nominal ledger.

KEY TERMS

- A **materials control account** (or **stores control account**) records the total cost of invoices received for each type of material (purchases) and the total cost of each type of material issued to various departments (the sum of the value of all materials requisition notes).

- A **wages control account** records the total cost of the payroll (plus employer's national insurance contributions) and the total cost of direct and indirect labour as recorded in the wages analysis sheets and charged to each production unit, job, or batch.

- A **production overhead control account** is a total record of actual expenditure incurred and the amount absorbed into individual units, jobs or batches. Subsidiary records for actual overhead expenditure items and cost records which show the overheads attributed to individual units or jobs must agree with or reconcile to the totals in the control account.

- A **work in progress control account** records the total costs of direct materials, direct wages and production overheads charged to units, jobs or batches, and the cost of finished goods which are completed and transferred to the distribution department. Subsidiary records of individual job costs and so on will exist for jobs still in production and for jobs completed.

Activity 7.2 **Level: Assessment**

The following data relate to the stores ledger control account of Fresh Ltd, an air freshener manufacturer, for the month of April 20X0.

	£
Opening stock	18,500
Closing stock	16,100
Deliveries from suppliers	142,000
Returns to suppliers	2,300
Cost of indirect materials issued	25,200

Tasks

(a) Calculate the value of the issue of direct materials during April 20X0.
(b) State the double entry to record the issue of direct materials in the cost accounts.

---

5 COST BOOKKEEPING SYSTEMS

5.1 There are two types of cost bookkeeping system, the **interlocking** and the **integrated.** Interlocking systems require **separate ledgers** to be kept for the cost accounting function and the financial accounting function, which means that the cost accounting profit and financial accounting profit have to be **reconciled.** Integrated systems, on the other hand, **combine the two functions in one set of ledger accounts.**

5.2 Modern cost accounting systems (computerised) integrate cost accounting information and financial accounting information and are known as **integrated systems.** You are much more likely to deal with integrated systems, and this is the system we shall be looking at in detail.

> **KEY TERM**
>
> An **integrated system** is a system where the cost accounting function and the financial accounting function are combined in one system of ledger accounts.

5.3 The following diagram shows a cost accounting system which uses absorption costing. The entries in the individual accounts have been simplified. Study the diagram carefully, and work through the double entries represented in the diagram. **Make sure that you understand the logic behind the flow of costs.**

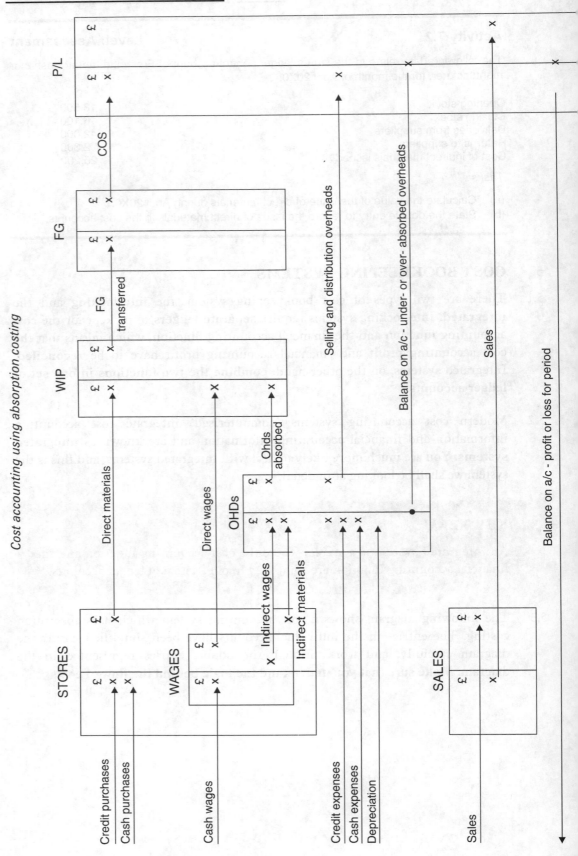

Cost accounting using absorption costing

Dealing with overheads

5.4 When an absorption costing system is in use, we know that the amount of overhead included in the cost of an item is **absorbed at a predetermined rate**. The entries made in the cash book and the nominal ledger, however, are the **actual amounts**.

5.5 As we saw in an earlier chapter, it is highly unlikely that the actual amount and the predetermined amount will be the same. The difference is called **under- or over-absorbed overhead**. To deal with this in the cost accounting books we need to have an account to collect under- or over-absorbed amounts for each type of overhead.

5.6 EXAMPLE: THE UNDER-/OVER-ABSORBED OVERHEAD ACCOUNT

Gnocci Ltd absorbs production overheads at the rate of £0.50 per operating hour and administration overheads at 20% of the production cost of sales. Actual data for one month was as follows.

Administration overheads	£32,000
Production overheads	£46,500
Operating hours	90,000
Production cost of sales	£180,000

What entries need to be made for overheads in the ledgers?

5.7 SOLUTION

PRODUCTION OVERHEAD CONTROL ACCOUNT

	£		£
		Absorbed into WIP	
Cash	46,500	(90,000 × £0.50)	45,000
		Under-absorbed overhead	1,500
	46,500		46,500

ADMINISTRATION OVERHEAD CONTROL ACCOUNT

	£		£
Cash	32,000	To cost of sales (£180,000 × 0.2)	36,000
Over-absorbed overhead	4,000		
	36,000		36,000

UNDER-/OVER-ABSORBED OVERHEAD ACCOUNT

	£		£
Production overhead	1,500	Administration overhead	4,000
Balance to profit and loss a/c	2,500		
	4,000		4,000

Less production overhead has been absorbed than has been spent so there is **under-absorbed production overhead of £1,500**. More administration overhead has been absorbed (into cost of sales, note, not into WIP) and so there is **over-absorbed administration overhead of £4,000**. The net over-absorbed overhead of £2,500 is a **credit in the profit and loss account**.

135

Activity 7.3 — Level: Assessment

PO Ltd absorbs production overheads using a direct labour hour rate. Data for last period are as follows.

Production overheads incurred – paid through bank account	£125,478
Depreciation of production machinery	£4,100
Direct labour hours worked	27,000
Production overhead absorption rate per direct labour hour	£5

Task

Prepare the production overhead control account for the period.

5.8 EXAMPLE: INTEGRATED ACCOUNTS

Shown below are the opening balances for the month of September 20X0 for Vermicelli Ltd, with a summary bank account and information obtained from the stores department, the payroll department and the production department. The provisions for depreciation are also given below. During the month goods costing £196,000 were sold (all on credit) for £278,000.

OPENING BALANCES - SEPTEMBER 20X0

	Dr £'000	Cr £'000
Raw materials stores account	30	
Work in progress account	20	
Finished goods account	60	
Debtors account	74	
Creditors account		85
Creditors for National Insurance & PAYE		19
Factory buildings account	250	
Provision for depreciation: factory buildings		20
Equipment account	320	
Provision for depreciation: equipment		170
Share capital account		100
Share premium account		20
Profit and loss reserve		290
Cash and bank account		50
	754	754

STORES REPORT - SEPTEMBER 20X0

	£'000
Materials received from suppliers and invoiced	40 (1)
Materials issued to production	32 (2)
Materials issued to production service departments	8 (3)
Materials issued to administrative departments	2 (4)

PAYROLL REPORT - SEPTEMBER 20X0

	Gross wages £'000	PAYE & employees' NI £'000	Net £'000	Employer's NI £'000
Direct wages (£5.50 per hour)	33 (a)	8	25	(2) a.
Production indirect wages	7 (b)	1	6	-
Administrative staff wages and salaries	10 (b)	3	7	1 (b)
Selling staff wages and salaries	10 (b)	3	7	1 (b)
	60	15 (c)	45 (d)	4

PRODUCTION REPORT - SEPTEMBER 20X0

Production overhead absorption rate	£12.50 per direct labour hour (e)
Cost of work completed in the month	£150,000 (f)

Prod OHD
33,000 ÷ £5.50   6,000 × 12.50 hrs
£75,000

CASH AND BANK ACCOUNT

	£'000		£'000
Debtors	(g) 290	Balance b/f	50 *overdrawn.*
		Wages and salaries	45 (d)
		Production overhead	15 (h)
		Administration overhead	8 (i)
		Selling overhead	20 (j)
		Creditor for national insurance and PAYE	19 (k)
		Creditors	45 (l)
		Balance c/f (surplus)	88
	290		290
Balance b/f	88		

PROVISIONS FOR DEPRECIATION - SEPTEMBER 20X0

	£'000
Factory buildings	2 m
Factory equipment	35 n
Office equipment	5 o
	42

Tasks

(a) Post the information given in the example to the integrated accounts of Vermicelli Ltd.

(b) Prepare a trial balance for Vermicelli Ltd, as at 30 September 20X0.

(c) Prepare a trading and profit loss account for Vermicelli Ltd for September 20X0.

5.9 SOLUTION

(a)

RAW MATERIALS STORES ACCOUNT

	£'000		£'000
Balance b/f	30	Work in progress account	32 (2)
(1) Creditors	40	Production overhead account	8 (3)
		Administration overhead account	2 (4)
		Balance c/f	28
	70		70
Balance b/f	28		

WAGES AND SALARIES ACCOUNT

	£'000		£'000
Bank	45 (d)	Work in progress	33 (a)
Creditor for national insurance and PAYE	15 (c)	Production overhead	7 (b)
		Administration overhead	10 (b)
		Selling overhead	10 (b)
	60		60

PRODUCTION OVERHEAD ACCOUNT

	£'000		£'000
Raw materials stores	8 (s)	Work in progress (note 1)	75 (e)
Wages and salaries	7 (b)		
Bank (expenses)	15 (h)		
Depreciation: buildings	2 (m)		
Depreciation: equipment	35 (n)		
Over-absorbed overhead to P + L	8		
	75		75

WORK IN PROGRESS ACCOUNT

	£'000		£'000
Balance b/f	20	Finished goods	150 (f)
Raw materials stores	32 (a)		
Wages and salaries	33 (a)		
Creditor for national insurance	2 (a)		
Production overhead	75 (e)	Balance c/f	12
	162		162
Balance b/f	12		

FINISHED GOODS ACCOUNT

	£'000		£'000
Balance b/f	60	Cost of sales	196
Work in progress (f)	150	Balance c/f	14
	210		210
Balance b/f	14		

COST OF SALES ACCOUNT

	£'000		£'000
Finished goods	196	Profit and loss account	196

ADMINISTRATION OVERHEAD ACCOUNT

	£'000		£'000
Raw materials stores	2 (u)	Profit and loss account	
Wages and salaries	10 (b)	(note 2)	26
Bank (expenses)	8 (i)		
Creditor for national insurance	1 (b)		
Depreciation	5 (o)		
	26		26

SELLING OVERHEAD ACCOUNT

	£'000		£'000
Wages and salaries	10(b)	Profit and loss account	31
Bank (expenses)	20(b)		
Creditor for national insurance	1		
	31		31

SALES ACCOUNT

	£'000		£'000
Profit and loss account	278	Debtors	278

TRADING AND PROFIT AND LOSS ACCOUNT

	£'000		£'000
Cost of sales	196	Sales	278
Gross profit c/d	82		
	278		278
Administration overhead	26	Gross profit b/d	82
Selling overhead	31	Over-absorbed overhead	8
Profit and loss reserve	33		
	90		90

DEBTORS ACCOUNT

	£'000		£'000
Balance b/f	74	Bank	290 (g)
Sales	278	Balance c/f	62
	352		352
Balance b/f	62		

CREDITORS ACCOUNT

	£'000		£'000
Bank	(l) 45	Balance b/f	85
Balance c/f	80	Raw materials stores	40 (l)
	125		125
		Balance b/f	80

CREDITORS FOR NATIONAL INSURANCE & PAYE

	£'000		£'000
Bank	(e) 19	Balance b/f	19
		Wages and salaries	15(c)
Balance c/f	19	Employer's contributions:	
		Work in progress	2 (a)
		Administration overhead	1 (b)
		Selling overhead	1 (b)
	38		38
		Balance b/f	19

FACTORY BUILDINGS ACCOUNT

	£'000		£'000
Balance b/f	250	Balance c/f	250

PROVISION FOR DEPRECIATION: FACTORY BUILDINGS

	£'000		£'000
Balance c/f	22	Balance b/f	20
		Charge for September 20X0	2 (m)
	22		22
		Balance b/f	22

EQUIPMENT ACCOUNT

	£'000		£'000
Balance b/f	320	Balance c/f	320

PROVISION FOR DEPRECIATION: EQUIPMENT

	£'000		£'000
Balance c/f	210	Balance b/f	170
		Factory equipment charge	35 (n)
		Office equipment charge	5 (o)
	210		210
		Balance b/f	210

SHARE CAPITAL ACCOUNT

	£'000		£'000
Balance c/f	100	Balance b/f	100

SHARE PREMIUM ACCOUNT

	£'000		£'000
Balance c/f	20	Balance b/f	20

PROFIT AND LOSS RESERVE

	£'000		£'000
Balance c/f	323	Balance b/f	290
		Profit and loss account	33
	323		323
		Balance b/f	323

(b)   The trial balance as at 30 September 20X0 is as follows.

	DR		CR
	£'000		£'000
Raw materials stores	28	Creditors	80
Work in progress	12	Creditor for national insurance	
Finished goods	14	and PAYE	19
Cash and bank	88	Provision for depreciation:	
Debtors	62	Factory buildings	22
Factory buildings	250	Equipment	210
Equipment	320	Share capital	100
		Share premium	20
		Profit and loss reserve	323
	774		774

Notes

(1) The amount of production overhead absorbed into WIP is calculated by multiplying the rate given (£12.50 per direct labour hour) by the number of direct labour hours, which was £33,000/£5.50 = 6,000.

$$£12.50 \times 6,000 = £75,000$$

(2) We are not told that administration and selling overheads are absorbed into units produced, so we must assume that the actual costs are charged in full in the period in which they are incurred. A 'vertical' profit and loss account may make this clearer.

(c) VERMICELLI LTD PROFIT & LOSS ACCOUNT
30 SEPTEMBER 20X0

	£'000	£'000
Sales		278
Opening stocks (30 + 20 + 60)	110	
Direct materials purchased (40 – 8 – 2)	30	
Wages and salaries (33 + 2)	35	
Production overhead absorbed	75	
	250	
Closing stocks (28 + 12 + 14)	(54)	
Cost of sales		196
Gross profit		82
Administration overhead	26	
Selling overhead	31	
Over-absorbed overhead	(8)	
		(49)
Net profit		33

ASSESSMENT ALERT

In an assessment, be prepared to complete partially completed cost accounts, and always make sure that your debits equal your credits!

Activity 7.4   Level: Pre-assessment

What would be the double entry to record the following events in an integrated accounts system?

(a) Materials costing £10,000 are purchased on credit and put into stock.
(b) Finished units costed at £50,000 are made available for sale.
(c) Materials valued at £5,000 are issued to the administration department.
(d) Indirect production wages of £20,000 are charged to the production department.

Activity 7.5   Level: Assessment

In the absence of the accountant you have been asked to prepare a month's cost accounts for Liverpool Ltd, a company which operates a costing system which is fully **integrated** with the financial accounts. The cost clerk has provided you with the following information.

(a) *Balances at beginning of month*

	£
Stores ledger control account	24,175
Work in progress control account	19,210
Finished goods control account	34,164
Creditors control account	15,187

(b) *Information relating to events during the month*

	£
Materials purchased	76,150
Materials issued from stores to production	29,630
Gross wages paid: direct workers	15,236
indirect workers	9,462
Payments to creditors	58,320
Selling and distribution overheads incurred	5,240
Other production overheads incurred but not yet paid for	16,300
Sales	75,400
Cost of finished goods sold	59,830
Cost of goods completed and transferred into finished goods store during the month	62,130

(c) The production overhead absorption rate is 150% of direct wages.

Task

Prepare the following accounts for the month.

Stores ledger control account
Work in progress control account
Finished goods control account
Production overhead control account
Creditors control account
Profit and loss account

Key learning points

- A **control account** is an account which records total cost, unlike an individual ledger account which records individual debits and credits.

- There are two main types of cost bookkeeping system, **interlocking systems** and **integrated systems.**

- An **integrated system** is one in which the cost accounting function and the financial accounting function are combined in one system of ledger accounts.

- The **wages control account** acts as a collecting place for wages before they are analysed into work in progress and production overhead control accounts.

- The **production overhead control account** acts as a collecting place for production overheads before they are absorbed into work in progress.

- Production overhead is absorbed into work in progress using the **predetermined overhead absorption rate.**

- Any balance remaining on the production overhead control account at the end of the period represents the **overhead under or over absorbed** during the period.

BPP
PUBLISHING

Quick quiz

1   What is a control account?

2   What are the two types of cost bookkeeping system?

3   What is the double entry for indirect materials issued to production?

4   What does it mean if the debit total on the production overhead control account is higher than the credit total?

Answers to quick quiz

1   An account which records total cost, as opposed to individual costs (which are recorded in individual ledger accounts).

2   Integrated and interlocking.

3   Debit Production overhead control account; Credit Materials stock account

4   Production overhead is under-absorbed.

8 Costing methods

This chapter contains

Learning objectives

On completion of this chapter you will be able to:

- Understand job and batch costing systems

- Deal with queries relating to job and batch costing systems

Performance criteria

6.1   (ii)   Information relating to direct costs is clearly and correctly coded, analysed and recorded

6.2   (iii)   Information relating to overhead costs is accurately and clearly recorded

Range statement

6.1.1 Direct costs: standard and actual material costs; standard and actual labour costs; standard and actual expenses

- Materials: raw materials; part finished goods; materials issued from stores within the organisation; deliveries

- Labour: employees of the organisation on the payroll; sub-contractors; agency staff

- Expenses: direct revenue expenditure

6.2.1 Overhead costs: standard and actual indirect material costs; standard and actual indirect labour costs; indirect expenses; depreciation charges

BPP
PUBLISHING

> ## Knowledge and understanding
>
> - Relationship between technical systems and costing systems – job, batch, unit systems
>
> - Understanding of the ways the accounting systems of an organisation are affected by its organisational structure, its administrative systems and procedures and the nature of its business transactions

1 INTRODUCTION

1.1 In this chapter we will be looking at two important costing methods: **job costing and batch costing.** These costing methods apply, as we discussed in Chapter 1, in situations where an organisation's output consists of separately identifiable units.

1.2 Job costing and batch costing systems can be distinguished from **unit costing systems,** as we saw in Chapter 1, because the latter apply when production consists of a continuous flow of identical units.

2 WHAT IS A COSTING METHOD?

> ### KEY TERM
>
> A **costing method** is a method of collecting costs which is designed to suit the way goods are processed or manufactured or the way that services are provided.

2.1 Each organisation's costing method will have unique features but **costing methods of firms in the same line of business will have common aspects.** On the other hand, organisations involved in completely different activities, such as hospitals and car part manufacturers, will use very different costing methods.

3 JOB COSTING

3.1 The aim of **job costing** is simply to collect the cost information shown below.

	£
Direct materials	X
Direct labour	X
Direct expenses	X
Direct cost	X
Production overhead	X
Total production cost	X
Administration overhead	X
Selling overhead	X
Cost of sales	X

To the final figure is added a '**mark-up**' and the total is the selling price of the job.

3.2 In other words, all we are doing is looking at one way of putting together the pieces of information that we have studied separately so far.

What is a job?

> **KEY TERM**
>
> A **job** is a cost unit which consists of a single order or contract.

3.3 With other methods of costing it is usual to produce for stock. Management therefore decide in advance how many units of each type, size, colour, quality and so on will be produced during the coming period.

3.4 These decisions will all be taken without taking into account the identity of the individual customers who will eventually buy the products.

3.5 In job costing on the other hand, production is usually carried out in accordance with the **special requirements** of each customer. It is therefore usual for each job to **differ in one or more respects from every other job**, which means that a separate record must be maintained to show the details of a particular job.

3.6 The work relating to a job is usually carried out within a factory or workshop and moves through processes and operations as a **continuously identifiable unit**. The term job may also be applied to work such as **property repairs**, and the job costing method may be used in the costing of **internal capital expenditure jobs** and **internal services**.

Procedure for the performance of jobs

3.7 The normal procedure in jobbing concerns involves the following.

(a) The prospective customer approaches the supplier and indicates the **requirements** of the job.

(b) A responsible official sees the prospective customer and agrees the **precise details of the items** to be supplied, for example the quantity, quality and colour of the goods, the date of delivery and any special requirements.

(c) The estimating department of the organisation then prepares an **estimate** for the job. This will include the following.

- The cost of the materials to be used

- The wages expected to be paid

- The amount for factory, administration, selling and distribution overhead

- The cost of any additional equipment needed specially for the job

- The supplier's profit margin

The total of these items will represent the **quoted selling price**.

(d) At the appropriate time, the job will be 'loaded' on to the factory floor. This means that as soon as all materials, labour and equipment are available and subject to the scheduling of other orders, the job will be started. In an efficient organisation, **the start of the job will be timed to ensure that while it will be ready for the customer by the promised date of delivery it will**

BPP PUBLISHING

not be loaded too early. Otherwise storage space will have to be found for the product until the date it is required by the customer.

Collection of job costs

3.8 Each job will be given a **number** to identify it. A separate record must be maintained to show the details of individual jobs. The process of collecting job costs may be outlined as follows.

(a) **Materials requisitions are sent to stores.**

(b) **The materials requisition note will be used to cost the materials issued to the job** concerned, and this cost may then be recorded on a **job cost sheet**. The cost may include items already in stock, at an appropriate valuation, and/or items specially purchased.

(c) **The job ticket is passed to the worker who is to perform the first operation.** The times of starting and finishing the operation are recorded on the ticket, which is then passed to the person who is to carry out the second operation, where a similar record of the times of starting and finishing is made.

(d) When the job is completed, the **job ticket is sent to the cost office**, where the time spent will be costed and recorded on the job cost sheet.

(e) The **relevant costs** of materials issued, direct labour performed and direct expenses incurred as recorded on the job cost sheet **are charged to the job account** in the work in progress ledger.

(f) **The job account is debited with the job's share of the factory overhead**, based on the absorption rate(s) in operation. If the job is incomplete at the end of an accounting period, it is valued at production cost in the closing balance sheet (where a system of absorption costing is in operation).

(g) **On completion of the job**, the job account is charged with the appropriate administration, selling and distribution overhead, after which **the total cost of the job can be ascertained.**

(h) The difference between the agreed selling price and the total actual cost will be the supplier's profit (or loss).

3.9 Here is a proforma job account, which will be one of the accounts in the work in progress control account.

JOB ACCOUNT

	£		£
Materials issued	X	Finished jobs	X
Direct labour	X		
Direct expenses	X		
Production overhead at predetermined rate	X		
Other overheads	X		X
	X		X

Activity 8.1   **Level: Pre-assessment**

What does the word 'job' mean when we talk about job costing? Give three examples.

Job cost sheet (or card)

3.10 An example of a job cost sheet is shown below.

3.11 When jobs are completed, **job cost sheets** are transferred from the **work in progress** category to **finished goods**. When delivery is made to the customer, the costs become a **cost of sale**. If the completed job was carried out in order to build up finished goods stocks (rather than to meet a specific order) the quantity of items produced and their value are recorded on **finished goods stores ledger cards**.

| JOB COST CARD | | | | | | | | | | | | | Job No. B641 | | | |

Customer	Mr J White				Customer's Order No.								Vehicle make	Peugot 205 GTE		
Job Description	Repair damage to offside front door												Vehicle reg. no.	G 614 SOX		
Estimate Ref. 2599					Invoice No.											
Quoted price £338.68					Invoice price £355.05								Date to collect 14.6.XO			

Material / Labour / Overheads

Date	Req. No.	Qty.	Price	Cost £	Cost p	Date	Emp-loyee	Cost Ctre	Hrs.	Rate	Bonus	Cost £	Cost p	Hrs	OAR	Cost £	Cost p
12.6	36815	1	75.49	75	49	12.6	018	B	1.98	6.50	-	12	87	7.9	2.50	19	75
12.6	36816	1	33.19	33	19	13.6	018	B	5.92	6.50	-	38	48				
12.6	36842	5	6.01	30	05						13.65	13	65				
13.6	36881	5	3.99	19	95												
Total C/F				158	68	Total C/F						65	00	Total C/F		19	75

Expenses

Date	Ref.	Description	Cost £	Cost p
12.6	-	N. Jolley Panel-beating	50	-
Total C/F			50	-

Job Cost Summary

	Actual £	Actual p	Estimate £	Estimate p
Direct Materials B/F	158	68	158	68
Direct Expenses B/F	50	00		
Direct Labour B/F	65	00	180	00
Direct Cost	273	68		
Overheads B/F	19	75		
	293	43		
Admin overhead (add 10%)	29	34		
= Total Cost	322	77	338	68
Invoice Price	355	05		
Job Profit/Loss	32	28		

Comments

Job Cost Card Completed by _____

Job costing and computerisation

3.12 **Job cost cards** exist in **manual** systems, but it is increasingly likely that in large organisations the job costing system will be **computerised**, using accounting software specifically designed to deal with job costing requirements. A computerised job accounting system is likely to contain the following features.

(a) Every job will be given a **job code number**, which will determine how the data relating to the job is stored.

(b) A **separate set of codes** will be given for the type of costs that any job is likely to incur. Thus, 'direct wages', say, will have the same code whichever job they are allocated to.

(c) In a sophisticated system, **costs can be analysed both by job** (for example all costs related to Job 456), **and by type** (for example direct wages incurred on all jobs). It is thus easy to compare actual and expected costs and to make comparisons between jobs.

(d) A job costing system might have facilities built into it which incorporate other factors relating to the performance of the job. In complex jobs, sophisticated planning techniques might be employed to ensure that the job is performed in the minimum time possible. **Time management features** therefore may be incorporated into job costing software.

Activity 8.2 **Level: Assessment**

Three of the following documents were used to establish the direct costs of job C1027. Identify the documents in question.

Stock card 8754/1262
Payroll (week-ending 26 September 20X0)
Factory electricity bill for the quarter to 29 September 20X0
GRN No 45725
M Bobb's clock card (w/e 26 September 20X0)
Materials requisition note no 20019
Industrial Refuse Ltd - weekly invoices for skip hire
M Bobb's time sheet (w/e 26 September 20X0)
Fred Davis - invoice for sub-contracting work 'per quotation'

---

4 JOB COSTING FOR INTERNAL SERVICES

4.1 **Job costing systems** may be used to control the costs of **internal service departments,** eg the maintenance department. A job costing system enables the cost of a specific job to be charged to a user department. Therefore instead of apportioning the total costs of service departments, each job done is charged to the individual user department.

4.2 An **internal job costing system** for service departments will have the following advantages.

(a) **Realistic apportionment.** The identification of expenses with jobs and the subsequent charging of these to the department(s) responsible means that costs are borne by those who incurred them.

(b) **Increased responsibility and awareness.** User departments will be aware that they are charged for the specific services used and may be more careful to use the facility more efficiently. They will also appreciate the true cost of the facilities that they are using and can take decisions accordingly.

(c) **Control of service department costs.** The service department may be restricted to charging a standard cost to user departments for specific jobs carried out or time spent. It will then be possible to measure the efficiency or inefficiency of the service department by recording the difference between the standard charges and the actual expenditure.

(d) **Budget information.** This information will ease the budgeting process, as the purpose and cost of service department expenditure can be separately identified.

Activity 8.3   Level: Assessment

East and West Ltd is a company that carries out jobbing work. One of the jobs carried out in May was job 2409, to which the following information relates.

Direct material Y:	400 kilos were issued from stores at a cost of £5 per kilo.
Direct material Z:	800 kilos were issued from stores at a cost of £6 per kilo. 60 kilos were returned.
Department P:	300 labour hours were worked, of which 100 hours were overtime.
Department Q:	200 labour hours were worked, of which 100 hours were overtime.

Overtime work is not normal in Department P, where basic pay is £4 per hour plus an overtime premium of £1 per hour. Overtime work was done in Department Q in May because of a request by the customer of another job to complete his job quickly. Basic pay in Department Q is £5 per hour and overtime premium is £1.50 per hour. Overhead is absorbed at the rate of £3 per direct labour hour in both departments.

Tasks

(a) Calculate the direct materials cost of job 2409
(b) Calculate the direct labour cost of job 2409
(c) Calculate the full production cost of job 2409 using absorption costing

---

ASSESSMENT ALERT

In an assessment, you may be asked to determine the amount of profit to be added to a job cost. Remember that profit may be expressed either as a percentage of job cost (such as 25% (25/100) mark up) or as a percentage of price (such as 20% (25/125) margin).

Activity 8.4   Level: Assessment

A curtain-making business manufactures quality curtains to customers' orders. It has three production departments (X, Y and Z) which have overhead absorption rates (per direct labour hour) of £12.86, £12.40 and £14.03 respectively.

Two pairs of curtains are to be manufactured for customers. Direct costs are as follows.

	Job TN8	Job KT2
Direct material	£154	£108
Direct labour	20 hours dept X	16 hours dept X
	12 hours dept Y	10 hours dept Y
	10 hours dept Z	14 hours dept Z

Labour rates are as follows: £3.80(X); £3.50 (Y); £3.40 (Z).

The firm quotes prices to customers that reflect a required profit of 25% on selling price.

Task

Calculate the total cost and selling price of each job.

5 BATCH COSTING

> ### KEY TERM
>
> A **batch** is a cost unit which consists of a separate, readily identifiable group of product units which maintain their separate identity throughout the production process.

5.1 The procedures for **costing batches** are very similar to those for costing jobs.

(a) The batch is treated as a **job** during production and the costs are collected in the manner already described in this chapter.

(b) Once the batch has been completed, the **cost per unit** can be calculated as the total batch cost divided by the number of units in the batch.

5.2 EXAMPLE: BATCH COSTING

A company manufactures model cars to order and has the following budgeted overheads for the year, based on normal activity levels.

	Budgeted overheads	Budgeted activity
Department	£	
Welding	6,000	1,500 labour hours
Assembly	10,000	1,000 labour hours

Selling and administrative overheads are 20% of production cost. An order for 250 model cars type XJS1, made as Batch 8638, incurred the following costs.

Materials	£12,000
Labour	100 hours welding shop at £2.50/hour
	200 hours assembly shop at £1/hour

£500 was paid for the hire of special X-ray equipment for testing the welds.

Task

Calculate the cost per unit for Batch 8638.

5.3 SOLUTION

The first step is to calculate the overhead absorption rate for the production departments.

Welding $= \dfrac{£6,000}{1,500} = $ £4 per labour hour

Assembly $= \dfrac{£10,000}{1,000} = $ £10 per labour hour

Total cost - Batch no 8638

	£	£
Direct material		12,000
Direct expense		500
Direct labour $100 \times 2.50 =$	250	
$200 \times 1.00 =$	200	
		450
Prime cost		12,950
Overheads $100 \times 4 =$	400	
$200 \times 10 =$	2,000	
		2,400
Production cost		15,350
Selling and administrative cost (20% of production cost)		3,070
Total cost		18,420

$$\text{Cost per unit} = \frac{£18,420}{250} = £73.68$$

Activity 8.5

Level: Assessment

Lyfsa Kitchen Units Ltd crafts two different sizes of standard unit and a DIY all-purpose unit for filling up awkward spaces. The units are built to order in batches of around 250 (although the number varies according to the quality of wood purchased), and each batch is sold to NGJ Furniture Warehouses Ltd.

The costs incurred in May were as follows.

	Big unit	Little unit	All-purpose
Direct materials purchased	£5,240	£6,710	£3,820
Direct labour			
Skilled (hours)	1,580	1,700	160
Semi-skilled (hours)	3,160	1,900	300
Direct expenses	£1,180	£1,700	£250
Selling price of batch	£33,180	£27,500	£19,500
Completed at 31 May	100%	80%	25%

The following information is available.

All direct materials for the completion of the batches have been recorded. Skilled labour is paid £5 per hour, semi-skilled £4 per hour. Administration expenses total £4,400 per month and are to be allocated to the batches on the basis of direct labour hours. Direct labour costs, direct expenses and administration expenses will increase in proportion to the total labour hours required to complete the little units and the all-purpose units. On completion of the work the practice of the manufacturer is to divide the calculated profit on each batch 20% to staff as a bonus, 80% to the company. Losses are absorbed 100% by the company.

Tasks

(a) Calculate the profit or loss made by the company on big units.

(b) Project the profit or loss likely to be made by the company on little units and all-purpose units.

(c) Comment on any matters you think relevant to management as a result of your calculations.

Key learning points

- **Job costing** is the costing method used where each cost unit is separately identifiable.

- Each job is given a **number** to distinguish it from other jobs.

- Costs for each job are collected on a **job cost sheet** or **job card.**

- Material costs for each job are determined from **materials requisition notes**.

- Labour times on each job are recorded on a **job ticket,** which is then costed and recorded on the job cost sheet.

- **Overhead** is absorbed into the cost of jobs using the predetermined overhead absorption rates.

- An **internal job costing system** can be used for costing the work of service departments.

- **Batch costing** is similar to job costing in that each batch of similar articles is separately identifiable. The **cost per unit** manufactured in a batch is the total batch cost divided by the number of units in the batch.

Quick quiz

1   What is a job?

2   How are the material costs for each job determined?

3   How would you calculate the cost per unit of a completed batch?

Answers to quick quiz

1   A cost unit which consists of a separately identifiable single order or contract.

2   From materials requisition notes, or from suppliers' invoices if materials are purchased specifically for a particular job.

3    $\dfrac{\text{Total batch cost}}{\text{Number of units in the batch}}$

Part D

Standard costing and variance analysis

9 Standard costing

This chapter contains

1   Introduction

2   Standard costs and standard costing

3   How standards are set

4   Performance standards

Learning objectives

On completion of this chapter you will be able to:

- Identify direct costs in accordance with organisational costing procedures

- Ensure that information relating to standard costs is clearly and correctly coded, analysed and recorded

- Calculate standard costs in accordance with organisational policies and procedures

Performance criteria

6.1 (i)   Direct costs are identified in accordance with the organisation's costing procedures

6.1 (ii)   Information relating to direct costs is clearly and correctly coded, analysed and recorded

6.1 (iii)   Direct costs are calculated in accordance with the organisation's policies and procedures

6.2 (ii)   Overhead costs are established in accordance with the organisation's procedures

6.2 (iii)   Information relating to overhead costs is accurately and clearly recorded

Range statement

6.1.1 Direct costs: standard and actual material costs; standard and actual labour costs; standard and actual expenses

- Materials: raw materials; part finished goods; materials issued from stores within the organisation; deliveries

- Labour: employees of the organisation on the payroll; sub-contractors; agency staff

- Expenses: direct revenue expenditure

6.2.1 Overhead costs: standard and actual indirect material costs; standard and actual indirect labour costs; indirect expenses; depreciation charges

Knowledge and understanding

- Procedures for establishing standard materials costs, use of technical and purchasing information

- Procedures for establishing standard labour costs: use of information about labour rates

- Methods of setting standards for expenses

- Principles and objectives of standard costing systems: variance reports

1 INTRODUCTION

1.1 In the last section of this Interactive Text we will turn our attention to **standard costing** and **variance analysis.**

1.2 In this chapter we will be looking at the **principles of standard costing** and at how **standard costs can be set** for each of the costs you have studied so far: materials, labour and expenses.

1.3 The remaining chapters will then go on to look at the calculation and interpretation of variances, and how they may be reported to management.

2 STANDARD COSTS AND STANDARD COSTING

What is a standard?

KEY TERM

A **standard** represents what we think should happen. It is our best 'guesstimate' of how long something will take to produce, what quantity of materials it will require, how much it will cost and so on.

2.1 The **materials standard** for a product is our best estimate of how much material is needed to make the product (standard materials usage) multiplied by our best estimate of the price we will have to pay for the material (standard materials price). For example, we might think that two square metres of material should be needed to make a curtain and that the material should cost £10 per square metre. The standard material cost of the curtain is therefore 2 × £10 = £20.

2.2 Likewise the **labour standard** for a product is an estimate of how many hours are needed to make the product multiplied by the amount the employee is paid per hour.

What is standard costing?

KEY TERM

Standard costing is the preparation of standard costs for use in the following situations.

- In costing as a means of valuing stocks and the cost of production. It is an alternative method of valuation to methods like FIFO, LIFO or replacement costing.

- In variance analysis, which is a means of controlling the business.

2.3 The main use of standard costs is in **variance analysis.** This involves comparing the standard cost with the actual cost to derive a difference, or **variance.** We will look at variance analysis in detail in the next chapter.

The standard cost card

2.4 A **standard cost card** can be prepared for each product or service. The card will normally show the following.

- The **quantity** and **price** of each **direct material** required
- The **time** and **rate** of each **grade of direct labour** required
- The **overhead recovery**
- The **full cost**
- The **standard selling price** and the **standard profit** per unit may also be shown.

ASSESSMENT ALERT

One of the tasks in the June 2001 Central Assessment required candidates to complete a standard stock card for motor oil. Standard stock cards show details of receipts and issues of stock, all of which are valued at **standard cost**.

2.5 A distinction should be made in the standard cost between the following overhead costs.

(a) **Fixed and variable production overheads,** unless variable overheads are insignificant in value, in which case all production overheads are regarded as fixed costs.

(b) **Production overhead and other overheads** (administration and marketing). In many costing systems, administration and marketing overheads are excluded from the standard unit cost, so that the standard cost is simply a standard production cost.

2.6 A simple standard cost card might therefore look like this.

		STANDARD COST CARD PRODUCT 1234		
DESCRIPTION	**QUANTITY**	**COST PER KG/HOUR/ETC**	**EXTENSION**	**TOTAL**
Materials			£	£
Flour	*3 kg*	*4.00*	*12.00*	
Water	*9 litres*	*2.00*	*18.00*	
SUB-TOTAL				*30.00*
Labour				
Duckers	*6 hrs*	*10.00*	*60.00*	
Divers	*8 hrs*	*11.00*	*88.00*	
SUB-TOTAL				*148.00*
Direct cost				*178.00*
Variable production o/h	*14 hrs*	*0.50*		*7.00*
Standard variable cost				*185.00*
Fixed production o/h	*14 hrs*	*4.50*		*63.00*
Standard full production cost				*248.00*
Administration o/h				*15.00*
STANDARD COST OF SALE				*263.00*
Standard profit				*40.00*
STANDARD SELLING PRICE				*303.00*

2.7 In a computer system cost cards could be assembled on a spreadsheet, or by means of a tailor-made programme drawing its information from a database.

Issue of raw material stock at standard cost

2.8 In Chapter 2, we considered the different methods of valuing materials issues and stocks. We briefly mentioned that issues and stock could be valued at a **pre-determined cost**, or what is known as a **standard cost**.

2.9 This method is therefore quite simple, since all issues and all closing stock will be valued at the same pre-determined cost.

For example, material A has a standard cost of £8 per unit, it therefore follows that:

(a) if 200 units of material A are issued, the issues will be valued at 200 × £8 = £1,600;

(b) if 700 units of material A are held in stock at the year end, the stock valuation of material A will be 700 × £8 = £5,600.

Activity 9.1   **Level: Pre-assessment**

(a)   In what senses is a standard cost a 'standard'?

(b)   Why is standard costing used?

3 HOW STANDARDS ARE SET

Establishing standard material costs

3.1 We have already seen that the standard materials cost for a unit of output is calculated as follows.

> **KEY TERM**
>
> **Standard materials cost** = standard materials usage × standard materials price

To set a standard materials cost we therefore need to establish the **standard materials usage** and the **standard materials price**.

Standard usage of materials

3.2 To ascertain how much material should be used to make a product, technical specifications have to be prepared. This will be done by experts in the production department. On the basis of these technical and engineering specifications and in the light of experience, a **bill of materials** will be drawn up which lists the **quantity of materials** required to make a unit of the product. These quantities can include **allowances for wastage** of materials if that is normal and unavoidable.

Standard prices of materials

3.3 The proper approach to setting a standard price for a particular material is to study the market for that material and become aware of any likely future trends. If your company makes apple pies, news of a disastrous apple crop failure clearly has implications for forecasting raw materials prices.

3.4 In practice it is not always possible or practicable to acquire full information. In such circumstances it is likely that **standard prices** would be set on the basis of **current prices** and any notification from suppliers of changes (for example a new catalogue or price list).

3.5 Sometimes businesses are able to enter into a contract stating that an agreed price will be charged for an agreed period. Obviously this reduces the uncertainty in the standard setting process.

3.6 Standards should also take into account any **discount** that may be available for bulk purchase. Management will need to consider whether it is economical to buy in sufficiently large quantities to earn the discounts, after considering the costs of holding the stock.

Establishing standard labour costs

3.7 In principle it is easy to set **standards for labour**.

(a) Find out how long it should take to produce a unit.
(b) Multiply this time by the rate that the person who produces the unit is paid.

> **KEY TERM**
>
> **Standard labour cost** = time it should take to produce a unit × standard labour rate

3.8 In practice, of course, it is not this straightforward. For example, an experienced worker may be able to do the job in less time than a novice, and two equally experienced workers may take a different length of time to do the same job. Some time must be spent **recording actual performance** before a realistic standard can be established.

3.9 EXAMPLE: LABOUR STANDARDS

Fix-a-car Ltd employs two female mechanics, Georgina, who is an apprentice, and Clarissa, who has given loyal service for ten years. The accountant is looking through last week's figures and decides to note down the time each mechanic took to perform each of ten MOT tests.

Georgina	*Clarissa*
Minutes	Minutes
63	30
55	28
50	35
57	25
49	32
52	33
58	29
57	31
70	30
69	27

Georgina is presently paid £4.50 per hour and Clarissa £8 per hour. Calculate the standard time for performing an MOT test and the standard labour cost for performing an MOT test.

3.10 SOLUTION

The total time taken for 20 MOT tests is 880 minutes, an average of 44 minutes per test. Georgina takes a total of 580 minutes and Clarissa 300 minutes. Multiplied by their respective hourly rates the total cost is £83.50 or an average of £4.18 per MOT.

We have therefore calculated the following for MOT tests.

Standard time	44 minutes
Standard labour cost per MOT test	£4.18

3.11 These figures have considerable shortcomings however.

(a) They take no account of the time of day when the work was performed, or the type or age of vehicle concerned.

(b) We cannot tell to what extent the difference in performance of the two mechanics is due to their relative experience and to what extent it is due to other factors: possibly Georgina does the more difficult jobs to gain experience, while Clarissa works on cars that she regularly maintains for established customers who ask for her.

3.12 On the other hand it is quite likely that a better controlled set of measurements would give very similar results to those obtained using historical figures. In a case like this there is probably very little point in trying to be more scientific and 'accurate'. Even if the garage performed 20 MOTs a day, the first set of figures would have to be quite significantly wrong for a more accurate estimation to make any significant difference to the accuracy of the costing.

3.13 If, however, we were dealing with a high volume business where, say, 10,000 units were produced an hour, then small differences in times and costs per unit (or batch or whatever) would have a considerable impact on the accuracy of the costing. In such cases, the taking of more precise measurements in controlled conditions and the use of **sophisticated statistical techniques** would be worthwhile.

3.14 How would these figures affect Georgina and Clarissa if they were used as standards? So far as Georgina is concerned a standard time of 44 minutes is a good target to aim at as she is expected to improve her performance, but she is not expected to be as fast as the more experienced mechanic Clarissa. For Clarissa the standard could be demotivating as she may not work so hard if she knows she has half as long again as she needs to do an MOT.

3.15 A 'time saved bonus' for MOT tests taking less than 44 minutes is a good idea in this case: Clarissa will not slack off if she is financially rewarded for her hard work, and Georgina has a further incentive to speed up her own work.

Work study and standard costs

3.16 The point about accuracy might be developed here. In the example no special effort was made to record the times taken to perform the MOT tests. The standard was calculated using **historical data**.

3.17 This approach is widely used in practice. It has two **advantages**.

(a) There is **no extra expense** in obtaining the information.

(b) The information is not distorted by employees who, knowing they are being measured, **work more slowly than usual** to ensure that easy standards are set.

3.18 The information is, however, **distorted by past inefficiencies** and 'engineered standards' are therefore considered to be preferable. These are based upon a detailed study of the operations involved in a task. You may have heard of '**time and motion studies**', and this is essentially what is involved although the phrase is rather dated. The most commonly used techniques are the following.

(a) **Analytical estimating**. This involves breaking down a job into fairly 'large' units and estimating a time for each unit.

(b) **Predetermined motion time study (PMTS)**. This approach uses times established for basic human motions and so the physical motions required to perform the task would first need to be ascertained by observation.

(c) **Synthetic timing.** This technique is used if it is not possible to actually measure how long a job takes, perhaps because the job is still at the drawing board stage.

3.19 The standard times established by such methods are adjusted to allow for any delays that are unavoidable, and also include an allowance for rest, relaxation, and other contingencies such as machine breakdowns.

Activity 9.2   Level: Assessment

After extensive work study Carter Ltd has established that all of its production processes are carried out by means of combinations from a set of 10 basic labour operations. A standard time for each operation has been calculated by taking the mean of all observations.

Operation	Time (hours)
1	1 ½
2	1
3	¼
4	2
5	½
6	2
7	3
8	1
9	¼
10	½

Operations 2, 6 and 10 can only be done by trade Y workers and operations 4 and 7 only by grade Z workers.

Grade	Basic wage (per hour)
X	£4.80
Y	£5.50
Z	£6.50

The company now wishes to establish standard direct labour costs for each of its seven major products and its two enhanced packages. The operations involved for each product are as follows.

Product	Operations per unit
A	2, 4, 5
B	2, 5, 6, 10
C	3, 6, 8, 9
Sharp C	1, 3, 4, 6
D	1, 2, 6, 7, 10
E	3, 4, 5, 10
F	1, 4, 9
F (augmented)	3, 6, 7, 8
G	1, 5, 9, 10

Task

Calculate the standard direct labour cost of one unit of each of the nine products.

Standard hour

KEY TERM

A **standard hour** is the amount of work achievable, at standard performance, in an hour.

3.20 A standard hour can be a useful measure in standard costing. It is particularly useful when trying to monitor output of a quantity of dissimilar items.

3.21 EXAMPLE: CALCULATING STANDARD HOURS OF OUTPUT

T Ltd makes two hand-made products: toy dolls and toy cars. The standard time allowances for the products and the output achieved in the latest two periods are as follows.

	Dolls	Cars
Standard time in hours per unit	2.5	1.0
Output in units:		
period 4	270	120
period 5	130	300

3.22 SOLUTION

The products are obviously dissimilar, so it is not very meaningful to simply add together dolls and cars to obtain a figure for total output in each period.

The standard hours produced are calculated as follows.

		Dolls Std. hour		Cars Std. hour	Total Std. hour
Period 4	(270 × 2.5)	675	(120 × 1.0)	120	795
Period 5	(130 × 2.5)	325	(300 × 1.0)	300	625

Thus, although the total number of units produced in period 5 was greater, in terms of **standard hours produced** the actual output was considerably lower than in period 4.

ASSESSMENT ALERT

In June 1999 candidates were asked to explain what is meant by standard hour. In June 2000 they were asked to determine the standard labour time in hours to prepare a number of dissimilar restaurant meals.

Activity 9.3   **Level: Assessment**

FF Ltd operates a fast food restaurant, preparing burger meals and chicken meals.

- The standard time to prepare a burger meal is 10 minutes

- The standard time to prepare a chicken meal is 15 minutes

The output for the last period was as follows.

- 2,400 burger meals prepared

- 1,300 chicken meals prepared

How many standard hours of output were achieved last period?

Establishing standard costs for expenses

3.23 Standard costs for some types of expense can be set with reasonable certainty. Others suffer from the same problems as material and labour.

(a) If a **contract** has been entered into (for cleaning, say) then the standard cost can be set at the amount specified in the contract.

(b) Certain expenses are like materials in that there is a **fluctuating market rate** for a specific quantity and the amount likely to be consumed can be determined by 'engineering' methods (studying the relationship between what is put in and what comes out). Examples are gas and electricity.

3.24 An advantage (for standard setting purposes) with many expenses is that they are **fixed over the period for which the standard is being set.** The annual buildings insurance premium, for example, will be known for certain at the beginning of the year. It will not turn out to have been different when the year's actual results are determined.

3.25 In other cases expenses can be made to conform to a standard. **Discretionary costs,** for example, **need only be incurred up to a certain level.** Suppose you had £10,000 to spend on staff training. Once £10,000 had been spent this would be the end of staff training for the year.

Standards and inflation

3.26 One point to bear in mind is that inflation should be considered when standards are being set. For example, when establishing standard material costs, it is unlikely that the **standard materials usage** of a unit of product will change from one year to the next. The only changes in usage that would arise would be due to fundamental changes in working practices. It is however, likely that the **standard materials price** will increase in line with **inflation**.

3.27 Similarly, when establishing standard labour costs, in general, the time it should take to do a job is unlikely to change from year to year. The **standard labour rate** is, however, likely to increase in line with **inflation**.

3.28 When revising standards therefore, it is important to take into account how inflation might have an effect on materials prices, labour rates and expenses.

Recording variances

3.29 Earlier in this chapter we mentioned that a major objective of a standard costing system is to **control** an organisation's costs and revenues.

3.30 The identification, analysis and reporting of **variances** enables managers to monitor whether standard performance is being achieved. The following types of question can be answered by a detailed analysis of variances.

- Are material prices higher or lower than in the standard cost?
- Is material wastage being kept at standard levels?
- Has it been necessary to pay higher wage rates than expected?

3.31 In addition to helping to monitor and control current operations, variance analysis can play a part in **setting standard costs for the future.**

3.32 Management may be able to identify persistent variances which are **uncontrollable.** This means that they cannot be corrected by management action. Other favourable variances, where costs are lower than standard, may arise each period and management may attempt to perpetuate them. Examples of persistent variances include the following.

- The electricity supply company has increased unit prices for electricity
- New working practices mean that fewer labour hours are required per unit

3.33 This type of variance is likely to continue for the foreseeable future and it can provide valuable information for **updating the standard cost.** The variance will help to signal the extent to which the standard requires alteration. A particular cost may not be causing any significant variances, and there may be no changes foreseen in terms of prices or operations. In this situation it may not be necessary to alter the standard cost for the forthcoming period.

3.34 Standards are usually updated once a year. However, a particular standard cost may be no longer achievable and may not represent a **realistic target for control purposes.** When this happens the standard might be updated on an **interim basis** part way through the year, so that it continues to represent a realistic yardstick for planning and control purposes.

4 PERFORMANCE STANDARDS

4.1 Do not forget that **standards are averages.** Even under ideal working conditions, it would be unrealistic to expect every unit of activity or production to take exactly the same time, using exactly the same amount of materials, and at exactly the same price. Some variations are inevitable, but for a reasonably large volume of activity, it would be fair to expect that on average, standard results should be achieved.

4.2 When we are assessing the **level of performance** expected in a standard, there are four different types of **performance standard** that an organisation could aim for.

KEY TERMS

- **Ideal standards** are based on the most favourable operating conditions, with no wastage, no inefficiencies, no idle time and no breakdowns. Variances from ideal standards are useful for pinpointing areas where a close examination may result in large savings, but they are likely to have an unfavourable motivational impact. Employees will often feel that the goals are unattainable and not work so hard.

- **Attainable standards** are based on efficient (but not perfect) operating conditions. Some allowance is made for wastage, inefficiencies, machine breakdowns and fatigue. If well-set they provide a useful psychological incentive, and for this reason they should be introduced whenever possible. The consent and co-operation of employees involved in improving the standard are required.

- **Current standards** are standards based on current working conditions (current wastage, current inefficiencies). The disadvantage of current standards is that they do not attempt to improve on current levels of efficiency, which may be poor and capable of significant improvement.

- **Basic standards** are standards which are kept unaltered over a long period of time, and may be out-of-date. They are used to show changes in efficiency or performance over an extended time period. Basic standards are perhaps the least useful and least common type of standard in use.

BPP PUBLISHING

Activity 9.4   Level: Assessment

Kingston Ltd makes one product, the tudor. Two types of labour are involved in the preparation of a tudor, skilled and semi-skilled. Skilled labour is paid £10 per hour and semi-skilled £5 per hour. Twice as many skilled labour hours as semi-skilled labour hours are needed to produce a tudor, four semi-skilled labour hours being needed.

A tudor is made up of three different direct materials. Seven kilograms of direct material A, four litres of direct material B and three metres of direct material C are needed. Direct material A costs £1 per kilogram, direct material B £2 per litre and direct material C £3 per metre.

Variable production overheads are incurred at Kingston Ltd at the rate of £2.50 per direct labour (skilled) hour.

A system of absorption costing is in operation at Kingston Ltd. The basis of absorption is direct labour (skilled) hours. For the forthcoming accounting period, budgeted fixed production overheads are £250,000 and budgeted production of the tudor is 5,000 units.

Task

Using the above information to draw up a standard cost card for the tudor.

ASSESSMENT ALERT

Make sure that you can draw up a standard cost card such as the one in activity 9.4 above - this is first the sort of task that you may be asked to complete in an assessment.

Activity 9.5   Level: Assessment

LW Ltd makes and sells a single product, G, with the following standard specification for materials.

	Quantity Kilograms	Price per kilogram £
Direct material L	10	30
Direct material W	6	45

It takes 30 direct labour hours to produce one unit of G with a standard direct labour cost of £5.50 per hour.

The annual sales/production budget is 1,200 units evenly spread throughout the year.

The annual budgeted production overhead, all fixed, is £252,000 and expenditure is expected to occur evenly over the year, which the company divides into twelve calendar months. Absorption is based on units produced.

The budgeted sales quantity in one particular month was actually sold for a total of £120,000 at the standard selling price.

Task

Calculate the standard product cost and the gross profit of each unit sold.

Activity 9.6   Level: Assessment

The following times were recorded for the performance of a task in the last month.

Worker	Time	Time
Lynn	1 hour 45 minutes	2 hours
Alison	2 hours 5 minutes	1 hour 55 minutes
Jed	1 hour 15 minutes	1 hour 15 minutes
Kate	2 hours 10 minutes	1 hour 30 minutes

Worker	Time	Time
Nick	1 hour 45 minutes	1 hour 37 minutes
Edmund	1 hour 39 minutes	1 hour 57 minutes
Bob	2 hours	1 hour 30 minutes
Roger	2 hours 15 minutes	1 hour 43 minutes
Tina	1 hour 20 minutes	1 hour 35 minutes
Tim	2 hours 20 minutes	2 hours 2 minutes
Clive	1 hour 35 minutes	1 hours 52 minutes
Graham	1 hour 59 minutes	2 hours 5 minutes
Barry	1 hour 40 minutes	2 hours
Glen	1 hour 57 minutes	1 hour 53 minutes

The standard time for the performance of the task is 2 hours and 30 minutes, but this was set several years ago when most staff were unfamiliar with the equipment in use. It is estimated that at least 15 minutes of idle time may be unavoidable.

Task

Determine four performance standards for the task in question.

Activity 9.7

Level: Assessment

The following information has been collected about the materials used by Sutton Ltd, an organisation which uses standard costing.

Material	Supplier	Information source	Unit cost £	20X2 standard £	20X3 standard £
AB30	4073	20X3 catalogue	1.74	1.68	
AB35	4524	20X2 catalogue	5.93	5.93	
		Invoice (10/X2)	6.05		
		Telephone enquiry to 4524	6.00		
BB29	4333	X2/X3 catalogue	15.72	15.00	
BB42	4929	Invoice (5/X2)	2.36	2.40	
	-	New supplier quotation (11/X2)	1.94		
CA19	4124	Contract to 12/X3	20.07	20.07	
		Invoice (12/X2)	21.50		
CD26	4828	-		2.50	

Sutton Ltd uses the materials in a variety of combinations to make four different products. Technical specifications for usage (in units of material per batch) have been determined as follows.

Material	Guildford	Dorking	Reigate	Coulsdon
AB30	20	20	10	5
AB35	-	10	-	-
BB29	-	-	4	-
BB42	8	5	-	12
CA19	20	9	-	5
CD26	6	-	3	-

Tasks

(a) What are the 20X2 standard materials costs for each product?

(b) As a last resort standard costs are set by adding the current annual rate of inflation to the most recent available price, but more certain information is used if it is available (for example, catalogue prices are usually guaranteed for 12 months). Your task is to calculate the new standard costs for 20X3. Very large quantities are used so it is important to calculate to the nearest penny. The RPI is 3.7%.

Key learning points

- A **standard** represents what we think should happen.

- A **standard cost** is a predetermined unit of cost.

- **Standard costing** is a means of valuing stocks and the issue of materials to production and a way of exercising control over a business.

- A **standard cost card** shows full details of the standard cost of a product.

- Setting **materials standards** involves determining how much material is needed to produce a product and the price of that material.

- Setting standard **labour times** is generally a matter of estimating how long it will take to do a piece of work. This can be done on a rough and ready basis or by detailed work study.

- **Standard costs** can be set for expenses just as they can for any other cost.

- Standards are basically set by developing an awareness of market conditions and by understanding technical requirements.

- Standards can also be set so as to encourage improvements in performance.

- **Inflation** should always be considered when setting standards.

Quick quiz

1   What details would you expect to see on a standard cost card?

2   What is the formula for standard materials cost?

3   What is the formula for standard labour cost?

4   What are the advantages of using historical data to calculate labour standards?

5   How would you explain the term standard hour?

6   List four types of performance standard.

7   How often are standard cost revisions usually made?

Answers to quick quiz

1   The quantity and price of direct material. The time and rate of each grade of direct labour. Overhead recovery, full cost, standard selling price and standard profit.

2   Standard materials usage × standard materials price.

3   Time that it should take to produce a unit × standard labour rate per hour.

4   No extra costs are involved in getting the information, and the information is not distorted by employees working more quickly or slowly than usual.

5   The quantity of work that could be produced in one hour, working at the standard rate of performance.

6   Ideal, attainable, current and basic.

7   Once a year.

10 Calculation of variances

This chapter contains

1 Introduction

2 Variances

3 Materials variances

4 Labour variances

5 Fixed overhead variances

6 Control ratios

7 The reasons for cost variances

Learning objectives

On completion of this chapter you will be able to:

- Calculate and analyse materials (usage and price) and labour (rate and efficiency) variances

- Calculate and analyse the following overhead variances

  ° Expenditure
  ° Efficiency
  ° Volume
  ° Capacity

Performance criteria

6.1 (iv) Standard costs are compared against actual costs and any variances are analysed

6.2 (vi) Standard costs are compared against actual costs and any variances are analysed

Range statement

6.1.1 Direct costs: standard and actual material costs; standard and actual labour costs; standard and actual expenses

6.1.2 Variance analysis: Materials variances: usage, price; Labour variances: rate, efficiency

6.2.3 Variance analysis: Overhead variances: expenditure, efficiency, volume, capacity; Fixed overhead variances: expenditure, volume, capacity, efficiency

Knowledge and understanding

- Basic analysis of variances: usage; price; rate; efficiency; expenditure; volume; capacity

- Methods of analysing materials usage: reasons for wastage

- The significance of and possible reasons for variances

- Control ratios of efficiency, capacity and activity.

1 INTRODUCTION

1.1 Having set **standards** (as described in the previous chapter), what are we going to do with them? We mentioned that we could use materials standards to value materials issues and materials stock. But what about labour standards? And standards for expenses? **The principal reason most organisations use standard costs is for control.**

1.2 In the previous chapter we introduced you to the term 'variance'. When costs are incurred they are compared with the estimated standard cost, and if there is a difference it is known as a **variance**. Generally, somebody will be responsible for a variance and will be asked to explain why it occurred.

1.3 The analysis of variances is a very important aspect of costing. Variance analysis simply aims to find the difference between what costs **were** and what they **should have been**. In this chapter you will be learning how the analysis is done.

2 VARIANCES

2.1 **Standards represent what should happen**. Suppose for example that 10,000 units of product X should require 10,000 kg of material A costing £10,000. This is therefore the standard for product X. Let us now consider the actual results for product X - 11,000 kg of material A costing £12,000 were required to make 10,000 units of product X. We can therefore deduce the following.

(a) We had to spend £2,000 more on materials than we should have to make 10,000 units of product X.

(b) We used 1,000 kg more of material A than we should have to make 10,000 units of product X.

2.2 These differences that we have identified are the **variances** that we were explaining above.

KEY TERMS

- A **variance** is the difference between an actual result and an expected standard cost or revenue.

- **Variance analysis** is the process by which the *total* difference between standard and actual results is analysed.

2.3 Variances may be either **favourable** or **adverse**.

- A **favourable** variance means that actual results were better than standard
- An **adverse** variance means that actual results were worse than standard

3 MATERIALS VARIANCES

Why materials variances arise

3.1 Standards are estimates: they are predictions of what will happen. However, the accuracy of these estimates will depend upon what happens after they have been set.

3.2 For example, suppose you are expecting a good coffee bean harvest, and therefore set a **standard material price** of £10 per kg of coffee. If your prediction is correct, and a good harvest results, then your standard of £10 will be correct. However, if your prediction is not correct, and prices are in fact £15 per kg of coffee beans, then **your standard will be inaccurate.**

3.3 If your standard is inaccurate, then the actual costs incurred will be different to the standard costs estimated - and this is where our **differences** or **variances** arise.

3.4 Think back to how the **materials standard cost** is calculated.

materials standard cost = standard usage × standard price

3.5 Now think about how a variance could arise. Consider the following.

- If actual usage were different to standard usage
- If actual price were different to standard price
- If actual usage **and** actual price were **both** different to standard

Calculating materials variances

3.6 EXAMPLE: MATERIALS VARIANCES

The following standards have been set for product LW.

	Standard price	Standard usage
Material A	£2.20 per kg	2kg per unit

In February, the actual production and material usage figures were as follows.

Actual production	10,000 units
Material A	21,000 kg costing £47,250

Task

Calculate the following variances for February.

(a) Material total variance
(b) Material price variance
(c) Material usage variance

3.7 SOLUTION

(a) **The material total variance**

	£
10,000 units of product LW should have cost ($\times$ £2.20 $\times$ 2kg)	44,000
but did cost	47,250
Material total variance	3,250 (A)

The (A) denotes an **adverse** variance. The variance is adverse because the units cost more than they should have cost.

Now we can analyse the material total variance into its two constituent parts: the **material price variance** and the **material usage variance**.

(b) **The material price variance**

This is the difference between the price that should have been paid for 21,000 kg, and the price that was paid.

	£
21,000 kg should have cost ($\times$ £2.20)	46,200
but did cost	47,250
Material price variance	1,050 (A)

The price variance is adverse because the price paid for the material was higher than standard.

(c) **The material usage variance**

This is the difference between how many kilograms of material A should have been used to produce 10,000 units of product LW and how many kilograms were used, valued at the standard price per kilogram.

10,000 units should have used ($\times$ 2 kg)	20,000 kg
but did use	21,000 kg
Material usage variance in kg	1,000 kg
$\times$ standard price per kg	$\times$ £2.20
Material usage variance	£2,200 (A)

The usage variance is adverse because more material was used than should have been used.

KEY TERMS

- The **material total variance** is the difference between what the output actually cost and what it should have cost, in terms of material. It can be divided into the following two sub-variances.

- The **material price variance** is the difference between the standard price and the actual price of the *actual* quantity of material used or purchased. In other words, it is the difference between what the material did cost and what it should have cost.

- The **material usage variance** is the difference between the standard quantity of materials that *should* have been used for the number of units *actually* produced, and the actual quantity of materials used, valued at the standard price per unit of material. In other words, it is the difference between how much material should have been used and how much material was used, valued at standard cost.

3.8 The variances from Paragraph 3.7 can be **summarised** as follows.

	£
Material price variance	1,050 (A)
Material usage variance	2,200 (A)
Material total variance	3,250 (A)

Adverse and favourable variances

3.9 All of the examples we have seen so far have been cases where **more money was paid out** or **more materials were used than expected**. These are called **adverse variances** because they have adverse consequences. They mean that **less profit** is made than we hoped.

3.10 Sometimes, of course, things will be cheaper than usual or we will use them more efficiently. When less money is paid than expected or fewer materials are used than expected the variances are said to be **favourable variances**. They mean that **more profit** is made than we hoped.

3.11 EXAMPLE: ADVERSE AND FAVOURABLE VARIANCES

It is now April and actual data for product LW is as follows.

Production	9,500 units
Material A	20,000 kg costing £42,000

Have a go at calculating the variances yourself before looking at the solution.

3.12 SOLUTION

(a) Let's begin by calculating the **material total variance**.

	£
9,500 units should have cost (9,500 × 2kg × £2.20)	41,800
but did cost	42,000
Material total variance	200 (A)

The (A) indicates that overall the variance is **adverse**.

(b) We can now go on to calculate the individual components of the total variance (ie the price and usage variances).

	£
20,000 kg should have cost (× £2.20)	44,000
but did cost	42,000
Material price variance	2,000 (F)

The (F) indicates that this is a **favourable** variance because less money was spent than expected.

9,500 units should use (× 2 kg)	19,000 kg
but did use	20,000 kg
Material usage variance in kg	1,000 kg (A)
× standard price per kg	× £2.20
Material usage variance in £	£2,200 (A)

The (A) indicates that this is an **adverse** variance, because more materials were used than standard for 9,500 units.

(c)   Let's check that the total variance is the sum of the two individual variances.

	£
Price variance	2,000 (F)
Usage variance	(2,200) (A)
Total variance	(200) (A)

Remember that adverse variances are **negative** (*less* profit) and favourable variances are **positive** (*more* profit).

Material variances and opening and closing stock

3.13   Suppose that a company uses raw material P in production, and that this raw material has a standard price of £3 per metre. During one month 6,000 metres are bought for £18,600, and 5,000 metres are used in production. At the end of the month, stock will have been increased by 1,000 metres. In variance analysis, the problem is to determine the material price variance. Should it be calculated on the basis of **materials purchased** (6,000 metres) or on the basis of **materials used** (5,000 metres)?

3.14   The answer to this problem depends on how **closing stocks** of the raw materials will be valued.

(a)   If they are **valued at standard price**, (1,000 units at £3 per unit) the **price variance is calculated on material purchases** in the period.

(b)   If they are **valued at actual cost** (FIFO) (1,000 units at £3.10 per unit) the **price variance is calculated on materials used in production** in the period.

3.15   A **full standard costing system** is usually in operation and therefore the price variance is usually calculated on **purchases** in the period. We will return to consider this aspect of variance analysis in more detail in the next chapter.

Activity 10.1   **Level: Assessment**

Calculate the material total variance and its sub-variances given the following information.

Product A has a standard direct materials cost of £10 (5 kg of material M). During April 100 units of product A were manufactured using 520 kg of material M at a cost of £1,025.

4   LABOUR VARIANCES

4.1   **Labour variances** are very similar to materials variances but they have different names. There are two types of sub-variance that you need to understand and calculate for labour. The 'money' variance is called the **rate variance** and the 'quantity' variance is called the **efficiency variance**.

KEY TERMS

- The **labour total variance** is the difference between what the output should have cost and what it did cost, in terms of labour. It can be divided into the following two sub-variances.

- The **labour rate variance** is the difference between the standard rate and the actual rate for the actual number of hours paid for. In other words, it is the difference between what the labour did cost and what it should have cost.

- The **labour efficiency variance** is the difference between the hours that *should* have been worked for the number of units *actually* produced, and the actual number of hours worked, valued at the standard rate per hour. In other words, it is the difference between how many hours should have been worked and how many hours were worked, valued at the standard rate per hour.

4.2 EXAMPLE: LABOUR VARIANCES

Suppose that the labour standard for the production of a unit of product B is as follows.

> 2 hours of grade S labour at £6 per hour = £12 per unit

During May 200 units of product B were made and the direct labour cost of grade S labour was £2,418 for 390 hours work.

Task

Calculate the following variances.

(a) The direct labour total variance
(b) The direct labour rate variance
(c) The direct labour efficiency variance

4.3 SOLUTION

(a) Let us begin by calculating the **direct labour total variance**.

	£
200 units of product B should have cost (× £12)	2,400
but did cost	2,418
Direct labour total variance	18 (A)

Having learned that direct labour costs were £18 more than they should have been, we can now look at why this happened.

(b) **Labour rate variance**. This variance is calculated by taking the number of labour hours 'purchased' ie paid for, and comparing what they did cost with what they should have cost.

	£
390 hours of grade S labour should cost (× £6)	2,340
but did cost	2,418
Labour rate variance	78 (A)

The variance is **adverse** because **actual rates of pay were higher than expected.**

(c) **Labour efficiency variance.** This variance is calculated by taking the amount of output produced (200 units of product B) and comparing how long it should have taken to produce them with how long it did take. The difference is the **efficiency variance**, expressed in hours of work. It should be converted into £ by applying the **standard rate per labour hour.**

200 units of product B should take (× 2 hours)	400 hrs
but did take	390 hrs
Labour efficiency variance in hrs	10 hrs (F)
× standard rate per hour	× £6
Labour efficiency variance in £	£60 (F)

The variance is **favourable** because the **labour force has been more efficient** than expected.

(d) **Summary**

	£
Labour rate variance	78 (A)
Labour efficiency variance	60 (F)
Direct labour total variance	18 (A)

Activity 10.2   Level: Assessment

Pogle Ltd manufactures one product, the clanger. The following direct standard costs apply to the clanger.

	£
Direct material 10 kgs at £5 per kg	50
Direct labour 5 hours at £6 per hour	30

In July production was 10,000 units and actual data for the month was:

(a) Actual materials consumed 106,000 kgs costing £530,500
(b) Actual labour hours worked 50,200 hours, costing £307,200

Task

Calculate the material price and usage variances, and the labour rate and efficiency variances.

---

5   FIXED OVERHEAD VARIANCES

5.1 You may have noticed that the method of calculating cost variances for variable cost items is essentially the same for labour and materials. Fixed overhead variances are very different. In an absorption costing system, they are **an attempt to explain the under- or over-absorption of fixed production overheads in production costs.** You should of course, know all about under/over absorption of fixed overheads. We looked at this topic in detail in Chapter 5. If you need reminding, however, skim through Section 7 of that chapter again.

5.2 You will find it easier to calculate and understand **fixed overhead variances**, if you keep in mind the whole time that you are trying to 'explain' (put a name and value to) any under- or over-absorbed overhead.

Remember that the **absorption rate** is calculated as follows.

$$\text{Overhead absorption rate} = \frac{\text{Budgeted fixed overhead}}{\text{Budgeted activity level}}$$

5.3 If either of the following are incorrect, then we will have an under or over absorption of overhead.

- The numerator (number on top) = budgeted fixed overhead
- The denominator (number on bottom) = budgeted activity level

5.4 The **fixed overhead total variance** may be broken down into two parts as follows.

- An **expenditure variance**
- A **volume variance**. This in turn may be split into two parts.

  - An **efficiency variance**
  - A **capacity variance**

The fixed overhead expenditure variance

5.5 The fixed overhead expenditure variance occurs if the numerator is incorrect. It measures the under- or over-absorbed overhead caused by the **actual total overhead** being different from the budgeted total overhead.

The fixed overhead volume variance

5.6 As we have already stated, the fixed overhead volume variance is made up of the following sub-variances.

- Fixed overhead efficiency variance
- Fixed overhead capacity variance

5.7 The fixed overhead efficiency and capacity variances measure the under- or over-absorbed overhead caused by the **actual activity level** being different from the budgeted activity level used in calculating the absorption rate.

5.8 There are two reasons why the **actual activity level** may be different from the **budgeted activity level** used in calculating the absorption rate.

(a) The workforce may have worked more or less efficiently than the standard set. This deviation is measured by the **fixed overhead efficiency variance.**

(b) The hours worked by the workforce could have been different to the original budgeted hours (regardless of the level of efficiency of the workforce) because of overtime and strikes etc. This deviation from the standard is measured by the **fixed overhead capacity variance.**

How to calculate the variances

5.9 In order to clarify the overhead variances which we have encountered in this section, consider the following definitions which are expressed in terms of how each overhead variance should be calculated.

KEY TERMS

- **Fixed overhead total variance** is the difference between fixed overhead incurred and fixed overhead absorbed. In other words, it is the under- or over-absorbed fixed overhead.

- **Fixed overhead expenditure variance** is the difference between the budgeted fixed overhead expenditure and actual fixed overhead expenditure.

- **Fixed overhead volume variance** is the difference between actual and budgeted production/volume multiplied by the standard absorption rate per **unit** or per **standard hour**.

- **Fixed overhead efficiency variance** is the difference between the number of hours that actual production should have taken, and the number of hours actually taken (that is, worked) multiplied by the standard absorption rate per **hour**.

- **Fixed overhead capacity variance** is the difference between the original budgeted hours of work and the actual hours worked, multiplied by the standard absorption rate per **hour**.

5.10 You should now be ready to work through an example to demonstrate all of the fixed overhead variances.

5.11 EXAMPLE: FIXED OVERHEAD VARIANCES

Suppose that a company budgets to produce 1,000 units of product E during August 20X3. The expected time to produce a unit of E is five hours, and the budgeted fixed overhead is £20,000. The standard fixed overhead cost per unit of product E will therefore be as follows.

5 hours at £4 per hour = £20 per unit

Actual fixed overhead expenditure in August 20X3 turns out to be £20,450. The labour force manages to produce 1,100 units of product E in 5,400 hours of work.

Task

Calculate the following variances.

(a) The fixed overhead total variance
(b) The fixed overhead expenditure variance
(c) The fixed overhead volume variance
(d) The fixed overhead efficiency variance
(e) The fixed overhead capacity variance

5.12 SOLUTION

All of the variances assess the under or over absorption of fixed overheads.

(a) **Fixed overhead total variance**

	£
Fixed overhead incurred	20,450
Fixed overhead absorbed (1,100 units × £20 per unit)	22,000
Fixed overhead total variance	1,550 (F)
(= under-/over-absorbed overhead)	

The variance is favourable because more overheads were absorbed than incurred.

(b) **Fixed overhead expenditure variance**

	£
Budgeted fixed overhead expenditure	20,000
Actual fixed overhead expenditure	20,450
Fixed overhead expenditure variance	450 (A)

The variance is adverse because actual expenditure was greater than budgeted expenditure.

(c) **Fixed overhead volume variance**

The production volume achieved was greater than expected. The fixed overhead volume variance measures the difference at the standard rate.

Actual production volume achieved	1,100 units
Budgeted production volume	1,000 units
Volume variance in units	100 units (F)
× standard absorption rate per unit	× £20
Fixed overhead volume variance	£2,000 (F)

The variance is **favourable** because output was greater than expected.

(i) The labour force may have worked efficiently, and produced output at a faster rate than expected. Since overheads are absorbed at the rate of £20 per unit, more will be absorbed if units are produced more quickly. This **efficiency variance** is exactly the same in hours as the direct labour efficiency variance, but is valued in £ at the standard absorption rate for fixed overhead.

(ii) The labour force may have worked longer hours than budgeted, and therefore produced more output, so there may be a **capacity variance**.

(d) **Fixed overhead efficiency variance**

The efficiency variance is calculated in the same way as the labour efficiency variance.

1,100 units of product E should take (× 5 hrs)	5,500 hrs
but did take	5,400 hrs
Fixed overhead efficiency variance in hours	100 hrs (F)
× standard fixed overhead absorption rate per hour	× £4
Fixed overhead efficiency variance in £	£400 (F)

The labour force has produced 5,500 standard hours of work in 5,400 actual hours. Therefore output is 100 standard hours (or 20 units of product E) higher than budgeted and the variance is **favourable**.

(e) **Fixed overhead capacity variance**

The capacity variance is the difference between the budgeted hours of work and the actual active hours of work.

Budgeted hours of work	5,000 hrs
Actual hours worked	5,400 hrs
Fixed overhead capacity variance in hours	400 hrs (F)
× standard fixed overhead absorption rate per hour	× £4
Fixed overhead capacity variance in £	£1,600 (F)

Since the labour force worked 400 hours longer than budgeted, we should expect output to be 400 standard hours (or 80 units of product E) higher than budgeted. Hence the variance is **favourable**.

The variances may be summarised as follows.

	£
Expenditure variance	450 (A)
Efficiency variance	400 (F)
Capacity variance	1,600 (F)
Over-absorbed overhead (total variance)	£1,550 (F)

ASSESSMENT ALERT

In general, a favourable cost variance will arise if actual results are less than expected results. Be aware, however, of the **fixed overhead volume variance** and the **fixed overhead capacity variance** which give rise to favourable and adverse variances in the following situations.

- A favourable fixed overhead volume variance occurs when actual production is **greater than** budgeted production

- An adverse fixed overhead volume variance occurs when actual production is **less than budgeted** production

- A favourable fixed overhead capacity variance occurs when actual hours of work are **greater than** budgeted hours of work

- An adverse fixed overhead capacity variance occurs when actual hours of work are **less than** budgeted hours of work

Activity 10.3   Level: Assessment

Constance & Co Ltd expected to produce 14,000 units of its product during September 20X3. The standard time for a unit of the product is 2 hours and the budgeted fixed production overhead was £70,000.

In the event the actual fixed overhead expenditure was £67,500. The number of hours worked was 28,400 and 12,000 units were produced.

Task

Calculate all of the fixed overhead variances for September 20X3.

Measuring activity in terms of standard hours

5.13 In Chapter 9 you learned that activity can be measured in terms of **standard hours.** This is particularly useful if an organisation produces dissimilar products.

5.14 When an organisation manufactures dissimilar products, standard hours must be used as the basis for calculating overhead variances. The method of calculation does not alter, as the following example will demonstrate.

5.15 EXAMPLE: FIXED OVERHEAD VARIANCES BASED ON STANDARD HOURS

The following information is provided for the machining department last period.

Budgeted overhead	£185,000
Budgeted machine hours	37,000
Actual machine hours	36,000
Standard machine hours produced	36,600
Actual overheads incurred	£205,000

Task

Calculate the fixed overhead variances for the machining department last period.

5.16 SOLUTION

Remember that the **method of calculation does not alter:** we simply use 'standard hours of production' in place of 'units of production'.

Fixed overhead absorption rate $= \dfrac{£185,000}{37,000} = £5$ per standard machine hour

Fixed overhead total variance

	£
Fixed overhead incurred	205,000
Fixed overhead absorbed (36,600 std hours × £5)	183,000
Fixed overhead total variance	22,000 (A)

Fixed overhead expenditure variance

	£
Budgeted fixed overhead expenditure	185,000
Actual fixed overhead expenditure	205,000
Fixed overhead expenditure variance	20,000 (A)

Fixed overhead volume variance

Actual production volume achieved	36,600 std hrs
Budgeted production volume	37,000 std hrs
Volume variance in std. hrs	400 std hrs (A)
× std. absorption rate per std. hour	× £5
Fixed overhead volume variance	£2,000 (A)

Check: Volume £2,000 (A) + Expenditure £20,000 (A) = Total £22,000 (A)

Fixed overhead efficiency variance

Standard time for output achieved	36,600 hours
Actual hours taken	36,000 hours
Fixed overhead efficiency variance in hours	600 hours (F)
× std. absorption rate per hour	× £5
Fixed overhead efficiency variance	£3,000 (F)

Fixed overhead capacity variance

Budgeted hours of work	37,000
Actual hours worked	36,000
Capacity variance in hours	1,000 hours (A)
× std. absorption rate per hour	× £5
Fixed overhead capacity variance	£5,000 (A)

Check: Efficiency £3,000 (F) + Capacity £5,000 (A) = Volume £2,000(A)

Activity 10.4   Level: Assessment

SH Ltd makes products S and H. Data for the products and for activity last period are as follows.

- Standard time allowances are 10 minutes per unit of product S and 20 minutes per unit of product H

- Budgeted overhead for the period = £4,500

- Actual overhead incurred during period = £5,200

- Budgeted production for period = 4,200 units of S; 2,400 units of H
- Activity achieved during period = 3,600 units of S; 3,000 units of H
- Hours worked during period = 1,800

Task

Calculate the following variances for the period

(a)   Fixed overhead expenditure variance
(b)   Fixed overhead volume variance
(c)   Fixed overhead capacity variance
(d)   Fixed overhead efficiency variance

Activity 10.5   Level: Assessment

Lynn Ltd produces and sells the Koob, the standard cost for one unit being as follows.

	£
Direct material A - 10 kilograms at £20 per kg	200
Direct material B - 5 litres at £6 per litre	30
Direct wages - 5 hours at £6 per hour	30
Fixed overhead	50
Total standard cost	310

The fixed overhead included in the standard cost is based on an expected monthly output of 900 units. Fixed overhead is absorbed on the basis of direct labour hours.

During April 20X3 the actual results were as follows.

Production	800 units
Material A	7,800 kg used, costing £159,900
Material B	4,300 litres used, costing £23,650
Direct wages	4,200 hours worked for £24,150
Fixed overhead	£47,000

Tasks

(a)   Calculate price and usage variances for each material.
(b)   Calculate labour rate and efficiency variances.
(c)   Calculate fixed overhead expenditure, volume, efficiency and capacity variances.

---

6   CONTROL RATIOS

Efficiency, capacity and activity (production volume) ratios

6.1   In Chapter 3 you saw how labour activity can be measured by ratios as follows.

- Efficiency ratio
- Capacity ratio
- Activity ratio or production volume ratio

Efficiency ratio	**Capacity ratio**	**Activity ratio**
$\dfrac{\text{Standard hours to make actual output}}{\text{Actual hours worked}}$	$\times \dfrac{\text{Actual hours worked}}{\text{Hours budgeted}}$	$= \dfrac{\text{Output measured in expec or standard hours}}{\text{Hours budgeted}}$

These ratios are usually expressed as percentages.

6.2   EXAMPLE: RATIOS

Rush and Fluster Ltd budgets to make 25,000 standard units of output (in four hours each) during a budget period of 100,000 hours.

Actual output during the period was 27,000 units which took 120,000 hours to make.

Task

Calculate the efficiency, capacity and activity (production volume) ratios.

6.3   SOLUTION

(a)   Efficiency ratio $\dfrac{(27,000 \times 4)\ \text{hours}}{120,000\ \text{hours}} \times 100\% =$ 90%

(b)   Capacity ratio $\dfrac{120,000\ \text{hours}}{100,000\ \text{hours}} \times 100\% =$ 120%

(c)   Activity ratio $\dfrac{(27,000 \times 4)\ \text{hours}}{100,000\ \text{hours}} \times 100\% =$ 108%

(d)   The production volume (activity) ratio of 108% (more output than budgeted) is explained by the 120% capacity working, offset to a certain extent by the poor efficiency (90% × 120% = 108%).

6.4   The ratios that we have calculated provide equivalent information to the **overhead variances,** but in a **non-monetary** form.

(a)   The **efficiency** ratio is equivalent to the **overhead efficiency variance.** The ratio of **below 100%** would be represented by an **adverse** efficiency variance. It is worth noting that the **labour efficiency variance** would also be adverse.

(b)   The **capacity** ratio is equivalent to the **overhead capacity variance.** The ratio of **above 100%** would be represented by a **favourable** capacity variance.

(c)   The **activity** or **production volume** ratio is equivalent to the **overhead volume variance.** The ratio of **above 100%** would be represented by a **favourable** volume variance.

7   THE REASONS FOR COST VARIANCES

7.1   There are many possible reasons for cost variances arising, as you will see from the following list of possible causes.

ASSESSMENT ALERT

This is not an exhaustive list. In an assessment you should review the information given and use your imagination and common sense to suggest possible reasons for variances.

Variance	Favourable	Adverse
(a) Material price	Unforeseen discounts received	Price increase
	More care taken in purchasing	Careless purchasing
	Change in material standard	Change in material standard
(b) Material usage	Material used of higher quality than standard	Defective material
		Excessive waste
	More effective use made of material	Theft
		Stricter quality control
	Errors in allocating material to jobs	Errors in allocating material to jobs
(c) Labour rate	Use of apprentices or other workers at a rate of pay lower than standard	Wage rate increase
		Use of higher grade labour
(d) Labour efficiency	Output produced more quickly than expected because of work motivation, better quality of equipment or materials, or better methods	Lost time in excess of standard allowed
		Output lower than standard set because of deliberate restriction, lack of training, or sub-standard material used
	Errors in allocating time to jobs	Errors in allocating time to jobs
(e) Overhead expenditure	Savings in costs incurred	Increase in cost of services used
	More economical use of services	Excessive use of services
		Change in type of services used
(f) Overhead capacity	Extra overtime was worked	Machine breakdowns
	More employees taken on	Shortage of materials
(g) Overhead efficiency	As for labour efficiency	As for labour efficiency

7.2 Once variances have been calculated, management have to decide whether or not to investigate their causes. It would be extremely **time consuming and expensive** to investigate every variance therefore managers have to decide which variances are significant.

7.3 A number of factors can be taken into account when deciding whether a variance is significant.

(a) **Materiality.** A standard cost is really only an **average** expected cost and is not a rigid specification. Small variations either side of this average are therefore bound to occur. The problem is to decide whether a variation from standard should be considered **significant** and worthy of investigation. **Tolerance limits** can be set and only variances which exceed such limits would require investigating.

(b) **Controllability.** Some types of variance may not be controllable even once their cause is discovered. For example, if there is a general worldwide increase in the price of a raw material there is nothing that can be done internally to control the effect of this.

(c) **The type of standard being used.**

(i) The efficiency variance reported in any control period, whether for materials or labour, will depend on the **efficiency level** set. If, for example, an **ideal standard** is used, variances will always be **adverse**.

(ii) A similar problem arises if **average price levels** are used as standards. If inflation exists, favourable price variances are likely to be reported at the beginning of a period, to be offset by adverse price variances later in the period as inflation pushes prices up.

(d) **Interdependence between variances.** Quite possibly, individual variances should not be looked at in isolation. One variance might be inter-related with another, and much of it might have occurred only because the other, inter-related, variance occurred too.

Interdependence between variances

7.4 When two variances are interdependent (interrelated) one will usually be adverse and the other one favourable. Here are some examples.

Materials price and usage

7.5 It may be decided to purchase cheaper materials for a job in order to obtain a **favourable price variance**. This may result in higher materials wastage and an **adverse usage variance**. If the cheaper materials are more difficult to handle, there might also be some **adverse labour efficiency** variance.

Labour rate and efficiency

7.6 If employees are paid higher rates for experience and skill, using a highly skilled team to do some work would incur an **adverse rate variance**, but should also obtain a **favourable efficiency variance**. In contrast, a **favourable rate variance** might indicate a larger-than-expected proportion of inexperienced workers in the workforce. This could result in an **adverse labour efficiency variance**, and perhaps poor materials handling and high rates of rejects too (**adverse materials usage variance**).

Activity 10.6   **Level: Assessment**

(a) Give two possible reasons for an adverse material price variance.

(b) What variances might arise if temporary student labour is used on a job?

Key learning points

- A **variance** is the difference between actual results and standard results. **Variance analysis** is the process by which the total difference between actual results and standard results is analysed.

- In general, a **favourable** variance arises when actual results are better than standard results, an **adverse** variance means that actual results were worse than standard.

- **Total**, **price** and **usage** variances may be calculated for materials.

- **Total**, **rate** and **efficiency** variances may be calculated for labour.

- **Fixed overhead variances** include the following.

  ○ **Expenditure** variance

  ○ **Volume** variance (which may be split into **efficiency** and **capacity**)

- When an organisation manufactures **dissimilar units, standard hours** must be used as the basis for calculating overhead variances.

- When considering the reasons why variances have occurred, it is important to remember that they should not be looked at in isolation, since there may be **interdependence between variances**.

Quick quiz

1   What is a material usage variance?

2   What do favourable variances mean in terms of profit?

3   List three possible reasons why an adverse material usage variance might occur.

4   The fixed overhead volume variance is broken down into which two sub-variances?

5   What is the fixed overhead total variance and what is it equivalent to?

6   Which of the following formulae is correct?

    (a)   Efficiency ratio × capacity ratio = activity ratio
    (b)   Efficiency ratio × activity ratio = capacity ratio
    (c)   Capacity ratio × activity ratio = efficiency ratio

Answers to quick quiz

1   The difference between the standard quantity of materials that should have been used for the number of units actually produced, and the actual quantity of materials used, valued at the standard price per unit of material.

2   They mean the actual profits are higher than standard profits.

3   • Material is defective
    • There is an excessive waste of material
    • Theft
    • Stricter quality control

4   The overhead efficiency variance and the overhead capacity variance.

5   It is the difference between fixed overhead incurred and fixed overhead absorbed. It is equivalent to the under- or over-absorbed overhead.

6   (a) Efficiency ratio × capacity ratio = activity ratio

11 Further aspects of variance analysis

This chapter contains

1   Introduction

2   Presenting variances in a report to management

3   Standard cost bookkeeping

Learning objectives

On completion of this chapter you will be able to:

- Compare standard costs against actual costs and analyse any variances

- Prepare standard cost reports with variances clearly identified and presented in an intelligible form

- Identify any unusual or unexpected results and report them to management

- Identify any reasons for significant variances and present explanations to management

- Produce the results of variance analysis and the explanations of specific variances for management

- Deal with any variance analysis queries

Performance criteria

6.1 (iv)   Standard costs are compared against actual costs and any variances are analysed

6.3 (i)   Standard cost reports with variances clearly identified are presented in an intelligible form

BPP PUBLISHING

6.3 (ii) Unusual or unexpected results are identified and reported to managers

6.3 (iii) Any reasons for significant variances from standard are identified and the explanations presented to management

6.3 (iv) The results of the analysis and explanations of specific variances are produced for management

6.3 (v) Staff working in operational departments are consulted to resolve any queries in the data

Range statement

6.1.1 Direct costs: standard and actual material costs; standard and actual labour costs; standard and actual expenses

6.1.2 Variance analysis: Materials variances: usage, price; Labour variances: rate, efficiency

6.3.1 Methods of presentation: written report containing analysis and explanation of specific variances; further explanations to managers

6.3.2 Types of variances: Overhead variances: expenditure, efficiency, volume, capacity; Materials variances: usage, price; Labour variances: rate, efficiency

Knowledge and understanding

- Principles and objectives of standard costing systems: variance reports

- The significance of and possible reasons for variances

1 INTRODUCTION

1.1 So far, we have considered how different types of variance are calculated without considering how they may be presented in a statement, or in a report to management. In this chapter we will be looking at how to prepare variance reports for management. The chapter will conclude with a review of how standard costs and variances are recorded in the bookkeeping system.

2 PRESENTING VARIANCES IN A REPORT TO MANAGEMENT

2.1 To demonstrate how variances may be presented in a report to management we will work through an example. This will give you some useful revision of the variance calculations you learned in Chapter 10.

2.2 EXAMPLE: PREPARING VARIANCE REPORTS

Dollar Princess Ltd manufactures one product, the opalette. The standard cost card for the product is as follows.

STANDARD COST CARD - OPALETTE

		£
Direct materials	0.5 kilos at £4 per kilo	2.00
Direct labour	2 hours at £5.00 per hour	10.00
Fixed overhead	2 hours at £3.70 per hour	7.40
Standard cost		19.40

Budgeted output for the month of June 20X0 was 5,100 units. Actual results for June 20X0 were as follows.

Production was 4,850 units

Materials consumed in production amounted to 2,300 kilos at a total cost of £9,800

8,500 labour hours were worked at a cost of £55,250

Fixed overheads amounted to £42,300

Task

Calculate all cost variances for the month ended 30 June 20X0 and present them in a variance report for management.

2.3 SOLUTION

		£
(a)	2,300 kg of material should cost (× £4)	9,200
	but did cost	9,800
	Material price variance	600 (A)

(b)	4,850 opalettes should use (× 0.5 kgs)	2,425 kg
	but did use	2,300 kg
	Material usage variance in kgs	125 kg (F)
	× standard price per kg	× £4
	Material usage variance in £	£ 500 (F)

		£
(c)	8,500 hours of labour should cost (× £5)	42,500
	but did cost	55,250
	Labour rate variance	12,750 (A)

(d)	4,850 opalettes should take (× 2 hrs)	9,700 hrs
	but did take	8,500 hrs
	Labour efficiency variance in hours	1,200 hrs (F)
	× standard rate per hour	× £5
	Labour efficiency variance in £	£6,000 (F)

		£
(e)	Budgeted fixed overhead (5,100 units × 2 hrs × £3.70)	37,740
	Actual fixed overhead	42,300
	Fixed overhead expenditure variance	4,560 (A)

		£
(f)	Actual production at standard rate (4,850 units × £7.40)	35,890
	Budgeted production at standard rate (5,100 units × £7.40)	37,740
	Fixed overhead volume variance	1,850 (A)

2.4 One way of presenting a standard cost report is as follows.

STANDARD COST REPORT

Month: June 20X0
Budgeted output: 5,100 units
Actual output: 4,850 units

	Adverse	Favourable	£	£
Direct materials				
Standard cost of actual output			9,700	
Direct material price variance	600			
Direct material usage variance		500		
Total direct material variance			100 (A)	
Actual direct materials cost				9,800
Direct labour				
Standard cost of actual output			48,500	
Direct labour rate variance	12,750			
Direct labour efficiency		6,000		
Total direct labour variance			6,750 (A)	
Actual direct labour cost				55,250
Fixed overhead				
Standard cost of actual output			35,890	
Fixed overhead expenditure variance	4,560			
Fixed overhead volume variance	1,850			
Total fixed overhead variance			6,410 (A)	
Actual fixed overhead cost				42,300
Total cost for period				107,350

Significance of variances

2.5 Once you have completed your variance report, it should be clear which variances, if any, are **significant**. Variances may be considered to be significant if they are more than a certain proportion of actual costs. For example, in Paragraph 2.4, we can calculate the following percentages in order to determine how significant each of the total variances are.

(a) $\dfrac{\text{Materials total variance}}{\text{Actual materials cost}} = \dfrac{£100}{9,800} = 1\%$

(b) $\dfrac{\text{Labour total variance}}{\text{Actual labour cost}} = \dfrac{£2,600}{16,800} = 16\%$

(c) $\dfrac{\text{Fixed overhead total variance}}{\text{Actual fixed overhead cost}} = \dfrac{£6,410}{42,300} = 15\%$

As a **general guideline,** if the variance as a percentage of actual costs is greater than, say, 5%, then it might be considered to be significant. However, each organisation may have its own levels of significance which may be greater or less than 5%.

2.6 The calculations in Paragraph 2.5 show that the labour and overhead total variances are significant. Significant variances should be investigated to find out why they have arisen.

Activity 11.1   Level: Assessment

Bradford Ltd manufactures one product, an alista, for which the standard cost is as follows.

STANDARD COST CARD - ALISTA

		£
Direct materials	1 kilo at £2 per kilo	2.00
Direct wages	4 hours at £6.00 per hour	24.00
Fixed overhead	3 hours at £3.50 per hour	10.50
Standard cost		36.50

Budgeted output for April was 8,000 units. Actual results for April were as follows.

Production was 9,000 units

Materials consumed in production amounted to 10,000 kilos at a total cost of £22,000

30,000 labour hours were worked at a cost of £182,000

Fixed overheads amounted to £82,000

Tasks

(a) Calculate all cost variances for April.
(b) Prepare a variance report for management.

2.7 The variance report that we have demonstrated so far in this chapter is just one form of presentation that can be used. You will come across a variety of different presentations in your work and in assessments. Try the following example, which demonstrates another presentation that may be used. This form of presentation highlights the total variances for each cost element. The example also demonstrates how to present a variance schedule.

2.8 EXAMPLE: VARIANCE ANALYSIS REPORTS

McIntosh plc uses a standard costing system and for the single product that the firm produces the following standard costs apply.

	£
Direct material 5 kgs at £2 per kg	10
Direct wages 4 hours at £6 per hour	24
Fixed overhead 4 hours at £2 per hour	8
Total standard cost	42

In September, 20X0 production is budgeted at 5,000 units and actual data for the month is as follows.

(a) Production 5,400 units
(b) Actual materials consumed 30,000 kgs, costing £57,000
(c) Actual labour hours worked 23,300, costing £145,000
(d) Actual fixed overhead cost £38,000

Tasks

(a) Prepare a variance report, detailing total materials, labour and overhead variances.

(b) Calculate all the material, labour and fixed overhead sub-variances of the total variances in your variance report.

(c) Prepare a report for management which includes a variance schedule and explanations of why the variances that you have calculated in (b) might have arisen.

2.9 SOLUTION

(a) McINTOSH PLC VARIANCE REPORT

Month   *September*

Budgeted output 5,000 units
Actual output   5,400 units

	Actual costs £	Output Units	Standard costs Unit cost £	Total standard cost £	Total variance £
Materials	57,000	5,400	10	54,000	3,000 (A)
Labour	145,000	5,400	24	129,600	15,400 (A)
Fixed overhead	38,000	5,400	8	43,200	5,200 (F)
	240,000		42	226,800	13,200 (A)

(b) (i)

	£
30,000 kgs should cost ($\times$ £2)	60,000
but did cost	57,000
Material price variance	3,000 (F)

(ii)

5,400 units should have used ($\times$ 5 kgs)	27,000 kgs
but did use	30,000 kgs
Material usage variance (in kgs)	3,000 kgs (A)
$\times$ standard cost per kg	$\times$ £2
Material usage variance (in £)	£6,000 (A)

(iii)

	£
23,300 hours should have cost ($\times$ £6)	139,800
but did cost	145,000
Labour rate variance	5,200 (A)

(iv)

5,400 units should take ($\times$ 4 hrs)	21,600 hrs
but did take	23,300 hrs
Labour efficiency variance (in hrs)	1,700 hrs (A)
$\times$ standard rate per hour	$\times$ £6
Labour efficiency variance (in £)	£10,200 (A)

(v)

	£
Budgeted fixed overhead ($4 \times £2 \times 5,000$)	40,000
Actual fixed overhead	38,000
Fixed overhead expenditure variance	2,000 (F)

(vi)

5,400 units should have taken ($\times$ 4 hrs)	21,600 hrs
but did take	23,300 hrs
Fixed overhead efficiency variance (in hrs)	1,700 hrs (A)
$\times$ standard rate per hour	$\times$ £2
Fixed overhead efficiency variance (in £)	£3,400 (A)

(vii)

Budgeted activity level	20,000 hrs
Actual activity level	23,300 hrs
Fixed overhead capacity variance (in hrs)	3,300 hrs (F)
$\times$ standard rate per hr	$\times$ £2
Fixed overhead capacity variance (in £)	£6,600 (F)

(c)

REPORT

To: McIntosh plc management
From: A Technician
Date: 15 October 20X0
Subject: Variance analysis report - September 20X0

This report contains a variance schedule which lists all of the cost variances for the period under consideration. Specific variances are explained where possible.

McINTOSH PLC
VARIANCE SCHEDULE

	(F)	(A)	
Cost variances	£	£	£
Materials price	3,000		
Materials usage		6,000	
Labour rate		5,200	
Labour efficiency		10,200	
Fixed overhead expenditure	2,000		
Fixed overhead efficiency		3,400	
Fixed overhead capacity	6,600		
	11,600	24,800	13,200 (A)

Possible explanation of variances

(a) **Favourable material price variance.** Unforeseen discounts may have been received by purchasing staff.

(b) **Adverse material usage variance.** The material may have been defective, or there may have been excessive waste during production.

(c) **Adverse labour rate variance** There may have been wage rate increases, or excessive overtime may have been worked (and charged to direct labour costs).

(d) **Adverse labour and overhead efficiency variance.** There may have been increased number of machine breakdowns (thus resulting in increased idle time).

(e) **Favourable fixed overhead expenditure variance.** There may have been more economical use of services.

(f) **Favourable fixed overhead capacity variance.** The workforce may have worked longer hours than expected, perhaps because of extra overtime hours.

(*Note.* There are many reasons for the above variances - we have only noted one or two specific reasons. Look back at the explanations given in Chapter 10 for a full range of possibilities.)

Activity 11.2　　　　　　　　　　　　　　　　　　　　　**Level: Assessment**

Ross Ltd uses a standard costing system and for the single product that the firm produces the following standard costs apply.

	£
Direct material 5 kgs at £3 per kg	15
Direct wages 4 hours at £4 per hour	16
Fixed overhead 4 hours at £1 per hour	4
Total standard cost	35

In April production is budgeted at 6,000 units and actual data for the month is as follows.

(a)   Production 6,200 units

(b)   Actual materials consumed 33,000 kgs, costing £97,000

(c)   Actual labour hours worked 25,800, costing £106,000

(d)   Actual fixed overhead cost £23,000

Tasks

(a)   Prepare a variance report, detailing total materials, labour and overhead variances.

(b)   Calculate all the material, labour and fixed overhead sub-variances of the total variances in your variance report.

(c)   Prepare a variance schedule for Ross Ltd for April.

ASSESSMENT ALERT

Variances are commonly assessed in Unit 6 Assessments. Make sure that you are able to calculate all of the variances covered in this Interactive Text and ensure that you are also able to comment on the possible causes of variances.

3   STANDARD COST BOOKKEEPING

3.1   Now that you know how to calculate variances and present them to management, you need to be able to incorporate them into a **standard cost bookkeeping system.** We looked at cost bookkeeping in detail in Chapter 7. Glance back at the chapter if you need to remind yourself of the main principles.

3.2   The general principle in standard cost bookkeeping is that cost variances should be recorded as **early as possible**. They are recorded in the relevant account **where they arise** and the appropriate double entry is taken to a variance account. Examples are as follows.

(a)   **Material price variances** are apparent when materials are purchased, and they are therefore recorded in the **stores account**. If a price variance is adverse, we should credit the stores account and debit a variance account with the amount of the variance.

(b)   **Material usage variances** do not occur until output is actually produced in the factory, and they are therefore recorded in the **work in progress account**. If a usage variance is favourable, we should debit the work in progress account and credit a variance account with the value of the variance.

3.3   There are some possible variations in accounting method between one organisation's system and others, especially in the method of recording overhead variances, but the following are the basic principles.

(a)   The **material price variance** is recorded in the **stores control account**.

(b)   The **labour rate variance** is recorded in the **wages control account**.

(c)   The following variances are recorded in the **work in progress account**.

●   Material usage variance
●   Labour efficiency variance

(d)   The **production overhead expenditure variance** will be recorded in the **production overhead control account**.

(e) The **production overhead volume variance** may be recorded in the **production overhead control account**. (*Note.* Alternatively, you may find the volume variance recorded in the **work in progress account**.)

(f) The balance of variances in the variance accounts at the end of a period may be **written off to the profit and loss account**.

3.4 The actual process is best demonstrated with an example. Work carefully through the one which follows, ensuring that you know how the various variances are recorded.

3.5 EXAMPLE: COST BOOKKEEPING AND VARIANCES

Zed operates an integrated accounting system and prepares its final accounts monthly. You are provided with the following information.

Balances as at 1 October

	£'000
Plant and machinery, at cost	600
Stock - raw materials	520
Wages payable	40
Stock - finished goods	132

Data for the month of October

Materials purchased on credit	400,000 kgs at £4.90 per kg
Issued to production	328,000 kgs
Direct wages incurred	225,000 hours at £4.20 per hour
Direct wages paid	£920,000
Production overhead incurred on credit	£1,490,000
Production and sales	39,000 units

Additional data

Depreciation provision	plant and machinery, 20% pa on cost
Stocks of raw materials and finished goods	maintained at standard

Standard data

Direct material price	£5.00 per kg
Direct material usage	8 kgs per unit
Direct wages	£4.00 per hour
Direct labour	6 hours per unit
Production overhead	absorbed at 150% of direct wages
Budgeted output	10,000 units per week

Required

(a) Calculate the appropriate variances for October.

(b) Show the following ledger accounts for October.

   (i)   Stores ledger control account
   (ii)   Direct wages control account
   (iii)   Production overhead control account
   (iv)   Work in progress control account
   (v)   Finished goods control account
   (vi)   Cost of sales control account
   (vii) Variances account

3.6 SOLUTION

(a) We will begin by determining the standard unit cost and calculating the variances.

Standard cost per unit	£
Direct materials (8 kgs × £5)	40
Direct labour (6 hrs × £4)	24
Production overhead (150% × £24)	36
	100

Direct material price variance	£'000
400,000 kgs should cost (× £5)	2,000
but did cost (400,000 × £4.90)	1,960
	40 (F)

Direct material usage variance	
39,000 units should use (× 8)	312,000 kgs
but did use	328,000 kgs
Variance in kg	16,000 kgs (A)
× standard price per kg	× £5
	£80,000 (A)

Direct labour rate variance	£'000
225,000 hours should cost (× £4)	900
but did cost (225,000 × £4.20)	945
	45 (A)

Direct labour efficiency variance	
39,000 units should take (× 6 hrs)	234,000 hrs
but did take	225,000 hrs
Variance in hours	9,000 hrs (F)
× standard cost per hour	× £4
	£36,000 (F)

Production overhead expenditure variance	£'000	£'000
Budgeted expenditure (10,000 units × 4 wks × £36)		1,440
Actual expenditure		
Incurred on credit	1,490	
Depreciation (20% × 1/12 × £600)	10	
		1,500
		60 (A)

Production overhead volume variance	£'000
Actual production at standard rate (39,000 × £36)	1,404
Budgeted production at standard rate (10,000 × 4 wks × £36)	1,440
	36 (A)

(b) (i)

STORES LEDGER CONTROL ACCOUNT

	£'000		£'000
Balance b/f	520	Work in progress	
Creditors		(328,000 × £5)	1,640
(400,000 × £4.90)	1,960	Balance c/d	880
Material price variance	40		
	2,520		2,520
Balance b/d	880		

Notes

(1) Materials are issued from store at standard price.

(2) The material price variance is recorded in this account.

(ii)

DIRECT WAGES CONTROL ACCOUNT

	£'000		£'000
Bank	920	Balance b/f	40
Balance c/d	65	Work in progress	
		(225,000 hrs × £4)	900
		Labour rate variance	45
	985		985
		Balance b/d	65

Notes

(1) Labour hours are charged to work in progress at the standard rate per hour.

(2) The labour rate variance is recorded in this account.

(iii)

PRODUCTION OVERHEAD CONTROL ACCOUNT

	£'000		£'000
Creditors	1,490	Work in progress	
Depreciation on plant		(39,000 × £36)	1,404
and machinery	10	*Production overhead*	
		expenditure variance	60
		Production overhead	
		volume variance	36
	1,500		1,500

Notes

(1) Production is charged with the standard rate for the units produced.

(2) The production overhead expenditure variance is shown in this account

(3) In this example, the production overhead volume variance is shown in the overhead account.

(iv)

WORK IN PROGRESS CONTROL ACCOUNT

	£'000		£'000
Stores ledger	1,640	Finished goods	
Direct wages	900	(39,000 × £100)	3,900
Production overhead	1,404	*Direct material usage*	
Direct labour		*variance*	80
efficiency variance	36		
	3,980		3,980

Notes

(1) Output is valued at standard production cost.

(2) The efficiency variances appear in this account.

(v)

FINISHED GOODS CONTROL ACCOUNT

	£'000		£'000
Balance b/f	132	Cost of sales (39,000 × £100)	3,900
Work in progress	3,900	Balance c/d	132
	4,032		4,032
Balance b/d	132		

(vi)

COST OF SALES CONTROL ACCOUNT

	£'000		£'000
Finished goods	3,900	Profit and loss	3,900

(vii)

VARIANCES ACCOUNT

	£'000		£'000
Wages (labour rate)	45	Stores (material price)	40
Production o'head WIP (expenditure)	60	WIP (labour efficiency)	36
Production o'head WIP (volume)	36	Profit and loss account	145
WIP (material usage)	80		
	221		221

3.7 The variances are recorded in a variances account as part of the double entry system. The balance on the account at the end of the period is written off to the profit and loss account. Sometimes a separate account is used for each variance, but the double entry principles would be the same.

Deriving variances from bookkeeping entries

3.8 In our example we calculated all of the variances before completing the accounts. In fact, the material price variance and the labour rate variance can sometimes be derived simply by preparing the accounts. Consider the following example.

3.9 EXAMPLE: DERIVING VARIANCES FROM BOOKKEEPING ENTRIES

B Ltd makes a single product and maintains a standard cost bookkeeping system. Extracts from the standard cost details and operating information for May are as follows.

Standard material price	£2 per kg
Standard labour rate	£8 per hour

Material stock at standard cost:
Opening balance, 1 May	£40,000
Closing balance, 31 May	£44,000

Material purchases during May	85,000 kg at a cost of £187,000
Materials issued to production during May	83,000 kg
Wages paid during May	9,000 hours at a cost of £68,400

Prepare the following accounts for May

- Stores ledger control account
- Direct wages control account

3.10 SOLUTION

STORES LEDGER CONTROL ACCOUNT

	£		£
Balance b/f	40,000	Work in progress (83,000 × £2 std)	166,000
Creditors	187,000	Material price variance (balancing figure)	17,000
		Balance c/f	44,000
	227,000		227,000
Balance b/f	44,000		

The material price variance of £17,000 was derived as a **balancing figure** in the account. It will be transferred as a debit to the variance account and therefore it is an **adverse variance.**

We can calculate the variance as a check. To do so you need to remember our discussion in Paragraph 3.14 of Chapter 10. Since material stock is valued at standard cost, the material price variance will be based on the **purchases** during the month.

	£
85,000 kg purchased should have cost (× £2)	170,000
but did cost	187,000
Material price variance	17,000 Adverse

Let's complete the direct wages control account now. The labour rate variance will be derived as a balancing figure.

DIRECT WAGES CONTROL ACCOUNT

	£		£
Bank	68,400	Work in progress (9,000 hrs × £8 std)	72,000
Labour rate variance (bal fig)	3,600		
	72,000		72,000

The labour rate variance of £3,600 (the balancing figure) will be transferred as a credit to the variance account and therefore it is a **favourable variance.**

We can check the labour rate variance by calculation.

	£
9,000 hours worked should have cost (× £8)	72,000
but did cost	68,400
Labour rate variance	3,600 (F)

Maintaining stores records at standard cost

3.11 In Chapter 2 we mentioned that materials stores record cards can be maintained at standard cost. If this is done the price variance is **extracted at the time of receipt** of material purchases.

Activity 11.3   **Level: Assessment**

The stores record card for material R is shown below. The record card shows both actual and standard cost and price variances are identified at the time of receipt. Stocks are valued at standard price of £7 per kg.

STORES RECORD CARD

Material: Material R

Code: RMM127

Date	Receipts					Issues	Balance	
	Quantity kg	Actual Price per kg £	Total Actual Cost £	Total Standard Cost £	Price Variance £	Quantity kg	Quantity kg	Total Standard Cost £
B/f at 1 Aug							250	1,750
8 Aug	360	7.30	2,628	2,520	108 (A)		610	4,270
10 Aug						400		
15 Aug	360	7.40	2,664					
19 Aug						500		
22 Aug	400	6.70						
30 Aug						200		
Total price variance								

Task

Complete the stores record card for August and show the total price variance for the month.

Key learning points

- A **variance report** is a report which summarises cost variances.

- The general principle in standard cost bookkeeping is that **cost variances should be recorded as early as possible.** They are recorded in the relevant account in which they arise and the appropriate double entry is taken to a variance account.

- The **material price variance** and **labour rate variance** can be derived from the bookkeeping records.

Quick quiz

1   If 3,000 kg of material A should have cost £9,000, but did cost £10,400, what is the materials price variance?

2   When preparing a statement that reconciles standard cost of production to actual cost of production, should you *add* or *subtract* an adverse variance to the standard cost of production in order to calculate the actual cost of production?

3   Material stocks are valued at standard cost within MC Ltd. Should the material price variance be based on the purchases for the period or on the usage for the period?

Answers to quick quiz

1   £1,400 (Adverse)

2   Add (since the actual costs of production are higher than standard costs when the sum of the cost variances is adverse).

3   The material price variance should be based on the purchases for the period.

Recording cost information case study

Recording cost information case study

1 INTRODUCTION

1.1 In this Interactive Text, we have looked in detail at the ways cost information is recorded. In this case study, we are going to bring all of your knowledge together by looking at a scenario which covers many of the practical aspects of recording cost information.

1.2 This case study is going to be centred around Mill Stream Cottage Guest House. The following details are relevant.

- The guest house is within close proximity to Gatwick Airport and is mainly used by air travellers.

- The guest house has ten twin bedrooms. The rooms and associated running costs are identical for each bedroom.

- The Mill Stream Cottage Guest House organises its operations into four cost centres.
    - Kitchen
    - Reception
    - Room changeovers
    - Administration

- A lavender presentation pack is left in each room for guests. Each pack contains
    - Soap
    - Toothpaste
    - Shower gel
    - Bubble bath
    - Moisturiser
    - Small lavender pillow

- Most guests use the packs or take them home with them.

- The standard usage of lavender presentation packs is two packs per room per night.

213

- The packs are purchased from a number of different suppliers and the standard purchase price is £2.50.

- The packs can also be sold as gifts at the guest house reception for £7.50 each.

1.3 The tasks covered in this case study are performed by the accounting technician.

1.4 The main aim of this case study is to show you how standard cost bookkeeping systems operate in practice, from receiving invoices to closing off ledger accounts.

1.5 We will start by looking at how to record and analyse direct costs.

2 RECORDING AND ANALYSING DIRECT COSTS

2.1 Mill Stream Cottage Guest House purchases the lavender presentation packs from a number of different suppliers, and packs are ordered weekly. The accounting technician keeps a record of the presentation packs received and issued on a stores record card.

2.2 The stores record card shows both the actual cost and the standard cost. It identifies any price variance which might arise **at the time of receipt** of the invoice.

2.3 Stocks of lavender presentation packs are valued at the standard cost of £2.50.

2.4 During June 2001, the accounting technician received the following four purchase invoices in respect of lavender presentation packs.

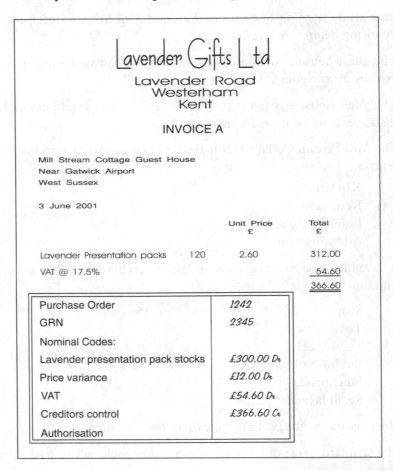

Lavender Gifts Ltd
Lavender Road
Westerham
Kent

INVOICE A

Mill Stream Cottage Guest House
Near Gatwick Airport
West Sussex

3 June 2001

		Unit Price £	Total £
Lavender Presentation packs	120	2.60	312.00
VAT @ 17.5%			54.60
			366.60

Purchase Order	1242
GRN	2345
Nominal Codes:	
Lavender presentation pack stocks	£300.00 Dr
Price variance	£12.00 Dr
VAT	£54.60 Dr
Creditors control	£366.60 Cr
Authorisation	

GIFTS 'R' US

Gifton Park
Reigate Hill
Surrey

INVOICE B

Mill Stream Cottage Guest House
Near Gatwick Airport
West Sussex

10 June 2001

	Unit Price £	Total £
Lavender Presentation packs 90	2.65	238.50
VAT @ 17.5%		41.74
		280.24

Purchase Order	*1250*
GRN	*2354*
Nominal Codes:	
Lavender presentation pack stocks	*£225.00 Dr*
Price variance	*£13.50 Dr*
VAT	*£41.74 Dr*
Creditors control	*£280.24 Cr*
Authorisation	

Lavender Gifts Ltd

Lavender Road
Westerham
Kent

INVOICE C

Mill Stream Cottage Guest House
Near Gatwick Airport
West Sussex

17 June 2001

	Unit Price £	Total £
Lavender Presentation packs 180	2.50	450.00
VAT @ 17.5%		78.75
		528.75

Purchase Order	*1290*
GRN	*2363*
Nominal Codes:	
Lavender presentation pack stocks	*£450.00 Dr*
Price variance	-
VAT	*£78.75 Dr*
Creditors control	*£528.75 Cr*
Authorisation	

Lavender Gifts Ltd
Lavender Road
Westerham
Kent

INVOICE D

Mill Stream Cottage Guest House
Near Gatwick Airport
West Sussex

24 June 2001

		Unit Price £	Total £
Lavender Presentation packs	240	2.45	588.00
VAT @ 17.5%			102.90
			690.90

Purchase Order	1299
GRN	2376
Nominal Codes:	
Lavender presentation pack stocks	£600.00 Dr
Price variance	£12.00 Cr
VAT	£102.90 Dr
Creditors control	£690.90 Cr
Authorisation	

2.5 When the invoices are received, the accounting technician stamps them with a grid as shown above so that she can analyse the costs before recording them in the standard cost bookkeeping system which is in operation. Look through the purchase invoices from Lavender Gifts Ltd and Gifts 'R' Us and make sure that you understand where all of the hand-written entries have come from.

2.6 For example, the hand written entries on Invoice A are derived as follows.

- The **purchase order number** shows that the accounting technician has checked that the goods were actually ordered.

- The **goods received note (GRN) number** shows that the accounting technician has checked that the goods were actually received.

- **Lavender presentation packs stocks:** 120 packs × £2.50 std = £300 debit.

- **Price variance:** should cost £300 – did cost £312 = £12 debit (adverse).

- **VAT** is not included in the cost of stock and is transferred to a separate account.

- **Creditors control** is credited with the total amount of the invoice.

2.7 It is very common for standard cost bookkeeping systems to extract price variances when invoices are received from suppliers. Such systems have the advantage of being able to report variances as soon as possible and then management can take any action which may be required.

2.8 Apart from using the presentation packs in guests' rooms, the packs are also sold as gifts in the reception area of Mill Stream Cottage Guest House. Sales of packs as gifts are shown in the following summary of till receipts.

SUMMARY OF TILL RECEIPTS – JUNE 2001		
Week No	*Number of Presentation Packs sold*	*Sales value* £
1 (7.6.01)	20	150.00
2 (14.6.01)	5	37.50
3 (21.6.01)	10	75.00
4 (28.6.01)	-	-

2.9 The number of packs used in guests' rooms during June 2001 is shown in the following table.

SUMMARY OF PRESENTATION PACKS USED IN GUESTS' ROOMS – JUNE 2001	
Week No	*Presentation Packs used*
1 (7.6.01)	130
2 (14.6.01)	95
3 (21.6.01)	105
4 (28.6.01)	60

2.10 The accounting technician likes to update the stores record cards for issues of presentation packs (sales or usage by guests) at the end of each week. She also updates the standard cost bookkeeping system. The next section of this case study will go on to look at

- Updating stores record cards
- Updating the standard cost bookkeeping system

3 STORES RECORD CARDS AND COST BOOKKEEPING ENTRIES

3.1 The invoices in Paragraph 2.4 and the summaries in Paragraphs 2.8 and 2.9 can be used to update the stores record card (or stock card) as shown below.

STORES RECORD CARD

Product: Lavender Presentation packs..............

| Date | Receipts | | | | | Issues | Balance | |
	Quantity	Actual Cost per pack £	Total Actual Cost £	Total Standard Cost £	Price Variance £	Quantity	Quantity	Total Standard Cost £
B/f at 1 June							50	125.00
3 June	120	2.60	312.00	300.00	12.00 (A)		170	425.00
7 June						150	20	50.00
10 June	90	2.65	238.50	225.00	13.50 (A)		110	275.00
14 June						100	10	25.00
17 June	180	2.50	450.00	450.00	-		190	475.00
21 June						115	75	187.50
24 June	240	2.45	588.00	600.00	12.00 (F)		315	787.50
28 June						60	255	637.50

3.2 Notice how straightforward it is to use a standard cost bookkeeping system.

- All stocks are valued at standard cost.

- Price variances are identified when invoices are received and not when the presentation packs are used.

For example, the value of stocks on 17 June 2001 can immediately be calculated as £475.00 (190 packs at £2.50 each).

3.3 The stores record card, the summary of till receipts and information on usage of presentation packs by guests can be used to update the standard cost bookkeeping system. The ledger accounts we shall be looking at in detail are as follows.

- Presentation packs stock control account
- Presentation packs price variance account
- VAT account
- Creditors' control account
- Cost of sales account– presentation packs sold
- Packs issued to guests' rooms account

Presentation packs stock control account

3.4 The main thing to remember with this account is that the balance b/f on 1 June and c/f on 28 June should agree to the figures on the stores record card.

PRESENTATION PACKS STOCK CONTROL ACCOUNT

		£			£
1.6.01	Stock b/f	125.00	7.6.01	Cost of sales – 20 presentation packs sold	50.00
3.6.01	Invoice A	300.00	7.6.01	130 packs issued to guests' rooms	325.00
10.6.01	Invoice B	225.00	14.6.01	Cost of sales – 5 presentation packs sold	12.50
17.6.01	Invoice C	450.00	14.6.01	95 packs issued to guests' rooms	237.50
24.6.01	Invoice D	600.00	21.6.01	Cost of sales – 10 presentation packs sold	25.00
			21.6.01	105 packs issued to guests' rooms	262.50
			28.6.01	60 packs issued to guests' rooms	150.00
				Balance c/f	637.50
		1,700.00			1,700.00

Presentation packs – price variance account

3.5 You can use either the invoices in Paragraph 2.4 or the stores record card in Paragraph 3.1 to prepare this ledger account.

PRESENTATION PACKS PRICE VARIANCE ACCOUNT

		£			£
3.6.01	Invoice A	12.00	24.6.01	Invoice D	12.00
10.6.01	Invoice B	13.50	28.6.01	Profit and loss a/c	13.50
		25.50			25.50

3.6 The total price variance is a **debit** of £13.50 which indicates an **adverse variance** (an expense in the profit and loss account).

VAT

3.7 The bookkeeping entries required for the VAT account can be found on the invoices in Paragraph 2.4.

VAT ACCOUNT

		£			£
3.6.01	Invoice A	54.60			
10.6.01	Invoice B	41.74			
17.6.01	Invoice C	78.75			
24.6.01	Invoice D	102.90			

Creditors' control account

3.8 As with the VAT account above, the information required to complete the creditors' control account is clearly marked on the invoices in Paragraph 2.4.

CREDITORS' CONTROL ACCOUNT

		£			£
			3.6.01	Invoice A	366.60
			10.6.01	Invoice B	280.24
			17.6.01	Invoice C	528.75
			24.6.01	Invoice D	690.90

Cost of sales account– presentation packs sold

3.9   This account can be completed at the same time as the presentation packs stock control account. When stocks are transferred to the gift shop for sale, the cost bookkeeping entries are as follows.

Step 1   Cr   Presentation packs stock control account (as in Paragraph 3.4)

Step 2   Dr   Cost of sales account – presentation packs sold

COST OF SALES – PRESENTATION PACKS SOLD

		£		£
7.6.01	Presentation packs stock control a/c	50.00		
14.6.01	Presentation packs stock control a/c	12.50		
21.6.01	Presentation packs stock control a/c	25.00		
		87.50		

At the end of an accounting period, the cost of sales of presentation packs sold is transferred to the profit and loss account.

Packs issued to guests' rooms account

3.10   This account can also be completed at the same time as the presentation packs stock control account. When the packs are taken out of store and used in guests' rooms, the cost bookkeeping entries are as follows.

Step 1   Cr   Presentation packs stock control account

Step 2   Dr   Packs issued to guests' rooms account

3.11   ### PACKS ISSUED TO GUESTS' ROOMS

		£		£
7.6.01	Presentation packs stock control a/c (130)	325.00		
14.6.01	Presentation packs stock control a/c (95)	237.50		
21.6.01	Presentation packs stock control a/c (105)	262.50		
28.6.01	Presentation packs stock control a/c (60)	150.00		
		975.00		

Standard cost card

3.12 Mill Stream Cottage Guest House prepares rooms every day so that they are ready for guests at short notice.

The standard cost bookkeeping system which is in place means that a **standard cost card** is prepared for the costs involved in cleaning and preparing the bedrooms (called a 'room changeover' cost).

STANDARD COST CARD SERVICE: ROOM CHANGEOVER			
	QUANTITY	UNIT PRICE	TOTAL
DIRECT MATERIALS		£	£
Lavender presentation packs	2	2.50	5.00
DIRECT LABOUR	MINUTES	HOURLY RATE	
		£	
Cleaning room	18	6.00	1.80
Cleaning laundry	30	6.00	3.00
PRIME COST			9.80
INDIRECT COST	48	3.00	2.40
TOTAL COST			12.20

3.13 During the four weeks ended 28 June 2001, Mill Stream Cottage Guest House carried out 205 room changeovers and issued 390 presentation packs for use in guests' rooms.

205 room changeovers should have used:

205 × 2 packs per room = 410 presentation packs

Since the standard usage of presentation packs for 205 room changeovers is more than the actual usage, the usage variance for presentation packs will be **favourable**.

We can now record the cost bookkeeping entries in the following accounts.

- Packs issued to guests' rooms
- Standard cost of changeovers – presentation packs
- Presentation packs – usage variance

3.14 The packs issued to guests' rooms account has so far been debited with the standard cost of the **actual usage.** We did this in Paragraph 3.11. The next step is to transfer the standard usage for 205 room changeovers to the standard cost of changeovers – presentation packs account.

PACKS ISSUED TO GUESTS' ROOMS

			£				£
7.6.01	Presentation packs stock control a/c (130)		325.00	28.6.01	Standard cost of packs for 205 room changeovers (205 × £5.00)		1,025.00
14.6.01	Presentation packs stock control a/c (95)		237.50				
21.6.01	Presentation packs stock control a/c (105)		262.50				
28.6.01	Presentation packs stock control a/c (60)		150.00				
28.6.01	Pack usage variance ★		50.00				
			1,025.00				1,025.00

★ This balancing figure represents the favourable usage variance of presentation packs

STANDARD COST OF CHANGEOVERS – PRESENTATION PACKS

		£		£
28.6.01	Packs issued to guests' rooms	1,025.00		

3.15 The usage variance for presentation packs is recorded in the usage variance account for presentation packs as shown below.

PRESENTATION PACKS – USAGE VARIANCE

		£			£
28.6.01	Profit and loss account	50.00	28.6.01	Packs issued to guests' rooms	50.00

3.16 You should now be able to see the chain of events that occurs when goods or services are purchased and how the purchase invoice feeds into the stores record card and the ledger accounts. You should also have a clear understanding of how the material price and usage variances are an integral part of the standard cost bookkeeping system.

3.17 Let's go on to have a look at cost bookkeeping entries and variances for labour.

4   COST BOOKKEEPING ENTRIES FOR LABOUR

4.1 As you should be aware by now, the main source of labour cost information is the **payroll** records.

4.2 A summary of the payroll records for June 2001 for Mill Stream Cottage Guest House is shown below.

PAYROLL RECORDS – SUMMARY FOR JUNE 2001		
ROOM CHANGEOVER	*Hours worked in June 2001*	*Gross cost* £
Direct labour		
Cleaning Rooms	70	455.00
Cleaning Laundry	100	620.00

During June 2001, the domestic staff carried out 205 room changeovers. This information can be used to record the labour costs and variances in the standard cost bookkeeping system operated by Mill Stream Cottage Guest House.

4.3 The ledger accounts that we will be preparing in this section are as follows.

- Payroll control account
- Standard cost of cleaning rooms account
- Standard cost of cleaning laundry account
- Total labour cost variance account
- Labour efficiency variance
- Labour wage rate variance

4.4 Let's start with the payroll control account.

Payroll control account

4.5 The payroll control account is debited with information provided in the payroll summary.

- Gross cost of cleaning rooms – debit payroll control account £455.00
- Gross cost of cleaning laundry – debit payroll control account £620.00

The credit entries in the payroll control account will be the corresponding standard costs of cleaning rooms and laundry.

PAYROLL CONTROL ACCOUNT

		£			£
28.6.01	Payroll	455.00	28.6.01	Standard cost of cleaning rooms (W1)	369.00
28.6.01	Payroll	620.00	28.6.01	Standard cost of cleaning laundry (W2)	615.00
			28.6.01	Total labour cost variance*	91.00
		1,075.00			1,075.00

* Balancing figure

Workings

(W1) **Standard cost of cleaning rooms**

$$205 \text{ changeovers} \times \frac{18 \text{mins}}{60 \text{mins}} \quad = \quad 61.5 \text{ hours}$$

$$61.5 \text{ hours} \times £6.00 \text{ per hour} \quad = \quad £369$$

(W2) **Standard cost of cleaning laundry**

$$205 \text{ changeovers} \times \frac{30 \text{mins}}{60 \text{mins}} \quad = \quad 102.5 \text{ hours}$$

$$102.5 \text{ hours} \times £6.00 \text{ per hour} \quad = \quad £615$$

Cost of cleaning rooms and laundry accounts

4.6 The standard cost of cleaning rooms and laundry are transferred to the corresponding accounts.

STANDARD COST OF CLEANING ROOMS ACCOUNT

		£		£
28.6.01	Payroll control	369.00		

STANDARD COST OF CLEANING LAUNDRY ACCOUNT

	£		£
28.6.01 Payroll control	615.00		

Total labour cost variance account

4.7 The balance on the payroll account represents the total labour cost variance – this figure of £91.00 needs to be debited to the total labour cost variance account where it can be analysed further.

TOTAL LABOUR COST VARIANCE ACCOUNT

		£			£
28.6.01	Payroll control account	91.00	28.6.01	Labour efficiency variance – cleaning rooms (W1)	51.00
28.6.01	Labour efficiency variance – cleaning laundry (W2)	15.00	28.6.01	Labour wage rate variance – cleaning rooms (W3)	35.00
			28.6.01	Labour wage rate variance – cleaning laundry (W4)	20.00
		106.00			106.00

Workings

(W1) The domestic staff should have spent 61.5 hours cleaning rooms (see W1 of payroll control account). They actually spent 70 hours cleaning rooms (see payroll records). The difference of 8.5 hours (70 – 61.5) valued at the standard rate of £6 per hour = £51 (A). The variance is adverse because more hours were spent cleaning rooms than should have been.

(W2) The domestic staff should have spent 102.5 hours cleaning laundry (see W2 of payroll control account). They actually spent 100 hours (see payroll records). The difference of 2.5 hours (100 – 102.5) valued at the standard rate of £6 per hour = £15 (F). The variance is favourable because less hours were spent cleaning laundry than expected.

(W3) The domestic staff should have been paid £420 (70 hours × £6) for cleaning rooms in June 2001 but they were actually paid £455. This represents an adverse variance of £455 – £420 = £35.

(W4) The domestic staff should have been paid £600 (100 hours × £6) for cleaning laundry in June 2001 but they were actually paid £620. This represents an adverse variance of £620 – £600 = £20.

4.8 You can also calculate the labour wage rate variances by comparing the average wage rates paid to domestic staff for cleaning rooms and laundry.

4.9 **Cleaning rooms**

Average wage rate	= £455 ÷ 70 hours	= £6.50 per hour
Standard wage rate		£6.00 per hour
Additional expense	= £6.50 – £6.00	= £0.50 per hour

When 70 hours are worked, this represents an adverse variance of 70 hours × £0.50 = £35 (as calculated previously).

4.10 Cleaning laundry

Average wage rate = £620 ÷ 100 hours = £6.20 per hour
Standard wage rate = £6.00 per hour

Additional expense = £6.20 – £6.00 = £0.20 per hour

When 100 hours are worked, this represents an adverse variance of 100 hours × £0.20 = £20 (as calculated previously).

Labour efficiency and wage rate variance account

4.11 Don't forget that the labour efficiency variance account and the labour wage rate variance account must also be prepared. We have already looked at how the individual entries are calculated.

LABOUR EFFICIENCY VARIANCE

	£			£
28.6.01 Total labour cost variance a/c	51.00	28.6.01 Total labour cost variance a/c		15.00
		28.6.01 Profit and loss account		36.00
	51.00			51.00

LABOUR WAGE RATE VARIANCE

	£		£
28.6.01 Total labour cost variance a/c	35.00	28.6.01 Profit and loss account	55.00
28.6.01 Total labour cost variance a/c	20.00		
	55.00		55.00

Alternative method

4.12 It is important that you understand how the individual labour variances arise. However, there is an alternative method of establishing the labour variances which involves the labour rate variance 'falling out' from the payroll account and the efficiency variance 'falling out' from the cost of cleaning rooms/laundry accounts. Have a look at the following ledger accounts.

PAYROLL CONTROL ACCOUNT

	£		£
28.6.01 Payroll	455.00	28.6.01 Standard rate for 70 hours cleaning rooms (× £6)	420.00
28.6.01 Payroll	620.00	28.6.01 Standard rate for 100 hours cleaning laundry (× £6)	600.00
		28.6.01 Labour rate variance to profit and loss account	55.00
	1,075.00		1,075.00

COST OF CLEANING ROOMS ACCOUNT

	£		£
28.6.01 Payroll control account	420.00	28.6.01 Standard cost of rooms cleaned $205 \times \frac{18\text{mins}}{60\text{mins}} \times £6.00$	369.00
		28.6.01 Labour efficiency variance to profit and loss account	51.00
	420.00		420.00

COST OF CLEANING LAUNDRY ACCOUNT

		£			£
28.6.01	Payroll control account	600.00	28.6.01	Standard cost of cleaning laundry	
28.6.01	Labour efficiency variance to profit and loss account	15.00		$205 \times \dfrac{30\,\text{mins}}{60\,\text{mins}} \times £6.00$	615
		615.00			615

4.13 You will notice that the individual variances which have dropped out of the ledger accounts above as balancing figures are exactly the same as those calculated earlier.

5 RECORDING AND ANALYSING FIXED COSTS

5.1 The budgeted overheads for Mill Stream Cottage Guest House are all treated as fixed costs. The following table shows budgeted fixed overheads for a four-week period (after allocation and apportionment).

Overhead	Total (after allocation and apportionment)
	£
Kitchen	500
Reception	300
Room changeovers	576
Administration	235
	1,611

5.2 The total budgeted labour hours for room changeovers during a four-week period is 192 hours.

5.3 The budgeted overhead for room changeovers after allocation and apportionment is £576. Therefore:

$$\text{Budgeted overhead absorption rate} = \frac{\text{Budgeted overheads for room changeovers}}{\text{Budgeted direct labour hours}}$$

$$= \frac{£576}{192}$$

$$= £3 \text{ per direct labour hour}$$

If you look back at the standard cost card in paragraph 3.12, you will see that the standard absorption rate for indirect costs is £3.00 per labour hour.

5.4 For room changeovers, therefore, we expect overheads to be £576 and we expect to work a total of 192 labour hours in a four-week period.

5.5 Standard cost bookkeeping systems allow indirect costs and variances to be analysed in detail in the ledger accounts.

5.6 If the actual overheads for room changeovers during a four-week period is £580, then we have an adverse overhead expenditure variance of £4.

£576 (budgeted overhead) – £580 (actual overhead) = £4 adverse

5.7 The budgeted volume in terms of the number of room changeovers can be calculated as follows.

Budgeted labour hours			192 hours
Budgeted labour hours per room changeover:			
Cleaning room	18 minutes		
Cleaning laundry	30 minutes		
	48 minutes	÷ 60	÷ 0.8 hours
∴ Budgeted number of room changeovers per period			240

5.8 Now we can calculate the overhead volume variance.

	£
Actual volume at standard rate (205 changeovers × £2.40)	492
Budgeted volume at standard rate (240 changeovers × £2.40)	576
Overhead volume variance	84 adverse

The variance is adverse because volume was lower than budgeted, and this would have led to an under absorption of overheads.

5.9 The overhead absorbed by 205 room changeovers = 205 × £2.40 = £492.

5.10 Let's have a look at the cost bookkeeping entries for the following items.

- Actual fixed overheads
- Absorbed fixed overheads
- Fixed overhead expenditure variance
- Fixed overhead volume variance

Total fixed overhead control account

5.11 This account has a credit entry which represents the actual fixed overheads that relate to the room changeovers. The debit on this account will be the total overheads for Mill Stream Cottage Guest House.

TOTAL FIXED OVERHEAD CONTROL

	£		£
		28.6.01 Room changeover fixed overheads (actual)	580

5.12 The entry which corresponds to this credit in the total fixed overhead control account is a debit in the room changeover fixed overhead control account.

In this account we can also post the following items.

- Fixed overhead expenditure variance (£4 (A))
- Overheads absorbed for room changeovers (£492)
- Fixed overhead volume variance (£84 (A))

ROOM CHANGEOVER FIXED OVERHEADS CONTROL

		£			£
28.6.01	Total fixed overhead control	580	28.6.01	Overhead absorbed for room changeovers	492
			28.6.01	Fixed overhead volume variance	84
			28.6.01	Fixed overhead expenditure variance	4
		580			580

5.13 The fixed overhead expenditure variance account can also be completed.

FIXED OVERHEAD EXPENDITURE VARIANCE ACCOUNT

		£			£
28.6.01	Room changeover fixed overhead control	4	28.6.01	Profit and loss account	4

Fixed overhead volume variance account

5.14 The fixed overhead volume variance of £84 adverse can be further analysed in the fixed overhead volume variance account. You will remember that the overhead volume variance can be subdivided as follows.

- Capacity variance
- Efficiency variance

5.15 The **capacity variance** is a measure of how well Mill Stream Cottage Guest House have used available direct labour hours. The budgeted hours were 192 but only 170 have actually been worked (see payroll records in Paragraph 4.2). There is therefore a shortfall in utilisation of 22 hours (192 – 170). The potential under absorption of overhead resulting from this shortfall is

22 hours × £3.00 (standard overhead absorption rate per hour) = £66 (A)

5.16 The **efficiency variance** can be calculated by comparing the standard labour hours for 205 room changeovers and the actual labour hours worked for 205 room changeovers.

	Hours
Standard labour hours (205 room changeovers)	164*
Actual labour hours (205 room changeovers)	170**
	6

* 61.5 + 102.5 = 164 (See (W1) and (W2) in Paragraph 4.5)
** Per payroll records (See Paragraph 4.2)

The domestic staff therefore worked 6 hours more than expected for 205 room changeovers. At a standard overhead absorption rate of £3 per hour, this gives rise to an efficiency variance of

6 hours × £3 per hour = £18 (A)

5.17 The volume variance can be proved as follows.

	£
Capacity variance	66 (A)
Efficiency variance	18 (A)
Volume variance	84 (A)

Fixed overhead volume variance

5.18 The fixed overhead volume variance account can now be completed.

FIXED OVERHEAD VOLUME VARIANCE

		£			£
28.6.01	Room changeover fixed overheads (volume variance)		28.6.01	Capacity variance	66
			28.6.01	Efficiency variance	18
		84			
		84			84

5.19 The corresponding entries can also be posted to the fixed overhead capacity variance account and the fixed overhead efficiency variance account. Remember that the balances on these accounts will be transferred to the profit and loss account at the end of the period.

FIXED OVERHEAD CAPACITY VARIANCE

		£			£
28.6.01	Fixed overhead volume variance account	66	28.6.01	Profit and loss account	66

FIXED OVERHEAD EFFICIENCY VARIANCE

		£			£
28.6.01	Fixed overhead volume variance account	18	28.6.01	Profit and loss account	18

5.20 Finally, we can look at the account which records the total standard costs of room changeovers. The costs involved are as follows.

- Cost of packs issued to guests' rooms
- Cost of cleaning rooms account
- Cost of cleaning laundry account
- Room changeover overheads

ROOM CHANGEOVER STANDARD COSTS

		£			£
28.6.01	Packs issued to guests' rooms	1,025	28.6.01	Transfer to profit and loss account	2,501★
28.6.01	Cost of cleaning rooms account	369			
28.6.01	Cost of cleaning laundry account	615			
28.6.01	Room changeover fixed overhead	492			
		2,501			2,501

★ This figure represents the standard cost of 205 room changeovers (205 × £12.20)

5.21 We have now completed our recording cost information case study and this should have helped you to consolidate your recording cost information knowledge.

It would be a good idea to come back to this case study in a couple of weeks time and actually work through the problems yourself without looking at the solutions. Good luck!

Answers to activities

BPP
PUBLISHING

Answers to Chapter 1 activities

Answer 1.1

Materials	*Labour*	*Expenses*
Saleable stocks	Petrol station staff	Heating
Carrier bags	Car park attendant	Lighting
Other packaging	Check-out staff	Telephone
Cleaning materials	Supervisors	Post
Bakery ingredients	Delicatessen staff	Stationery
	Bakery staff	Rent
	Shelf fillers	Business rates
	Warehouse staff	Water rates
	Cleaners	Vehicle running costs
	Security staff	Advertising
	Administrative staff	Discounts
	Managers	Bank charges
	Delivery staff	Waste disposal
	Maintenance staff	

Answer 1.2

(a) Variable
(b) Fixed
(c) Fixed
(d) Fixed
(e) Variable

Answer 1.3

Helping hand. Think about the type of production process involved and how costs would be collected.

- **A baker** would probably use batch costing. The cost units (loaves, cakes) are identical but would be produced in separately identifiable batches.

- **A transport company** would use unit costing, probably using a cost unit such as the tonne-kilometre (the cost of carrying one tonne for one kilometre).

- **A plumber** would use job costing, since every plumbing job is a separately identifiable cost unit.

- **An accountancy firm** would use job costing, since each client would require a different amount of time from employees of different skills.

- **A paint manufacturer** would use unit costing since the total costs incurred would be averaged over all the tins of paint produced in a period.

Answer 1.4

(a) A **cost unit** is a unit of product (or service) for which costs are ascertained.

(b) A **functional cost** is one that relates to a 'function' or area of operations of a business, for example production, administration, research, distribution and so on.

(c) A **fixed cost** is one that does not increase or decrease when a different number of units are produced.

(d) A **standard cost** is an estimate of what a cost should be on average in the future.

(e) An **indirect cost** is a cost that cannot be identified with one particular cost unit.

(f) An **overhead** is another name for an indirect cost (as explained in (e)).

Answers to activities

(g) A **cost centre** is a location, a function (a person or a department), an activity or a piece of equipment which incurs costs that can be attributed to cost units.

(h) A **variable cost** is one that increases when more units are made and decreases when fewer units are made.

(i) A **direct cost** is one that can be traced directly to a cost centre or cost unit.

Answers to Chapter 2 activities

Answer 2.1

(a) Metal, rubber, plastic, glass, fabric, oil, paint, glue

(b) Cereals, plastic, cardboard, glue. You might have included sugar and preservatives and so on, depending upon what you eat for breakfast

(c) Sand, gravel, cement, bricks, plaster, wood, metal, plastic, glass, slate

(d) You will have to mark your own answer. If you work for a service organisation like a firm of accountants, you could view the paper (and binding) of sets of accounts sent out to clients as raw materials, although in practice such materials are likely to be regarded as indirect costs

Answer 2.2

Direct materials can be traced directly to specific units of production, whereas indirect materials cannot.

Answer 2.3

(a) Direct
(b) Direct
(c) Indirect
(d) Direct
(e) Direct

Answer 2.4

Raw materials are goods purchased for incorporation into products for sale, but not yet issued to production. Work in progress is the name given to the materials while they are in the course of being converted to the final product. Finished goods are the end products when they are ready to be sold.

Answer 2.5

(a) The name and address of the ordering organisation
(b) The date of the order
(c) The order number
(d) The address and date for delivery and collection
(e) Details of the goods or services ordered

Answer 2.6

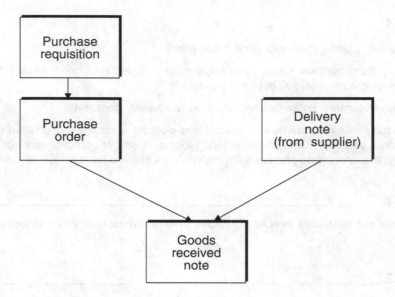

Answer 2.7

(a) FIFO

Date of issue	Quantity	Value		Cost of issues
	Units		£	£
4 May	200	100 at £2.00	200	
		100 at £2.10	210	
				410
11 May	400	300 at £2.10	630	
		100 at £2.12	212	
				842
20 May	100	100 at £2.12		212
				1,464
Closing stock value	200	100 at £2.12	212	
		100 at £2.40	240	
				452
				1,916

The cost of materials issued plus the value of closing stock equals the cost of purchases plus the value of opening stock (£1,916).

(b) LIFO

Date of issue	Quantity	Value		Cost of issues
	Units		£	£
4 May	200	200 at £2.10		420
11 May	400	300 at £2.12	636	
		100 at £2.10	210	
				846
20 May	100	100 at £2.40		240
				1,506
Closing stock value	200	100 at £2.10	210	
		100 at £2.00	200	
				410
				1,916

The cost of materials issued plus the value of closing stock equals the cost of purchases plus the value of opening stock (£1,916).

(c) Cumulative weighted average

Date	Received Units	Issued Units	Balance Units	Total stock value £	Unit cost £	Price of issue £
Opening stock			100	200	2.00	
3 May	400			840	2.10	
			500*	1,040	2.08	
4 May		200		(416)	2.08	416
			300	624	2.08	
9 May	300			636	2.12	
			600*	1,260	2.10	
11 May		400		(840)	2.10	840
			200	420	2.10	
18 May	100			240	2.40	
			300*	660	2.20	
20 May		100		(220)	2.20	220
Cost of issues						1,476
Closing stock			200	440	2.20	440
						1,916

* A new unit stock value is calculated whenever a new receipt of materials occurs.

The cost of materials issued plus the value of closing stock equals the cost of purchases plus the value of opening stock (£1,916).

Answer 2.8

(a) FIFO has the disadvantage that if stocks are quite old they may be issued to production at a price which is well below the current market price. This gives the wrong message to production managers.

(b) LIFO has the advantage that stock will be issued to production at a cost close to market value, thereby helping production managers gain a realistic idea of costs.

(c) The weighted average method involves less cumbersome calculations than the other methods, but the issue price rarely represents an actual price that could be found in the market.

Answer 2.9

	Cost centre code no.	Expenditure code no.
Issue of packing materials to production	300	100
Issue of raw materials to machining centre	100	100
Issue of lubricating oils to maintenance	400	200
Issue of cleaning materials to finishing centre	200	200

Answer 2.10

(a) Stock quantities delivered may not have matched the quantity shown on the Goods Received Note, which is used to update the stock records.

(b) The quantity of stock issued to production may not have matched the quantity on the Material Requisition.

(c) Stock may have been returned to stores without documentation.

(d) There may be other errors in the stock records (for example casting errors).

(e) Stock may have been destroyed or broken without a record being made.

(f) Stock may have been stolen.

Answer 2.11

(a) Reorder quantity $= \sqrt{\dfrac{2cd}{h}}$

$= \sqrt{\dfrac{2 \times \text{ordering costs} \times \text{annual demand}}{\text{Stockholding costs}}}$

$= \sqrt{\dfrac{2 \times 200 \times 4{,}000}{10}}$

$= 400 \text{ kg}$

(b) Reorder level $= \text{maximum usage} \times \text{maximum lead time}$

$= 600 \times 3$

$= 1{,}800 \text{ kg}$

(c) Maximum stock level $= \text{reorder level} + \text{reorder quantity} - (\text{minimum usage} \times \text{minimum lead time})$

$= 400 + 1{,}800 - (100 \times 1)$

$= 2{,}100 \text{ kg}$

Answer 2.12

(a) Reorder level
$= \text{maximum usage} \times \text{maximum lead time}$
$= 600 \text{ kg} \times 3 \text{ weeks}$
$= 1{,}800 \text{ kg}$

(b) Minimum stock level
$= \text{reorder level} - (\text{average usage} \times \text{average lead time})$
$= 1{,}800 \text{ kg} - (500^* \text{ kg} \times 2 \text{ weeks})$
$= 800 \text{ kg}$

(c) Maximum stock level
$= \text{reorder level} + \text{reorder quantity} - (\text{minimum usage} \times \text{minimum lead time})$
$= 1{,}800 \text{ kg} + 1{,}732 \text{ kg} - (400 \text{ kg} \times 1 \text{ week})$
$= 3{,}132 \text{ kg}$

* Average usage $= (600 + 400) \div 2 = 500 \text{ kg}$

Answer 2.13

Helping hand. Study the completed values of the issues to determine what stock pricing method is in use. Check the balances and order quantities against the control levels given on the stores record card.

STORES RECORD CARD

Material: **A4 paper, white** .... Maximum Quantity: **140 boxes** ....
Code: ....**PWA4**.............................. Minimum Quantity: ..**40 boxes** ....
Re-order Level: ....**60 boxes** ....
Re-order Quantity: ....**80 boxes** ....

Date	Receipts				Issues				Stock balance		
	Document number	Qty	Price £ per box	Total £	Document number	Qty	Price £ per box	Total £	Qty	Price £ per box	Total £
1/11									60	2.30	138.00
									20	2.32	46.40
									80		184.40
3/11					389	30	2.30	69.00	30	2.30	69.00
									20	2.32	46.40
									50		115.40
5/11	123	100	2.33	233.00					30	2.30	69.00
									20	2.32	46.40
									100	2.33	233.00
									150		348.40
8/11					397	40			10	2.32	23.20
						30	2.30	69.00	100	2.33	233.00
						10	2.32	23.20	110		256.20
						40		92.20			
9/11					401	30					
						10	2.32	23.20			
						20	2.33	46.60			
						30		69.80	80	2.33	186.40
12/11	137	80	2.35	188.00					80	2.33	186.40
									80	2.35	188.00
									160		374.40

Stock has risen above the maximum level on two occasions. On 5 November the excess was caused by ordering 100 boxes instead of the pre-set level of 80 boxes. On 12 November, the correct quantity was ordered (80 boxes) but the order was placed before the stock level had reached the pre-determined reorder level of 60 boxes.

Answers to Chapter 3 activities

Answer 3.1

The direct labour cost is the gross basic wage, £1,327.42.

Answer 3.2

(a) From the information given, the only way of analysing Walter's time is as so many hours of 'general foreman duties'. In other words his work is so diverse that it is not possible to trace it as a direct cost to individual jobs.

It would be more appropriate to ensure that details of the individual jobs were recorded in such a way that Walter's time could be equitably split between them. For example a job requiring 20 men is likely to require twice as much of Walter's attention as a job requiring 10 men.

(b) Peter's time may at first seem to be as difficult to analyse as Walter's, but in fact it is probable that he could fill in a daily or weekly time sheet, splitting out his time between the various types of work that he does. For example he may spend 3 hours at the counter in the morning, and 1 hour filing and 2 hours dealing with correspondence in the afternoon.

Answer 3.3

The answer is neither or both! Payroll is interested in any work that employees have done that might earn them bonuses or give rise to deductions, and it may be the job of costing to provide this information. Costing in turn is interested in the basic rates due to different types of worker and this information is more likely to be held in the payroll department.

In other words the two departments are interdependent and require a common pool of information.

Answer 3.4

Job 249

Employee	Hours	Rate £	Total £
George	14	8.20	114.80
Paul	49	7.40	362.60
			477.40

Job 250

Employee	Hours	Rate £	Total £
George	2	8.20	16.40
John	107	5.30	567.10
Ringo	74	6.50	481.00
			1,064.50

Answer 3.5

Units per hour	Processors	Finishers
Total units	12,000	10,000
Total hours	40	35
Units per hour	300	286

Time per unit		
Total hours	40	35
Total units	12,000	10,000

Time for one unit	12 seconds	12.6 seconds

Cost per unit

$\dfrac{\text{Total wages}}{\text{Total units}}$	$\dfrac{40 \times 6 \times £6.40}{12,000}$	$\dfrac{35 \times 4 \times £9.00}{10,000}$
Cost per 100 units	£12.80	£12.60

Helping hand. If you expressed time per unit in terms of hours per unit consider that a figure like '0.02 of an hour' means very little to most people, because we think of time in the units in which it is generally measured. Likewise £0.128 or even 12.8p is less meaningful than the figure for 100 units because 12.8p cannot be made up from actual coins. If you said '£1.28 for 10 units', this is fine.

Answer 3.6

To code overtime premium, we would need to know the reason why the overtime was worked. The premium would be a direct labour cost if the overtime was worked at the specific request of a customer. Otherwise, and more usually, the overtime premium would be an indirect labour cost.

Answer 3.7

OPERATION CARD

Operators Name Shah, L	Total Batch Quantity -
Clock No 7142	Start Time -
Pay week No 17 Date W/E XX/XX/XX	Stop Time -

Part No 713/V	Works Order No 14 AB
Opertion Drilling	Special Instructions -

Quantity Produced	No Rejected	Good Production	Rate	£
Monday 173	14	159	50p	79.50
Tuesday 131	2	129	40p	51.60
Wednesday 92	-	92	20p	18.40
Thursday 120	7	113	30p	33.90
Friday 145	5	140	40p	56.00

Insector ND	Operative LS
Foreman AN	Date XX/XX/XX

PRODUCTION CANNOT BE CLAIMED WITHOUT A PROPERLY SIGNED CARD

		£
Gross wage	=	79.50
		51.60
		18.40
		33.90
		56.00
		239.40

Answer 3.8

	£
Time rate = 35 hours × £8	280
Time allowed for 90 units (× 0.5 hour) = 45 hours	
Therefore time saved = 10 hours	
Bonus = 40% × 10 hours × £8	32
Total gross wages	312

Answer 3.9

(a) Overtime
(b) Piecework
(c) Bonus for saving time
(d) Group bonus
(e) Profit sharing schemes

Answer 3.10

Helping hand. To decide on the correct code numbers, read the instructions carefully, and then make two decisions for each cost.

- Which cost centre should be charged with the labour cost?
- Is the labour cost a direct cost or an indirect cost?

WEEKLY TIME SHEET

Name J. Wain   Staff number 17254   Week ending 091201

	M	T	W	T	F	TOTAL Hours	£	CODE
Direct time								
Finishing	5	4		1	3	13	143	10100
Packing			6	3		9	99	20100
Direct total	5	4		7	6	22	242	
Administration								
Budget meeting	2			1		3	33	
Total admin	2			1		3	33	30200
Training and courses								
First Aid course		3				3	33	
Total training		3				3	33	40200
Holidays, sickness								
Holiday			7			7	77	
Total leave			7			7	77	30200
TOTAL	7	7	7	7	7	35	385	

Signed ......RS...... Authorised ......LW......

Answer 3.11

(a) Piecework is a system of payments according to the amount of work performed. Differential piecework involves paying a different rate for different levels of production.

(b) A group bonus scheme is appropriate where each individual's contribution to overall performance is highly diverse and overall performance is not within any one person's control. Group bonuses are likely to encourage team effort. They are simpler to administer than individual bonuses.

Answers to Chapter 4 activities

Answer 4.1

Capital expenditure is expenditure which results in the acquisition of fixed assets or an improvement in their ability to earn income. *Revenue* expenditure is expenditure which is incurred either for the purpose of the trade or to maintain the *existing* earning capacity of fixed assets.

For example:

Expense	Cost	Capital/revenue
Ford Transit van purchased for use in the business	£8,000	Capital
Sign-painting of company name, logo and telephone number on van	£500	Capital
Petrol for van	£500	Revenue
New engine, replacing old one which blew up	£1,000	Revenue

Answer 4.2

(a) Capital expenditure

(b) Depreciation of a fixed asset is revenue expenditure.

(c) The legal fees associated with the purchase of a property may be added to the purchase price and classified as capital expenditure. The cost of the leasehold premises in the balance sheet of the business will then include the legal fees.

(d) Capital expenditure (enhancing an existing fixed asset)

(e) Revenue expenditure

(f) Capital expenditure

(g) If customs duties are borne by the purchaser of the fixed asset, they may be added to the cost of the machinery and classified as capital expenditure.

(h) Similarly, if carriage costs are paid for by the purchaser of the fixed asset, they may be included in the cost of the fixed asset and classified as capital expenditure.

(i) Installation costs of a fixed asset are also added to the fixed asset's cost and classified as capital expenditure.

(j) Revenue expenditure

Answer 4.3

(a) Yes. The annual depreciation charge for the fork-lift truck is an indirect revenue expense to be shared (65:35) between the warehouse and the production department. In other words it is a *cost* of these departments.

(b) (i) The machine is used exclusively for one product and therefore the whole of the depreciation charge is traceable *directly* to that product. Depreciation is thus a direct expense in this case.

    (ii) At the current rate of usage it looks as though the machine will last ten years but it will not be needed after the fourth year of its life and so straight line depreciation over four years seems the most appropriate charge.

$$\text{Depreciation charge} = \frac{\text{Cost} - \text{residual value}}{\text{Useful life}} = \frac{£4,000 - £800}{4 \text{ years}}$$

$$= £800 \text{ per annum}$$

Answers to activities

Answer 4.4

Straight line method

$$\text{Depreciation per annum} = \frac{\text{Cost} - \text{residual value}}{\text{Expected life}}$$

$$= \frac{£(75,000 - 5,000)}{5 \text{ years}}$$

$$= £14,000$$

Reducing balance method

	£
Capital cost	75,000
Year 1 charge (£75,000 × 42%)	31,500
	43,500
Year 2 charge (£43,500 × 42%)	18,270
	25,230
Year 3 charge (£25,230 × 42%)	10,597
	14,633
Year 4 charge (£14,633 × 42%)	6,146
	8,487
Year 5 charge (£8,487 × 42%)	3,565
	4,922

Answer 4.5

	£	Code
Strange (Properties) Ltd	4,000.00	0120
Yorkshire Electricity plc	1,598.27	0060
Dudley Stationery Ltd	275.24	0100
Dora David (Cleaner)	125.00	0040
BPP Publishing Ltd	358.00	0030
AAT	1,580.00	0160
British Telecom	1,431.89	0170
Kall Kwik (Stationers)	312.50	0100
Interest to 31.3.X3	2,649.33	0020
L & W Office Equipment	24.66	0090
Avis	153.72	0190
Federal Express	32.00	0100
Starriers Garage Ltd	79.80	0070

Answer 4.6

The following expenses may be chargeable directly to clients.

	£	
Kall Kwik (Stationers)	312.50	Photocopying costs: say 200 sets of accounts to be sent to shareholders?
Avis	153.72	The cost of renting a car to travel on a client's business?

The following expenses *may* be chargeable directly to departments.

	£	
Dudley Stationery Ltd	275.24	If this type of stationery is used exclusively by one department.
L & W Office Equipment	24.66	If the item is used exclusively by one department.
Starriers Garage Ltd	79.80	The car is probably used by a specific employee.

Federal Express expenses could also fall into this category. The remaining items need to be split between departments. Training costs and AAT subscriptions could be split according to the specific staff involved, rent according to the floor area occupied and so on. (The next chapter goes into this in more detail.)

Answers to Chapter 5 activities

Answer 5.1

(a) Absorption costing is a method of determining a product cost that includes a proportion of all production overheads incurred in the making of the product and possibly a proportion of other overheads such as administration and selling overheads.

(b) (i)   To value stock
    (ii) To fix selling prices
    (iii) To compare the profitability of different products

(c) (i)   Allocation of costs to cost centres
    (ii) Apportionment of costs between cost centres
    (iii) Absorption of costs into cost units

Answer 5.2

Analysis of apportionment of overhead costs, using the repeated distribution method.

	Basis	Forming £	Machines £	Assembly £	Maintenance £	General £	Total £
Directly allocated overheads:							
Repairs, maintenance		800	1,800	300	200	100	3,200
Departmental expenses		1,500	2,300	1,100	900	1,500	7,300
Indirect labour		3,000	5,000	1,500	4,000	2,000	15,500
Apportionment of other overheads:							
Rent, rates	1	1,600	3,200	2,400	400	400	8,000
Power	2	200	450	75	25	0	750
Light, heat	1	1,000	2,000	1,500	250	250	5,000
Dep'n of plant	3	2,500	6,000	750	750	0	10,000
Dep'n of fixtures	4	50	25	100	50	25	250
Insurance of plant	3	500	1,200	150	150	0	2,000
Insurance of buildings	1	100	200	150	25	25	500
		11,250	22,175	8,025	6,750	4,300	52,500
Apportion maintenance		1,350	3,375	1,350	(6,750)	675	
						4,975	
Apportion general		995	2,985	498	497	(4,975)	
Apportion maintenance		99	249	99	(497)	50	
Apportion general		10	30	5	5	(50)	
Apportion maintenance		1	3	1	(5)	-	
		13,705	28,817	9,978	0	0	52,500

Basis of apportionment:

1   floor area
2   effective horsepower
3   plant value
4   fixtures value

Answer 5.3

Machine shop A: $\dfrac{£57,168}{7,200}$ = £7.94 per machine hour

Machine shop B: $\dfrac{£63,000}{18,000}$ = £3.50 per machine hour

Assembly: $\dfrac{£46,592}{20,800}$ = £2.24 per direct labour hour

Answer 5.4

(a) Possible bases of overhead absorption include the following.

    (i)   A percentage of direct materials costs
    (ii)   A percentage of direct labour costs
    (iii)   A percentage of total direct costs
    (iv)   A rate per machine hour
    (v)   A rate per direct labour hour
    (vi)   A rate per unit
    (vii)   A percentage of factory cost (for administration overhead)
    (viii) A percentage of sales or of factory cost (for selling and distribution overhead)

Anything else that gives a fair share of the costs to cost units is also a possibility.

(b)   (i) $\dfrac{£108,000}{90,000}$ = £1.20 per direct labour hour

      (ii) $\dfrac{£108,000}{90,000 \times £5}$ × 100% = 24% of direct labour cost

Answer 5.5

	Domestic	Industrial
Direct labour cost per unit	£180	£80
Rate per hour	£10	£10
Direct labour hours per unit	18	8
Production volume (units)	20,000	20,000
Total labour hours	360,000	160,000

Absorption rate = $\dfrac{\text{Total overhead}}{\text{Total labour hours}}$ = $\dfrac{£1,040,000}{(360,000 + 160,000)}$ = £2.00 per hour

	Domestic £	Industrial £
Direct materials	28.00	40.00
Direct labour	180.00	80.00
Direct expenses	40.00	200.00
Direct cost	248.00	320.00
Production overhead (18 × £2.00)/(8 × £2.00)	36.00	16.00
	284.00	336.00

Answer 5.6

Direct apportionment method	Production 1 £	Production 2 £	Service 1 £	Service 2 £
	97,428	84,947	9,384	15,823
Apportion Service 1 costs (20 : 15)	5,362	4,022	(9,384)	–
	102,790	88,969	-	15,823
Apportion Service 2 costs (3 : 8)	4,315	11,508	-	(15,823)
	107,105	100,477	-	-

Answer 5.7

Repeated distribution method	Production 1 £	Production 2 £	Service 1 £	Service 2 £
	97,428	84,947	9,384	15,823
Apportion Service 1 costs (20:15:5)	4,692	3,519	(9,384)	1,173
	102,120	88,466	-	16,996
Apportion Service 2 costs (3:8:1)	4,249	11,331	1,416	(16,996)
	106,369	99,797	1,416	-
Reapportionment (20:15:5)	708	531	(1,416)	177
	107,077	100,328	-	177
Reapportionment (3:8:1)	44	118	15	(177)
	107,121	100,446	15	-
Reapportionment (20:15)	9	6	(15)	-
	107,130	100,452	-	-

Answer 5.8

Step-down method	Production 1 £	Production 2 £	Service 1 £	Service 2 £
	97,428	84,947	9,384	15,823
Apportion Service 1 costs (20:15:5)	4,692	3,519	(9,384)	1,173
	102,120	88,466	-	16,996
Apportion Service 2 costs (3:8)	4,635	12,361	-	(16,996)
	106,755	100,827	-	-

Answer 5.9

The production overhead absorption rate is calculated in advance of a period using estimates of both the total overhead likely to be incurred and the total quantity of the chosen basis.

$$\frac{\text{Total production overhead}}{\text{Total basis}} = \text{Production overhead absorption rate}$$

If either figure turns out to be incorrectly estimated (as it almost certainly will) the estimated absorption rate will have been either too high or too low, and hence over or under absorption of overheads will have occurred.

Answer 5.10

Helping hand. You could try to answer this activity by considering how the value of a simple fraction like 4 divided by 2 would increase or decrease as the value of the denominator or numerator varied. Remember that if the actual rate is more than the estimated rate there will be under absorption and vice versa.

(a) Under (because actual production overheads are higher than standard).
(b) Over (because actual hours are higher than standard).
(c) Over (because actual production overheads are lower than standard).
(d) Under (because actual hours are lower than standard).

Helping hand. If you find it difficult to do this by inspection, there is nothing wrong with calculating the estimated rate (£5.98) and then the actual rate in each case (£6.00; £5.97; £5.90; £6.08), but having done this make sure that you can explain in non-numerical terms what has happened. For example, in (c) lower overheads and a higher number of active hours have led to over absorption.

Answer 5.11

(a) A predetermined rate gives a constant overhead cost per unit rather than a fluctuating rate. This is more useful costing information in the long term.

(b) If selling prices were based on full cost plus a percentage mark up, the fluctuating costs which would result from the use of an actual rate would lead to variations in selling prices from period to period. High prices would be charged when demand for the product was at its lowest (because overhead costs would be spread over a smaller number of units) and this would be likely to lead to an even greater fall off in demand. A predetermined rate avoids these problems.

(c) Actual overhead costs are not known in full until the end of a period, which may be too late for costing and price-setting purposes. Predetermined rates are, by nature, known in advance.

Answer 5.12

Capacity means the volume of production that an organisation is capable of achieving. It is usually qualified by an adjective and expressed in hours of production.

(a) Full capacity is the maximum number of hours that could be worked in ideal conditions.
(b) Practical capacity is full capacity less an allowance for hours lost unavoidably.
(c) Budgeted capacity is the number of hours an organisation plans to work in a period.

Answer 5.13

Direct labour hours per unit of product M = £50/£5 = 10

Total cost per unit	£ per unit
Direct material	21.00
Direct labour	50.00
Total direct cost	71.00
Production overhead (£2 × 10 hours)	20.00
Total production cost	91.00
Non-production overhead (10% × £91.00)	9.10
Total cost	100.10

Answer 5.14

Activity based costing is similar to traditional absorption costing in that it attempts to ascribe to cost units a proportion of overheads. However, it is fairer than absorption costing in that there is an attempt to do this on the basis of what actually caused the cost to be incurred rather than according to some arbitrarily chosen basis. In many circumstances for example overheads will not be reduced if fewer labour hours are worked since their level is not connected to the number of labour hours. They might be significantly reduced if production runs were longer (there would be fewer set ups) and this might entail longer working hours.

Answer 5.15

(a) There is no reason why the total labour hours should be the same as the total machine hours, even if labour's role is confined solely to operating machines. For example the totals could be arrived at as follows.

175 workers × 52 weeks × 5 days × 7 hours = 318,500 hours

350 machines × 52 weeks × 5 days × 7 hours = 637,000 hours

This is just one of an infinite number of possibilities. Labour time and machine time could be almost completely unrelated.

(b) $\dfrac{\text{Total overhead}}{\text{Total labour hours}} = \dfrac{£859,329}{318,500} = £2.70 \text{ per hour}$

Total labour hours for the assimilator = 12 hours × 20,000 units = 240,000 hours

Therefore overheads absorbed by the assimilator = 240,000 × £2.70 = £648,000

Other products absorb the remainder of the overheads.

	£
Total overhead	859,329
Assimilator	(648,000)
Other products	211,329

(c) A machine hour rate would be more appropriate for the assimilator since it takes more machine hours than labour hours to produce an assimilator and the machine running cost is a larger proportion of the total cost.

(d)   Rate per hour = $\dfrac{£859,329}{637,000}$ = £1.35 per hour

It takes 22 machine hours to make one assimilator.

22 × £1.35 = £29.70 per unit

Answer 5.16

(a)

	Squeegess	Imbibulator
Direct labour cost	£90	£40
Rate per hour	£5	£5
Hours per unit	18	8
Production volume	10,000	10,000
Total labour hours	180,000	80,000

$$\dfrac{\text{Total overhead}}{\text{Total labour hours}} = \dfrac{£1,000,000}{(180,000 + 80,000)} = \underline{£3.85 \text{ per hour}}$$

	Squeegess £	Imbibulator £
Direct materials	14.00	20.00
Direct labour	90.00	40.00
Direct expenses	20.00	100.00
Direct cost	124.00	160.00
Production overhead (18 × £3.85)/(8 × £3.85)	69.30	30.80
	193.30	190.80

(b)   The unit costs are probably not fair because the Squeegess's costs are mainly labour based whereas the Imbibulator's costs appear to be mainly machine based. Because a labour hour basis is used the Squeegess has a much higher overhead cost than the Imbibulator. A separate absorption rate for each product would be fairer, but we would need to know what part of the total overhead incurred related to the Squeegess and what part to the Imbibulator.

Answers to Chapter 6 activities _____

Answer 6.1

(a) Mixed (semi-fixed)
(b) Fixed
(c) Fixed
(d) Variable
(e) Variable

Answer 6.2 _____

Helping hand. You may have thought of different, perfectly acceptable, types of cost.

Graph (c). Vehicle hire costs, where a rate is paid per mile travelled, subject to a maximum hire cost per period.

Graph (d). Photocopier rental cost, where the rental is fixed up to a certain number of copies per period. Once the number of copies exceeds that level, a constant charge is paid per copy taken.

Answer 6.3 _____

(a)

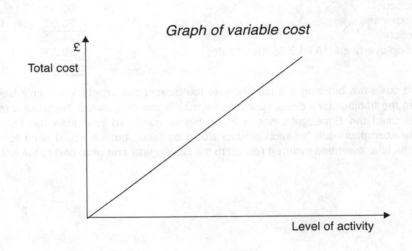

Graph of variable cost

(b)

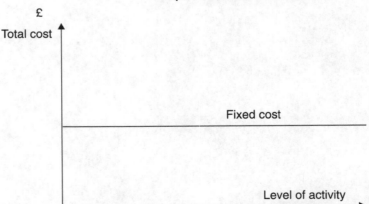

Graph of fixed cost

(c)

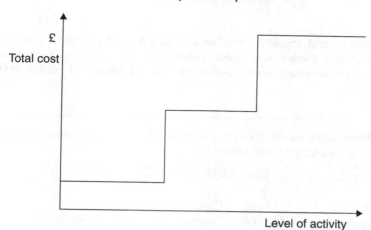

Graph of step cost

Answer 6.4

Step 1

Period with highest activity   =   month 2
Period with lowest activity   =   month 4

Step 2

Total cost at high activity level   =   £115,000
Total cost at low activity level   =   £97,000
Total units at high activity level   =   8,000
Total units at low activity level   =   6,000

Step 3

$$\text{Variable cost per unit} = \frac{\text{Total cost at high activity level} - \text{total cost at low activity level}}{\text{Total units at high activity level} - \text{total units at low activity level}}$$

$$= \frac{£(115,00 - 97,000)}{8,000 - 6,000} = \frac{£18,000}{2,000} = £9 \text{ per unit}$$

Step 4

Fixed costs   =   (Total cost at high activity level) – (total units at high activity level × variable cost per unit)

            =   £115,000 – (8,000 × £9) = £115,000 – £72,000   =   £43,000

Therefore, the costs in month 5 for output of 7,500 units are as follows

	£
Variable costs (7,500 × £9)	67,500
Fixed costs	43,000
Total costs	110,500

 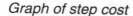

Answers to Chapter 7 activities

Answer 7.1

Entries in a wages control account would include total cost of payroll plus employer's national insurance contributions. Entries would also include transfers to work in progress accounts in respect of direct labour, and transfers to overhead accounts in respect of indirect labour.

Answer 7.2

(a) *Helping hand.* Since we are given no information on the issue of direct materials we need to construct a stores ledger control account.

STORES LEDGER CONTROL ACCOUNT

	£		£
Balance b/f	18,500	Creditors/cash (returns)	2,300
Creditors/cash	142,000	Overhead accounts (indirect materials)	25,200
		WIP (balancing figure)	116,900
		Balance c/f	16,100
	160,500		160,500

The value of the issue of direct materials during April 20X0 was £116,900.

(b) The issue of direct materials would therefore be recorded as follows.

DR	WIP control account	£116,900
CR	Stores ledger control account	£116,900

Answer 7.3

Helping hand. The depreciation provision is a production overhead cost incurred which is debited to the production overhead control account.

PRODUCTION OVERHEAD CONTROL ACCOUNT

	£		£
Bank account	125,478	Work in progress (27,000 × £5)	135,000
Depreciation	4,100		
Profit and loss account	5,422		
	135,000		135,000

The production overhead is over absorbed by £5,422. This amount is transferred, at the end of the period, as a credit in the profit and loss account.

Answer 7.4

			£	£
(a)	DEBIT	Materials stock	10,000	
	CREDIT	Creditors		10,000
(b)	DEBIT	Finished goods stock	50,000	
	CREDIT	Work in progress stock		50,000
(c)	DEBIT	Administration overhead/indirect materials	5,000	
	CREDIT	Materials stock		5,000
(d)	DEBIT	Production overhead control	20,000	
	CREDIT	Wages control		20,000

Answer 7.5

STORES LEDGER CONTROL ACCOUNT

	£		£
Opening balance b/f	24,175	Work in progress control	
Creditors control		(materials issued)	29,630
(materials purchased)	76,150	Closing stock c/f	70,695
	100,325		100,325

WORK IN PROGRESS CONTROL ACCOUNT

	£		£
Opening balance b/f	19,210	Finished goods control	
Stores ledger account		(cost of goods transferred)	62,130
(materials issued)	29,630	Closing stock c/f	24,800
Wages control			
(direct wages)	15,236		
Production overhead control			
(overhead absorbed			
15,236 × 150%)	22,854		
	86,930		86,930

FINISHED GOODS CONTROL ACCOUNT

	£		£
Opening balance b/f	34,164	Profit and loss account	
Work in progress control		(cost of sales)	59,830
(cost of goods completed)	62,130	Closing stock c/f	36,464
	96,294		96,294

PRODUCTION OVERHEAD CONTROL ACCOUNT

	£		£
Wages control (indirect	9,462	Work in progress control	
workers wages)		(overheads absorbed)	22,854
Creditors control (other		Profit and loss account (under-	
overheads incurred)	16,300	absorbed overhead) (bal.)	2,908
	25,762		25,762

CREDITORS CONTROL ACCOUNT

	£		£
Cash account (payments)	58,320	Opening balance b/f	15,187
Creditors c/f	49,317	Stores ledger control	
		(materials purchased)	76,150
		Production overhead control	
		(other overheads)	16,300
	107,637		107,637

PROFIT AND LOSS ACCOUNT

	£		£
Finished goods control		Sales	75,400
(cost of goods sold)	59,830		
Gross profit c/f	15,570		
	75,400		75,400
Selling and distribution		Gross profit b/f	15,570
overheads	5,240		
Production overhead control			
(under-absorbed overhead)	2,908		
Net profit c/f	7,422		
	15,570		15,570

Answers to Chapter 8 activities

Answer 8.1

A job is a cost unit which consists of a single order (or contract) usually carried out in accordance with the special requirements of each customer. This means that each job will be at least slightly different from every other job and so separate records must be maintained to show the details of a particular job.

Helping hand. You may have compiled a totally different list of examples of jobs.

Examples are numerous.
(a) A haircut
(b) The Channel Tunnel
(c) A tailor-made suit
(d) An audit
(e) Jobs done by domestic plumbers, builders and so on

Answer 8.2

The documents most likely to be needed to establish *direct* costs are the materials requisition note, M Bobb's time sheet and the sub-contractor's invoice.

Details of materials used could probably, but not necessarily, have been obtained from the stock card too. The payroll would not be analysed in sufficient detail. The cost of electricity is not (so far as we are told) *directly* traceable to the job in question. The GRN and the clock card are of no relevance. The skip hire invoice appears to be an ongoing cost, not directly traceable to this job.

Answer 8.3

(a)

	£
Direct material Y (400 kilos × £5)	2,000
Direct material Z (800 – 60 kilos × £6)	4,440
Total direct material cost	6,440

(b)

	£
Department P (300 hours × £4)	1,200
Department Q (200 hours × £5)	1,000
Total direct labour cost	2,200

Overtime premium will be charged to overhead in the case of Department P, and to the job of the customer who asked for overtime to be worked in the case of Department Q.

(c)

	£
Direct material cost	6,440
Direct labour cost	2,200
Production overhead (500 hours × £3)	1,500
	10,140

Answer 8.4

Helping hand. Note that the profit margin is given as a percentage on selling price. If profit is 25% on selling price, this is the same as $33^1/_3\%$ (25/75) on cost.

		Job TN8 £		Job KT2 £
Direct material		154.00		108.00
Direct labour: dept X	(20 × 3.80)	76.00	(16 × 3.80)	60.80
dept Y	(12 × 3.50)	42.00	(10 × 3.50)	35.00
dept Z	(10 × 3.40)	34.00	(14 × 3.40)	47.60
Total direct cost		306.00		251.40
Overhead: dept X	(20 × 12.86)	257.20	(16 × 12.86)	205.76
dept Y	(12 × 12.40)	148.80	(10 × 12.40)	124.00
dept Z	(10 × 14.03)	140.30	(14 × 14.03)	196.42
Total cost		852.30		777.58
Profit		284.10		259.19
Quoted selling price		1,136.40		1,036.77

Answer 8.5

(a) *Big units*

	£	£
Direct materials		5,240
Direct labour		
Skilled 1,580 hours at £5	7,900	
Semi-skilled 3,160 hours at £4	12,640	
		20,540
Direct expenses		1,180
Administrative expenses		
4,740 hours at £0.50 (see below)*		2,370
		29,330
Selling price		33,180
Calculated profit		3,850
Divided: Staff bonus 20%		770
Profit for company 80%		3,080

*Administrative expenses absorption rate $= \dfrac{£4,400}{8,800}$ per labour hour

$= £0.50$ per labour hour

(b)

		Little units £	£		All-purpose £	£
Direct materials			6,710			3,820
Direct labour						
Skilled	1,700 hrs at £5	8,500		160 hrs at £5	800	
Semi-skilled	1,900 hrs at £4	7,600		300 hrs at £4	1,200	
Direct expenses		1,700			250	
Administration						
expenses:	3,600 hrs at £0.50	1,800		460 hrs at £0.50	230	
		19,600			2,480	
Costs to						
completion	20/80 × 19,600	4,900		75/25 × 2,480	7,440	
			24,500			9,920
Total costs			31,210			13,740
Selling price			27,500			19,500
Calculated						
profit/(loss)			(3,710)			5,760
Divided: Staff bonus 20%			-			1,152
(Loss)/profit for company			(3,710)			4,608

Note that whilst direct labour costs, direct expenses and administration expenses increase in proportion to the total labour hours required to complete the little units and the all-purpose units, there will be no further material costs to complete the batches.

(c)   Little units are projected to incur a loss. There are two possible reasons for the loss.

(i)   The estimation process may be inadequate. For example, it may have been incorrect to assume that the make-up of the costs to completion is the same as the make-up of the costs already incurred. It is possible that all of the skilled work has already been carried out and only unskilled labour is required to complete the batch.

(ii)   The loss is a result of inadequate estimating. If so, the estimation procedure should be reviewed to prevent recurrence.

(iii)   It is the result of a lack of cost control. If this is the case, appropriate action should be taken to exercise control in future.

Answers to Chapter 9 activities

Answer 9.1

(a) A standard cost is standard in two senses.

    (i)   It is a uniform cost that is applied to all like items, irrespective of their actual cost.

    (ii) It is a measure of expected performance, that is, a standard to be achieved.

(b) Standard costing is used for two main reasons.

    (i)   As a means of valuing stocks and the cost of production.

    (ii) In variance analysis, which is a means of controlling the business.

Answer 9.2

Helping hand. This activity is a test of your ability to analyse information in a way that avoids laborious computations as much as a test of your understanding of standard setting. The operation is done by grade X labour at £4.80 per hour unless otherwise indicated.

Operation	Grade	Rate £	Time Hours	Cost £
1			1.50	7.20
2	Y	5.50	1.00	5.50
3			0.25	1.20
4	Z	6.50	2.00	13.00
5			0.50	2.40
6	Y	5.50	2.00	11.00
7	Z	6.50	3.00	19.50
8			1.00	4.80
9			0.25	1.20
10	Y	5.50	0.50	2.75

	A £	B £	C £	Sharp C £	D £	E £	F £	Augmented F £	G £
1				7.20	7.20		7.20		7.20
2	5.50	5.50			5.50				
3			1.20	1.20		1.20		1.20	
4	13.00			13.00		13.00	13.00		
5	2.40	2.40				2.40			2.40
6		11.00	11.00	11.00	11.00			11.00	
7					19.50			19.50	
8		4.80						4.80	
9		1.20					1.20		1.20
10		2.75			2.75	2.75			2.75
Standard cost	20.90	21.65	18.20	32.40	45.95	19.35	21.40	36.50	13.55

Answer 9.3

Helping hand. Read the data carefully. The standard times are provided in terms of **minutes**. You need to convert your final answer to **hours.**

Standard hours produced		Standard hours
Burger meals: $\dfrac{2,400\times10 \text{ minutes}}{60}$ =		400
Chicken meals: $\dfrac{1,300\times15 \text{ minutes}}{60}$ =		325
Total standard hours produced		725

BPP PUBLISHING

Answer 9.4

STANDARD COST CARD - PRODUCT TUDOR

Direct materials	Cost	Requirement	£	£
A	£1 per kg	7 kgs	7	
B	£2 per litre	4 litres	8	
C	£3 per m	3 m	9	
				24
Direct labour				
Skilled	£10 per hour	8 hours	80	
Semi-skilled	£5 per hour	4 hours	20	
				100
Standard direct cost				124
Variable production overhead	£2.50 per hour	8 hours		20
Standard variable cost of production				144
Fixed production overhead	£6.25 (W) per hour	8 hours		50
Standard full production cost				194

Working

$$\text{Overhead absorption rate} = \frac{£250,000}{5,000 \times 8} = £6.25 \text{ per skilled labour hour}$$

Answer 9.5

Standard product cost and gross profit

	£
Direct material L	300
Direct material W	270
Direct labour	165
Direct cost	735
Production overhead (£252,000/1,200)	210
Total product cost	945
Selling price (£120,000/(1,200/12))	1,200
Gross profit	255

Answer 9.6

(a) The *ideal standard*, based on the most favourable operating conditions, seems to be one hour. This is the time achieved by Jed less the 15 minutes idle time (since we are not sure it is *completely* unavoidable). However, in view of the other performances it seems unlikely that anybody could achieve this. Further investigation should be made to determine whether Jed's two attempts include idle time or not: it may be that they were rare occasions when idle time was avoided.

(b) The *current standard* can be taken as the average (the arithmetic mean) of all the times recorded.

Worker	Time Minutes	Time Minutes
Lynn	105	120
Alison	125	115
Jed	75	75
Kate	130	90
Nick	105	97
Edmund	99	117
Bob	120	90
Roger	135	103
Tina	80	95
Tim	140	122
Clive	95	112
Graham	119	125
Barry	100	120
Glen	117	113
	1,545	1,494

Arithmetic mean $= \dfrac{(1{,}545 + 1{,}494)}{2 \times 14} = 108.5$ minutes $= 1$ hour 48 minutes

(c) An *attainable standard* is one that makes some allowance for wastage and inefficiencies. Simply by looking at the times we can see that most come roughly in the range 1 hour 40 minutes to 2 hours. (1 hour 35 minutes to 2 hours if you do know how to calculate quartiles). A reasonably attainable standard would therefore be 1 hour 40 minutes or slightly less, giving most staff something to aim for.

(d) The *basic standard* is given in the question as 2 hours and 30 minutes. This is clearly very outdated and of little value.

Answer 9.7

(a)

Material	Standard cost £	Guildford £	Dorking £	Reigate £	Coulsdon £
AB30	1.68	33.60	33.60	16.80	8.40
AB35	5.93	-	59.30	-	-
BB29	15.00	-	-	60.00	-
BB42	2.40	19.20	12.00	-	28.80
CA19	20.07	401.40	180.63	-	100.35
CD26	2.50	15.00	-	7.50	-
Total standard materials cost		469.20	285.53	84.30	137.55

(b)

Material	Supplier	Information source	Unit cost £	20X2 standard £	20X3 standard £	Note
AB30	4073	20X3 catalogue	1.74	1.68	1.74	(i)
AB35	4524	20X2 catalogue	5.93	5.93		
		Invoice (10/X2)	6.05		6.27	(ii)
		Telephone enquiry to 4524	6.00			
BB29	4333	X2/X3 catalogue	15.72	15.00	16.30	(iii)
BB42	4929	Invoice (5/X2)	2.36	2.40		
	-	New supplier quotation (11/X2)	1.94		2.01	(iv)
CA19	4124	Contract to 12/X3	20.07	20.07	20.07	(v)
		Invoice (12/X2)	21.50			
CD26	4828	-		2.50	2.59	(vi)

Notes

(i) AB30 is costed on the basis of the 20X3 catalogue price which is assumed to be guaranteed for 12 months.

(ii) AB35's new standard cost is on the basis of the most recent invoiced cost plus 3.7%. (The telephone enquiry figure is suspiciously 'round'.)

(iii) BB29's current standard cost looks like an underestimate. Do not allow this to influence your calculation for 20X3.

(iv) BB42 should be bought from the new supplier, on the evidence available. The standard cost is £1.94 plus 3.7%.

(v) For CA19 the contractually agreed price should be used as the standard cost. Enquiries should be made as to why this was not the cost invoiced in December 20X2.

(vi) In the absence of other information 3.7% is added to the 20X2 standard cost for CD26.

Answers to Chapter 10 activities

Answer 10.1

Helping hand. Don't forget to indicate whether your calculated variance is adverse or favourable.

	£
100 units should cost (× £10)	1,000
but did cost	1,025
Material total variance	25 (A)

	£
520 kg should cost (× £2)	1,040
but did cost	1,025
Material price variance	15 (F)

100 units should use (× 5kg)	500 kgs
but did use	520 kgs
Material usage variance (in kgs)	20 kgs (A)
× standard price (per kg)	× £2
Materials usage variance (in £)	£40 (A)

Answer 10.2

	£
106,000 kgs should cost (× £5)	530,000
but did cost	530,500
Materials price variance	500 (A)

10,000 units should have used (× 10 kgs)	100,000 kgs
but did use	106,000 kgs
Material usage variance (in kilos)	6,000 kgs (A)
× standard price per kilo	× £5
Material usage variance (in £)	£30,000 (A)

	£
50,200 hours should have cost (× £6)	301,200
but did cost	307,200
Labour rate variance	6,000 (A)

10,000 units should take (× 5 hours)	50,000 hrs
but did take	50,200 hrs
Labour efficiency variance (in hours)	200 hrs (A)
× standard rate per hour	× £6
Labour efficiency variance (in £)	£1,200 (A)

Answer 10.3

The overhead absorption rate is $\dfrac{£70,000}{14,000}$ = £5 per unit, or £2.50 per hour

	£
Total fixed overhead incurred	67,500
Total fixed overhead absorbed (12,000 units × £5)	60,000
Under-absorbed overhead = total variance	7,500 (A)

	£
Budgeted fixed overhead expenditure	70,000
Actual fixed overhead expenditure	67,500
Expenditure variance	2,500 (F)

12,000 units should have taken (× 2 hrs)	24,000 hrs
but did take	28,400 hrs
Efficiency variance (in hrs)	4,400 hrs (A)
× standard absorption rate per hour	× £2.50
Efficiency variance (in £)	£11,000 (A)
Budgeted activity level	28,000 hrs
Actual activity level	28,400 hrs
Capacity variance (in hrs)	400 hrs (F)
× standard absorption rate per hour	× £2.50
Capacity variance (in £)	£1,000 (F)

Summary

	£
Expenditure variance	2,500 (F)
Efficiency variance	11,000 (A)
Capacity variance	1,000 (F)
Total variance	7,500 (A)

Answer 10.4

Helping hand. The first step is to calculate the budgeted overhead absorption rate per standard hour produced. To do this you need to convert the budgeted production output into standard hours.

Budgeted standard hours of production:

	Std hours
Product S (4,200 × 10 minutes/60)	700
Product H (2,400 × 20 minutes/60)	800
	1,500

$$\text{Budgeted overhead absorption rate} = \frac{£4,500}{1,500} = £3 \text{ per standard hour}$$

(a)

	£
Budgeted overhead expenditure	4,500
Actual overhead expenditure	5,200
Overhead expenditure variance	700 (A)

(b)   Actual production volume achieved:

	Std hours
Product S (3,600 × 10 minutes/60)	600
Product H (3,000 × 20 minutes/60)	1,000
	1,600

Overhead volume variance:

Actual production volume achieved	1,600 std hrs
Budgeted production volume	1,500 std hrs
Volume variance in std hrs	100 std hrs (F)
× absorption rate per std hour	× £3
Overhead volume variance	£300 (F)

(c)

Budgeted hours of work	1,500 hours
Actual hours worked	1,800 hours
Capacity variance in hours	300 hours (F)
× absorption rate per hour	× £3
Overhead capacity variance	£900 (F)

(d)

Standard time for output achieved	1,600 hours
Actual time taken	1,800 hours
Efficiency variance in hours	200 hours (A)
× absorption rate per hour	× £3
Overhead efficiency variance	£600 (A)

Check: Efficiency variance £600 (A) + Capacity variance £900 (F) = Volume variance £300(F).

Answer 10.5

(a) *Price variance - A*

	£
7,800 kgs should have cost (× £20)	156,000
but did cost	159,900
Price variance	3,900 (A)

Usage variance - A

800 units should have used (× 10 kgs)	8,000 kgs
but did use	7,800 kgs
Usage variance in kgs	200 kgs (F)
× standard price per kilogram	× £20
Usage variance in £	£4,000 (F)

Price variance - B

	£
4,300 litres should have cost (× £6)	25,800
but did cost	23,650
Price variance	2,150 (F)

Usage variance - B

800 units should have used (× 5 l)	4,000 Litres
but did use	4,300 Litres
Usage variance in litres	300 (A)
× standard price per litre	× £6
Usage variance in £	£1,800 (A)

(b) *Labour rate variance*

	£
4,200 hours should have cost (× £6)	25,200
but did cost	24,150
Rate variance	1,050 (F)

Labour efficiency variance

800 units should have taken (× 5 hrs)	4,000 hrs
but did take	4,200 hrs
Efficiency variance in hours	200 hrs (A)
× standard rate per hour	× £6
Efficiency variance in £	£1,200 (A)

(c) Overhead absorption rate per labour hour = £50/5 = £10
Budgeted overhead expenditure = £50 × 900 = £45,000
Actual output in standard hours = 800 × 5 = 4,000 standard hours

Fixed overhead expenditure variance

	£
Budgeted fixed overhead expenditure	45,000
Actual fixed overhead expenditure	47,000
Fixed overhead expenditure variance	2,000 (A)

Fixed overhead volume variance

Actual production volume achieved	800 units
Budgeted production volume	900 units
Volume variance in units	100 units (A)
× standard absorption rate per unit	× £50
Fixed overhead volume variance	£5,000 (A)

Fixed overhead efficiency variance

From labour efficiency variance:	
Efficiency variance in hours	200 hours (A)
× standard absorption rate per hour	× £10
Fixed overhead efficiency variance	£2,000 (A)

Fixed overhead capacity variance

Budgeted hours of work (900 units × 5 hrs)	4,500 hrs
Actual hours worked	4,200 hrs
Capacity variance in hours	300 hrs (A)
× standard absorption rate per hour	× £10
Fixed overhead capacity variance	£3,000 (A)

Answer 10.6

(a) Two possible reasons are a price increase and careless purchasing (failing to take a discount, using the wrong supplier and so on). A third is that a higher quality of material was purchased deliberately.

(b) The temporary labour is likely to be paid a lower rate than standard, leading to a favourable labour rate variance. However, the temporary staff are likely to be less efficient than experienced staff, resulting in an adverse labour efficiency variance and perhaps an adverse material usage variance also.

Answers to Chapter 11 activities

Answer 11.1

			£
(a)	(i)	10,000 kg of material should cost (× £2)	20,000
		but did cost	22,000
		Materials price variance	2,000 (A)

	(ii)	9,000 alistas should use (× 1 kg)	9,000 kg
		but did use	10,000 kg
		Material usage variance in kg	1,000 kg (A)
		× standard price per kg	× £2
		Material usage variance in £	£2,000 (A)

			£
	(iii)	30,000 hours of labour should cost (× £6)	180,000
		but did cost	182,000
		Labour rate variance	2,000 (A)

	(iv)	9,000 alistas should take (× 4 hrs)	36,000 hrs
		but did take	30,000 hrs
		Labour efficiency variance in hours	6,000 hrs (F)
		× standard rate per hour	× £6
		Labour efficiency variance in £	£36,000 (F)

			£
	(v)	Budgeted fixed overhead (8,000 units × 3 hrs × £3.50)	84,000
		Actual fixed overhead	82,000
		Fixed overhead expenditure variance	2,000 (F)

	(vi)	Actual production volume	9,000 units
		Budgeted production volume	8,000 units
		Volume variance in units	1,000 units (F)
		× standard overhead absorption rate per unit	× £10.50
		Fixed overhead volume variance	£10,500 (F)

STANDARD COST REPORT FOR APRIL

Budgeted output   8,000 units
Actual output   9,000 units

	Adverse	Favourable	£	£
Direct materials				
Standard cost of actual output			18,000	
Direct material price variance	2,000			
Direct material usage variance	2,000			
Total direct material variance			4,000 (A)	
Actual direct materials cost				22,000
Direct labour				
Standard cost of actual output			216,000	
Direct labour rate variance	2,000			
Direct labour efficiency variance		36,000		
Total direct labour variance			34,000 (F)	
Actual direct labour cost				182,000
Fixed overhead				
Standard cost of actual output			94,500	
Fixed overhead expenditure variance	2,000			
Fixed overhead volume variance		10,500		
Total fixed overhead variance			12,500 (F)	
Actual fixed overhead cost				82,000
Total cost for period				286,000

Answer 11.2

(a)   ROSS LTD VARIANCE REPORT

Month   April

Budgeted output   6,000 units
Actual output   6,200 units

	Actual costs £	Output Units	Standard costs Unit cost £	Total cost £	Total variance £
Materials	97,000	6,200	15	93,000	4,000 (A)
Labour	106,000	6,200	16	99,200	6,800 (A)
Fixed overhead	23,000	6,200	4	24,800	1,800 (F)
	226,000		35	217,000	9,000 (A)

(b)   (i)

	£
33,000 kgs should cost ($\times$ £3)	99,000
but did cost	97,000
Material price variance	2,000 (F)

(ii)

6,200 units should have used ($\times$ 5 kgs)	31,000 kgs
but did use	33,000 kgs
Material usage variance (in kgs)	2,000 kgs (A)
$\times$ standard price per kg	$\times$ £3
Material usage variance (in £)	£6,000 (A)

(iii)

	£
25,800 hours should have cost ($\times$ £4)	103,200
but did cost	106,000
Labour rate variance	2,800 (A)

(iv)

6,200 units should take ($\times$ 4 hrs)	24,800 hrs
but did take	25,800 hrs
Labour efficiency variance (in hrs)	1,000 hrs (A)
$\times$ standard rate per hour	$\times$ £4
Labour efficiency variance (in £)	£4,000 (A)

(v)

	£
Budgeted fixed overhead (4 $\times$ £1 $\times$ 6,000)	24,000
Actual fixed overhead	23,000
Fixed overhead expenditure variance	1,000 (F)

(vi)

6,200 units should have taken ($\times$ 4 hrs)	24,800 hrs
but did take	25,800 hrs
Fixed overhead efficiency variance (in hrs)	1,000 hrs (A)
$\times$ standard rate per hour	$\times$ £1
Fixed overhead efficiency variance (in £)	£1,000 (A)

(vii)

Budgeted activity level	24,000 hrs
Actual activity level	25,800 hrs
Fixed overhead capacity variance (in hrs)	1,800 hrs (F)
$\times$ standard rate per hr	$\times$ £1
Fixed overhead capacity variance (in £)	£1,800 (F)

BPP PUBLISHING

(c) ROSS LTD
VARIANCE SCHEDULE FOR APRIL

	(F) £	(A) £	£
Cost variances			
Materials price	2,000		
Materials usage		6,000	
Labour rate		2,800	
Labour efficiency		4,000	
Fixed overhead expenditure	1,000		
Fixed overhead efficiency		1,000	
Fixed overhead capacity	1,800		
	4,800	13,800	9,000 (A)

Answer 11.3

Helping hand. Study the entries that have already been completed on the record card. The stock balance is valued at the standard price of £7 per kg. The price variance column is the difference between the actual cost of receipts and the standard cost of the receipts, calculated at £7 per kg.

STORES RECORD CARD

Material: Material R
Code: RMM127

Date	Receipts					Issues	Balance	
	Quantity kg	Actual Price per kg £	Total Actual Cost £	Total Standard Cost £	Price Variance £	Quantity kg	Quantity kg	Total Standard Cost £
B/f at 1 Aug							250	1,750
8 Aug	360	7.30	2,628	2,520	108 (A)		610	4,270
10 Aug						400	210	1,470
15 Aug	360	7.40	2,664	2,520	144 (A)		570	3,990
19 Aug						500	70	490
22 Aug	400	6.70	2,680	2,800	120 (F)		470	3,290
30 Aug						200	270	1,890
Total price variance					132 (A)			

List of key terms and index

These are terms which we have identified throughout the text as being KEY TERMS. You should make sure that you can define what these terms mean; go back to the pages highlighted here if you need to check.

BPP PUBLISHING

Index

BPP PUBLISHING

See overleaf for information on other
BPP products and how to order

AAT Order

To BPP Publishing Ltd, Aldine Place, London W12 8AW
Tel: 020 8740 2211. Fax: 020 8740 1184
E-mail: Publishing@bpp.com Web:www.bpp.com

Mr/Mrs/Ms (Full name) _____

Daytime delivery address _____

Postcode _____

Daytime Tel _____

E-mail _____

	5/02 Texts	5/02 Kits	Special offer	8/02 Passcards	Tapes
FOUNDATION (£14.95 except as indicated)				Foundation	
Units 1 & 2 Receipts and Payments	☐	☐		£6.95 ☐	£10.00 ☐
Unit 3 Ledger Balances and Initial Trial Balance	☐				
Unit 4 Supplying Information for Mgmt Control	☐				
Unit 20 Working with Information Technology (£9.95) (6/02)	☐				
Unit 22/23 Healthy Workplace/Personal Effectiveness (£9.95)	☐				
INTERMEDIATE (£9.95)					
Unit 5 Financial Records and Accounts	☐	☐	All	£5.95 ☐	£10.00 ☐
Unit 6 Cost Information	☐	☐	Inter'te Texts	£5.95 ☐	£10.00 ☐
Unit 7 Reports and Returns	☐	☐	and Kits (£65)	£5.95 ☐	
Unit 21 Using Information Technology	☐	☐	☐	£5.95 ☐	
TECHNICIAN (£9.95)					
Unit 8/9 Core Managing Costs and Allocating Resources	☐	☐	Set of 12	£5.95 ☐	£10.00 ☐
Unit 10 Core Managing Accounting Systems	☐	☐	Technician		
Unit 11 Option Financial Statements (A/c Practice)	☐	☐	Texts/Kits	£5.95 ☐	£10.00 ☐
Unit 12 Option Financial Statements (Central Govnmt)	☐	☐	(Please	£5.95 ☐	
Unit 15 Option Cash Management and Credit Control	☐	☐	specify titles	£5.95 ☐	
Unit 16 Option Evaluating Activities	☐	☐	required)	£5.95 ☐	
Unit 17 Option Implementing Auditing Procedures	☐	☐	(£100)	£5.95 ☐	
Unit 18 Option Business Tax (FA02)(8/02 Text & Kit)	☐	☐	☐	£5.95 ☐	
Unit 19 Option Personal Tax (FA 02)(8/02 Text & Kit)	☐	☐		£5.95 ☐	
TECHNICIAN 2001 (£9.95)					
Unit 18 Option Business Tax FA01 (8/01 Text & Kit)	☐	☐			
Unit 19 Option Personal Tax FA01 (8/01 Text & Kit)	☐	☐			
SUBTOTAL	£	£	£	£	£

TOTAL FOR PRODUCTS £ _____

POSTAGE & PACKING

Texts/Kits	First	Each extra
UK	£2.00	£2.00
Europe*	£4.00	£2.00
Rest of world	£20.00	£10.00
Passcards		
UK	£2.00	£1.00
Europe*	£2.50	£1.00
Rest of world	£15.00	£8.00
Tapes		
UK	£1.00	£1.00
Europe*	£1.00	£1.00
Rest of world	£4.00	£4.00

£ ☐ (per line)

TOTAL FOR POSTAGE & PACKING £ _____
(Max £10 Texts/Kits/Passcards)

Grand Total (Cheques to *BPP Publishing*) I enclose
a cheque for (incl. Postage) £ _____
Or charge to Access/Visa/Switch
Card Number ☐☐☐☐☐☐☐☐☐☐☐☐

Expiry date _____ Start Date _____

Issue Number (Switch Only) _____

Signature _____

We aim to deliver to all UK addresses inside 5 working days; a signature will be required. Orders to all EU addresses should be delivered within 6 working days. All other orders to overseas addresses should be delivered within 8 working days. * Europe includes the Republic of Ireland and the Channel Islands.

REVIEW FORM & FREE PRIZE DRAW

All original review forms from the entire BPP range, completed with genuine comments, will be entered into one of two draws on 31 January 2003 and 31 July 2003. The names on the first four forms picked out on each occasion will be sent a cheque for £50.

Name: _____   Address: _____

_____

_____

How have you used this Interactive Text?
(Tick one box only)

☐ Home study (book only)

☐ On a course: college _____

☐ With 'correspondence' package

☐ Other _____

Why did you decide to purchase this Interactive Text? *(Tick one box only)*

☐ Have used BPP Texts in the past

☐ Recommendation by friend/colleague

☐ Recommendation by a lecturer at college

☐ Saw advertising

☐ Other _____

During the past six months do you recall seeing/receiving any of the following?
(Tick as many boxes as are relevant)

☐ Our advertisement in *Accounting Technician* magazine

☐ Our advertisement in *Pass*

☐ Our brochure with a letter through the post

Which (if any) aspects of our advertising do you find useful?
(Tick as many boxes as are relevant)

☐ Prices and publication dates of new editions

☐ Information on Interactive Text content

☐ Facility to order books off-the-page

☐ None of the above

Have you used the companion Assessment Kit for this subject?　☐ **Yes**　☐ **No**

Your ratings, comments and suggestions would be appreciated on the following areas

	Very useful	Useful	Not useful
Introductory section (How to use this Interactive Text etc)	☐	☐	☐
Chapter topic lists	☐	☐	☐
Chapter learning objectives	☐	☐	☐
Key terms	☐	☐	☐
Activities and answers	☐	☐	☐
Key learning points	☐	☐	☐
Quick quizzes and answers	☐	☐	☐
List of key terms and index	☐	☐	☐
Icons	☐	☐	☐

	Excellent	Good	Adequate	Poor
Overall opinion of this Text	☐	☐	☐	☐

Do you intend to continue using BPP Interactive Texts/Assessment Kits? ☐ Yes　☐ No

Please note any further comments and suggestions/errors on the reverse of this page.

The BPP author of this edition can be e-mailed at: lynnwatkins@bpp.com

Please return to: Nick Weller, BPP Publishing Ltd, FREEPOST, London, W12 8BR

REVIEW FORM & FREE PRIZE DRAW (continued)

Please note any further comments and suggestions/errors below

FREE PRIZE DRAW RULES

1   Closing date for 31 January 2003 draw is 31 December 2002. Closing date for 31 July 2003 draw is 30 June 2003.

2   Restricted to entries with UK and Eire addresses only. BPP employees, their families and business associates are excluded.

3   No purchase necessary. Entry forms are available upon request from BPP Publishing. No more than one entry per title, per person. Draw restricted to persons aged 16 and over.

4   Winners will be notified by post and receive their cheques not later than 6 weeks after the relevant draw date.

5   The decision of the promoter in all matters is final and binding. No correspondence will be entered into.